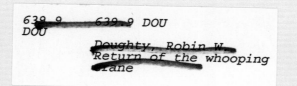

"As we came to know the species intimately, through daily association with the group wintering on the Texas Coast, we were impressed by the fact that the Whooping Crane walks a good deal more than it flies . . . This predilection for walking has not been stressed sufficiently in the literature" (Robert P. Allen, *The Whooping Crane,* p. 87). Shown here are Red/white/Red—Orange and nil—high silver. Photograph by John Jefferson.

Return of the Whooping Crane

by Robin W. Doughty

 UNIVERSITY OF TEXAS PRESS   AUSTIN

Number Fifteen
The Corrie Herring Hooks Series

Copyright © 1989 by the University of Texas Press
All rights reserved
Printed in Japan

First Edition, 1989

Requests for permission to reproduce material from this work should
be sent to Permissions, University of Texas Press, Box 7819, Austin,
Texas 78713-7819.

♾ The paper used in this publication meets the minimum
requirements of American National Standard for Information
Sciences—Permanence of Paper for Printed Library Materials,
ANSI Z39.48-1984.

The research for and publication of this book were made possible in
part by a grant from Conoco, Incorporated.

LIBRARY OF CONGRESS
CATALOGING-IN-PUBLICATION DATA

Doughty, Robin W.
    Return of the whooping crane / by Robin W. Doughty. — 1st ed.
        p.   cm.—(Corrie Herring Hooks series ; no. 15)
    Bibliography: p.
    Includes index.
    ISBN 0-292-79041-4 (alk. paper)
    1. Whooping crane.   2. Birds, Protection of.   I. Title.
II. Series: Corrie Herring Hooks series ; 15.
QL696.G84D68   1989
639.9′7831—dc19   89-31124
                                                            CIP

TITLE PAGE: Three whooping cranes head off to a distant
roost site from which they will command a broad horizon
while standing in a shallow lagoon or slough for the night.
Photograph from Entheos.

To FRANK JOHNSON, who guarded cranes for thirteen winter seasons, and to JIM LEWIS, who has worked to secure seasons for cranes to come.

Contents

Preface

About one hundred years ago, cranes wintered in large flocks on the Bolsón de Mapimí, a vast, sparsely settled tableland in northern Mexico. Visiting hunters blasted at these and other waterbirds, noting that because sandhill cranes were unused to being hunted they were quite tame. In that area, one sportsman, Theodore S. Van Dyke, observed the largest number of whooping cranes he had ever seen. They were foraging on swaths of cotton and corn irrigated by the River Nazas. The handsome white cranes strutted with the smaller sandhills but more often kept to themselves, making their presence known by calls, which sounded to Van Dyke like "the blast of a silver horn."

Van Dyke longed to work within shotgun range of a whooping crane. One day, clutching his gun, the avid hunter lay down in a wet patch of grain and was covered over by corn stalks. He ignored passing flights of ducks, let sandhill crane squadrons sail overhead unscathed, and even allowed tasty snipe to run within a few feet of his motionless body. Finally, the haunting sound of whooping cranes betrayed the arrival of his trophies. Tracking their calls, Van Dyke waited, straining to catch the delicate tracery of wingbeats as they drew nearer. Then, he scrambled up and swung his shotgun at the first white crane, which clawed the air barely thirty feet away. "It seemed wicked," he recalled, "to spoil anything so rare and so beautiful as that sight." It was the shot of a lifetime. His first barrel caused the big crane to fold up suddenly and plunge earthward; the second blast cut down its mate "in a revolving whirl of white, black, and carmine."

Van Dyke was jubilant. He had bagged a pair of whooping cranes, the most suspicious of all game birds. In a few seconds a man had caused two whoopers to "relax [their] hold on the warm sunlight."[1]

We no longer tolerate the hunter's panache and selfish desire to possess the whooping crane as a trophy. Van Dyke admired the bird's beauty; he drew strength from his encounter with the crane, but he could not resist killing it. Tempering this need to possess and subjugate, we have begun to cherish and love cranes and the places in which they exist. We are learning to respect whooping cranes for what they are and for the spirit of indomitability and wildness they represent. Today, crane researchers are engaged in creating opportunities for the whooping crane to build back its numbers. Experts are growing wiser in the ways of cranes and by doing so will ensure that our children may hear that special bugle ringing from remote marshlands.

I am extremely fortunate in having talked with biologists and other enthusiasts who have guided me to literature about cranes and to areas frequented by these lovely giants. Aransas National Wildlife biologist Tom Stehn, a key person who understands and appreciates whoopers, devotes most of his winter duties to observing cranes, checking on their well-being and noting interactions between members of the wild flock. I have been privileged to accompany Tom on many excursions through the Aransas Refuge. He has shown me where to look for whooping cranes, how to approach them, and what to deduce from their activities and vocalizations. Tom has unflagging enthusiasm for his task of crane guardian and has been most generous in sharing his knowledge and experiences with me.

Other dedicated researchers, including David Blankinship, Mary Anne Bishop, and Howard Hunt, have investigated the whooper's world. I have learned a great deal from their publications and in discussing their work. The Aransas National Wildlife Refuge staff have made my own experiences with cranes more rewarding. I am grateful to the late manager, Frank Johnson, and to his successor, Brent Giezentanner, for permission to visit back areas on the refuge. They also made files and reports available to me. Assistant manager Ken Schwindt,

Louise Frasier, Barry Jones, and other staff members always extended a cordial welcome and were most generous in answering innumerable queries. Pedro Ramirez offered data about water traffic through the refuge.

I thank Robert S. Jones, director of the University of Texas Marine Science Institute at Port Aransas, for permission to spend several months on the coast close to cranes and wetlands. Kathy Finnegan, Helen Garrett, and Rick Tinnin provided logistical assistance. Tony and Lynn Amos were most helpful in introducing me to plants and animals of the Texas beach and barrier islands; I thank Tony especially for his willingness to have me along on his dawn "beach obs."

For the past twenty years scientists at the National Wildlife Research Center at Patuxent near Laurel, Maryland, have reared and bred cranes. I am grateful to James W. Carpenter and David H. Ellis for permission to visit the crane pens and observe rearing procedures. I thank George Gee for talking with me about crane reproduction and physiology. Scott G. Hereford, Kathy O'Malley, Bruce Williams, Roddy Gabel, and other staff involved with day-to-day schedules were most kind in introducing me to Canus, Ghostbird, and other crane "characters" in the Patuxent flock. Richard and Marty Jachowski welcomed me to the Chesapeake Bay area.

I am grateful to Roderick Drewien for his kindnesses in helping me observe cranes at Grays Lake and along the "western" migration track, in providing me with reports about foster experiments in Idaho, and in generously sharing important information about whoopers from his unique expertise. Elwood Biseau, Wendy Brown, Gene Barney, Jerry D. French, Dale Stahlecker, Jan M. Ward, Will and Jennifer Swearingen, and Bill and Anne deBuys offered important input and support.

I am indebted to Canadian Wildlife Service biologist Ernie Kuyt, premier researcher and "custodian" of the Wood Buffalo breeding grounds, for his comments and assistance. Brian W. Johns, also with the Canadian Wildlife Service, has increased my understanding of crane movements in Saskatchewan. I acknowledge Whooping Crane Conservation Association secretary-treasurer Jerome J. Pratt and trustee R. Lorne Scott for their welcome to the annual meeting in Regina, Saskatchewan, in September 1987. I received assistance from Fred G. Bard, F. Graham Cooch, Fred W. Lahrman, and others at that important gathering of crane enthusiasts.

Another meeting of crane experts, under the auspices of the Fifth North American Crane Workshop, Kissimmee Prairie, Florida (February 1988), brought to light new information and insights. I thank Craig Faanes, Paul J. Currier, Gary Lingle, and Kenneth J. Strom for information about cranes on Nebraska's Platte River. Janet McMillen, Alan Bennett, and Stephen Nesbitt provided details about reintroduction sites east of the Mississippi River. Ray McCracken added specific material about the Kissimmee Prairie, as did Mary Anne Bishop, who made helpful suggestions about the manuscript.

George and Kyoko Archibald, Claire M. Mirande, Scott Swengel, and Robert Horwich were helpful in my visit to the International Crane Foundation, Baraboo, Wisconsin, and gave me invaluable information about crane species worldwide and about particular techniques for releasing cranes into the wild. George was generous in making suggestions for improving the text.

I acknowledge the assistance of Christopher Perrins, Edward Grey Institute for Field Ornithology, and Linda Birch, Alexander Library, Department of Zoology, Oxford University, for permission to use archives and to consult reprints. Dan Luten gave me helpful information and unstinting encouragement.

In Texas, I thank the Conoco Foundation for its generous support, which enabled me to take a sabbatical leave, without which the entire endeavor would not have been possible. I appreciate assistance from the University of Texas University Research Institute for a grant to conduct research and travel. Colleagues and staff in the Department of Geography at the University of Texas at Austin have given me longstanding support. I thank Barbara Brower, Anne Buttimer, and Barbara Parmenter for their helpful suggestions. Barbara Parmenter assisted in every phase of the project and gave me the benefit of her insight and creative imagination. I thank Beverly Beaty-Benadom, Cherie Smith, Bob Wolfkill, Gary Whalen, and Carol Vernon for typing the manuscript and making changes in the many drafts. I appreciate the note about sources from Lewis L. Gould, Department of History, University of Texas at Austin, and information supplied by Bruce Thompson and the late Floyd Potter, Texas Parks and Wildlife Department, and by R. H. "Dick" Cory of Austin, Texas.

Finally, I should like to express my sincere thanks to James C. Lewis, whooping crane coordinator, U.S. Fish and Wildlife Service, for his patience and imperturbability. Jim welcomed me in New Mexico, invited me to accompany him on several crane-related sorties, and responded to my pesterings with humor and wry wit. He was most helpful in putting me into contact with other experts and brought his talents as an editor to improving this manuscript. I owe him a debt of gratitude.

"The sight of a Whooping Crane in the air is an experience packed with beauty and drama. We see the broad sweep of the great wings in their stiff, almost ponderous mo- tion, the flash of sunlight on the satin white plumage" (Robert P. Allen, *The Whooping Crane,* p. 87). Photograph from Entheos.

CRANE SEASON

The edge of summer   turns
   on swallow   flicker,
      fits   cap on gull
shouts willet   echo

      and calls quits
to   whooping crane
   picnics.   No more winter
crabs   and wolfberry!

   Wingslant carries   white
hungry   things to grain
   and grasshopper.   Clouds
   fling snow,   tug wing

to ground   birds as
   they pass.   Flight end
is bison home   where
      wolf   howls play with

silence,   brown bears
   roll, and rusty young
      will try new wings
for long day   turnaround.

Part loosely wing the region; part more wise,
In common, ranged in figure, wedge their way,
Intelligent of seasons, and set forth
Their airy caravan; high over seas
Flying, and over lands, with mutual wing
Easing their flight: so steers the prudent crane.
                              —JOHN MILTON
                                 Paradise Lost

Introduction

It is the last day of October, and a dawn mist hangs over Goose Lake's unruffled water. Thin vapor conceals stirring birds. Only a muffled clamor topped by a falsetto yelp betrays the existence of several hundred sandhill cranes and speckled-bellied geese.

As a new day grows, ranks of sandhills step into the light. At first smudges in gray, the dawning sun turns dim shapes more russet. Finally, brighter light shows picket fences of birds strung across the lake, each line with another behind. Staring hard in our direction, every crane stands like an upright spike, relaxes, then bends back into that characteristic hourglass figure, head and neck filling out at its body and tapering again into long thin legs anchored in a water sheen.

Immediately, a large white object shows in a medley of browns. A loafing pelican perhaps? It moves, uncoils itself into a crane shape, and rises loftier than cousins— America's tallest bird at four and one-half feet—a whooping crane. We searched for it yesterday in milo fields. Lost among feeding sandhills whose darker plumage occasionally flashed gray in sun slant, this whooping crane had eluded us. Today on Goose Lake it is whiter than mist—almost a pelican white but in a different contour. Quietly, this crane is poised on the water's edge circled by a hundred relatives whose ranks begin to diminish as birds flap over a thicket of mesquite surrounding their marsh roost.

An early arrival, the whooping crane acts as if still on migration although winter quarters on Gulf salt marshes are barely eight miles away. Soon, it will link up with a hundred or so similar endangered cranes following a Plains flight path, who feast on grain and often associate with brown sandhills like this one on Goose Lake. In small flocks, families and pairs, whooping cranes are headed toward the Texas Aransas National Wildlife Refuge. This is a lone bird, a subadult too young to nest or claim space on tidal flats. Refuge staff had reports of its presence and are checking for distinguishing leg bands.

They mark it on a list of birds that they hope will complete a long, exhausting 2,500-mile journey from subarctic wildland.

This crane wears yellow and red bands. It is a female, who will pass one or two more winter seasons in Texas with similar-age birds before forming lifelong bonds that will make her a parent. She and her mate will guide a rusty-plumaged youngster from Canada's bush toward Gulf coast marshes. Tomorrow or maybe next week this white crane should leave companion sandhills and complete her journey. Setting down on bay shore she will bugle home others of her kind.

By 6:30 A.M. sandhills are streaming toward grain stubble southwest of Austwell. One or two dozen take to the air at once, while others look on impassively, aware of tumult but reluctant to quit a secure, familiar sleeping place. Languor does not deter the whooping crane, and in the middle of the exodus it, too, joins the steady stream.

On this day Goose Lake is for ducks and cranes. Large flights of geese have not yet swung down from northern skies. A few dot its surface but fail to outnumber squadrons of teal, shoveler, and gadwall. Hundreds of cranes, including the single whooper, have mingled with these ducks and use this wetland as a safe roost after they forage in nearby grain fields. On the bank a meadowlark pumps its yellow chest to welcome daybreak. A Le Conte's sparrow responds—a tiny, rotund friar giving morning benediction. But Yellow–Red is long gone; already she is gleaning milo three miles away, a conspicuous exclamation mark on the corrugated black earth of the Texas coast.

Cranes are marvelously shaped birds. Their sharp eyes, upright stance, long legs, and serpentine neck enable them to see great distances. They are capable of striding across marshes, swamps, and tidal flats faster than a person can walk, making them exceptionally

Locations for the Whooping Crane (based on U.S. Fish and Wildlife Service, *Whooping Crane Recovery Plan*, 1986; Robert P. Allen, *The Whooping Crane*)

difficult to approach. Goose Lake is a good habitat for such tall birds. Beyond its fringe of mesquite is an expanse of flat, grass-filled prairie on which intruders or potential predators are clearly visible to resting birds. In the shallows of this and other aquatic habitats cranes find sanctuary; they pass hours of darkness standing in water away from shore. Nothing can get near without being detected.

Goose lake also provides access to a range of foods, including grains, roots, and insects in nearby fields and mollusks, fish, and amphibia in surrounding marshes. Cranes pick up or seize these items with straight, powerful bills. Such a weapon can stab a coyote, wolf, or other predator close to a nest or chick. Proverbially wary, a crane may drop its narrow body into low cover and remain undetected on its nest, or it may swing into the air and, thrusting head and neck forward with legs trailing, make off speedily with strong, sustained wingbeats.

Nine of the world's fifteen crane species are migratory. Some, like the sandhills and whooper on Goose Lake, travel hundreds, even thousands, of miles along traditional pathways across the northern continents, covering up to several hundred miles in a day. By the arrival and departure of such familiar birds, ancient farmers took note of month and season. Mention of regular crane movements is recorded in the Old Testament's Jeremiah 8:7: "Yea, the stork in the heaven knoweth her appointed times; and the turtle and the crane and the swallow observe the time of their coming; . . ." There were dates in a calendar when people looked for these large, conspicuous birds. A thousand years before Christ, Homer's *Iliad* spoke of crane migrations. Lengthy flights took place usually in spring and fall when rippling voices of these majestic creatures pealed out to Greek and Roman listeners who spied distant chevrons spiraling against a backdrop of clouds. In spring, sonorous calls from returning cranes were a signal to begin ploughing.

Cranes were also weather prophets. Reportedly, they were able to summon storms with their cries, but, in fact, rain and contrary winds often grounded flocks. In fall, for some observers the early passage of cranes spelled early winter. When "winging long-necks" turned back from a sea crossing, sailors left harbors reluctantly, knowing that a storm was likely to strike. Theophrastus noted that when crane flocks departed and did not return it was a sign of fair weather. Others agreed; Aratus, for example, stated that "cranes also before a gentle calm steadily pursue one direction all together, and when the weather is fine will not be carried in dis-

ordered flight."

Greek and Roman writers believed cranes to be wise, intelligent, and sociable, capable of giving support to fatigued or wounded companions. They believed that cranes propped their bills against those in front and gained rest. They also argued that these strong, big birds carried on their backs small, weaker flying species. They carried wagtails, for example, or larks or finches to winter quarters by lifting them across seas and inhospitable deserts. Classical authors also noted other fables concerning how tall, bold cranes battled with diminutive pygmies after a beautiful maiden was transformed into a crane and attacked by her human countrymen.[1]

Bird scholar Edward A. Armstrong describes a "crane dance," mentioned in Greek literature and practiced throughout Europe and much of Asia, as a form of fertility rite associated with spring warmth. Simple folk commonly regarded birds as wiser than humans, noted Armstrong. Cranes had godlike powers. They carried spring into the winter landscape and extended promise of fertility and blessings from a sun whose red emblem glowed as a spot on their crowns. By emulating courtship dances of this powerful bird, in bowing, running, and jumping, people participated in a renewal of life. They abrogated to themselves the joys and passions of springtime cranes.

Several Asian crane species figure prominently in Oriental iconography. Cranes stand for happiness, fidelity, and a long life and continue to be esteemed in Japan and China. One of the more common crests, in Japan, for example, consists of a circular figure showing the head of a crane. This motif currently is the insignia for Japan Airlines.[2]

The Scientific View

The whooping crane is a member of the Gruidae, or Crane family, one of a dozen in the bird order Gruiformes, which includes button quails, rails and coots, limpkins, bustards, and so on, totaling about two hundred species. Lanky and similar-color storks, herons, and egrets, which look like cranes superficially, belong to another bird order and differ in structure and appearance, vocalizations, and social patterns, including nesting in colonies.

The name Gruidae is derived originally from the Greek *geranos* and probably refers to gutteral, rippling sounds made by common cranes. Loud trumpeting calls of many species, used for assertiveness, to give warning, and to claim territory, come from a long, coiled windpipe fitted into a hollow in the breastbone. The whoop-

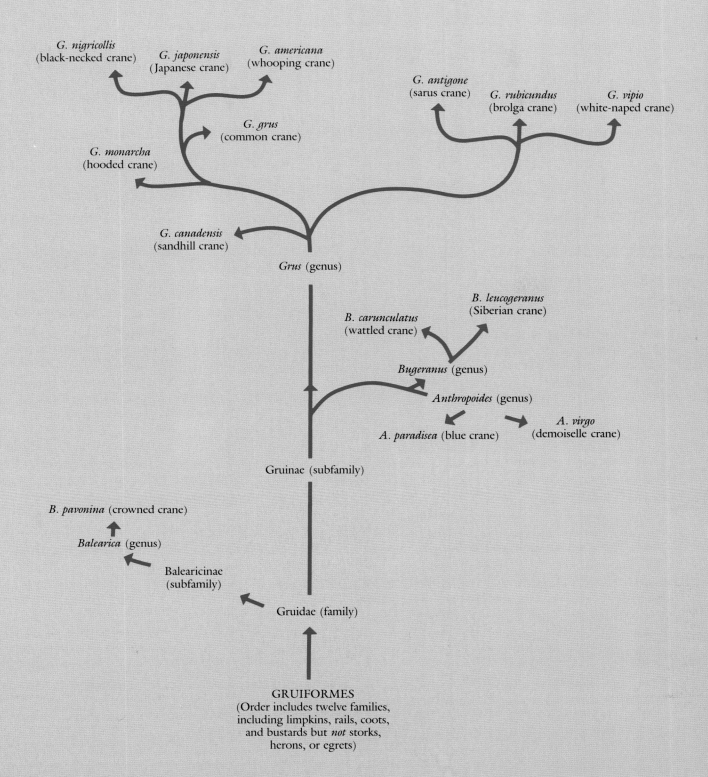

Crane Phylogeny and Classification

ing crane's windpipe is longest of all, taller than the height of the bird itself and wound up tightly inside its sternum; it enables calls to be carried long distances.

Members of the Gruidae family are terrestrial. Cranes nest, sleep, and feed in open, often marshy places, in which they pick up a range of plant and animal foods. Generally, they are colored white, gray, or brown; sexes look alike and both partners share in incubation and tending of one or two young. Pairs establish lifelong bonds, maintained and reinforced by courtship dances and nuptial displays.

The Gruinae subfamily to which the whooping crane is linked has three genera: *Anthropoides* with two species, *Bugeranus* with two species, and *Grus,* formerly with ten species, now revised to nine. The latter includes the whooping crane, *Grus americana,* and the sandhill crane, *Grus canadensis.* An older subfamily, Balearicinae, contains the widely dispersed and relatively abundant crowned cranes of Africa.

In the most recent survey of the natural history of the world's cranes, author Paul A. Johnsgard defines four genera and fourteen species. He accepts a classification similar to one proposed in the early 1930s but amended by ornithologist George Archibald. Archibald argues that genus *Balearica* (Africa's crowned crane), which is placed in the oldest subfamily, should be split into two species and that the very rare Siberian crane should be shifted from one genus to another. This revision makes a total of fifteen cranes worldwide.

DNA researcher Carey Krajewski substantially agrees with Archibald. He concurs that *Balearica* is the most ancient genus and that the Siberian crane is the most primitive member of the subfamily Gruinae, deserving its own genus. Other members comprise the genus *Grus.*

Johnsgard begins his study of cranes with the crowned crane by noting that fossil evidence suggests that *Balearica* "or one closely resembling the crowned crane" lived at least 10 million years ago and is "a more generalized type than are the other modern genera." Oldest fossil bones resemble those of crowned cranes; however, remains of cranes or of cranelike birds go back up to 54 million years in geological time.[3]

Fossilized bone remnants of whooping cranes date back to the Pleistocene Ice Age and come from as far afield as La Brea Tar Pits in Los Angeles, California, and the area near Melbourne, Florida. A fragment of tibia from Idaho's Snake River region is even earlier, from late Pliocene before the onset of the Ice Age.

Crane expert Robert Porter Allen compiled a list of thirty-five U.S. states, six Canadian provinces and districts, and four states in Mexico for which he discovered records of whooping cranes. He suggested that, although "the Pleistocene may have been its heyday," the crane was widespread in North America during late prehistoric well into historic times.

Whoopers probably ranged from Utah's Great Salt Lake across the continent into New England and down the Atlantic seaboard. In Mexico, they occurred in Tamaulipas and in high interior tablelands as far south as Jalisco. Northward, whoopers reached into Canada's districts of Keewatin and Mackenzie. Over the past century or so this aboriginal range has shrunk dramatically as agriculturalists reclaimed vast marshes used for nesting and more and more hunters prized the big, white, elusive birds as food and valuable trophies.[4]

The whooping crane is one of three species of cranes colored predominantly and conspicuously white. All three are migratory and all three exist in greatly reduced numbers. In addition to *Grus americana,* whose black-tipped wing feathers relieve the overall gleaming white in adult plumaged birds, there is a similar-patterned Siberian crane. Two, perhaps three, distinct populations of this latter species nest exclusively in the USSR. Several hundred breed in northeast Siberia's Yakutia and winter in the Yangtze Valley of eastern China. Another much smaller group, consisting of fewer than fifty individuals, summers along the lower reaches of the Ob River in western Siberia and takes a long arcing track southward through Afghanistan, where people hunt them, to winter quarters in northern India. A handful of Siberian cranes also pass winter months on the Caspian Sea lowlands in Iran. Their nesting place, possibly west of the Ural Mountains, remains unknown.

Superficially, the Siberian crane looks like the whooping crane but has a larger bare, red-colored area from the base of its bill to behind the eye. Its legs are pink, not black. The Siberian's voice is more gooselike or whistling in pitch and not as loud or bugling as that of its white counterpart in North America. Human keepers also consider it more aggressive.

The third white-colored crane is the so-called Tancho or red-crowned or Japanese crane, nearest relative of the whooping crane. This bird nests in wetlands of northeastern China and southeastern USSR and migrates to winter habitat in China and Korea. About four hundred Tanchos also reside in the northeastern portion of Japan's island of Hokkaido, and perhaps an additional one thousand or so are on mainland Asia.

In flight, the Japanese crane shows black on trailing

secondary wing feathers, not on primaries as do the other white species. Cheeks, neck, and throat of males are ashy black, paler in females, and form an elegant broad collar or neck band. This Asian crane, unlike its Siberian counterpart, is slightly taller than the whooping crane. But all three species are a good four or five inches shorter than the world's tallest flying bird, India's sarus crane, which stands about five and one-half feet tall and weighs as much as twenty-five pounds, compared with approximately fifteen pounds for a whooper.[5]

Most crane species inhabit Eurasia. China possesses seven or possibly eight species; the Soviet Union has seven, although some species, like the Siberian crane, are extremely localized or occur irregularly. Japan has three species, plus four others that may turn up very rarely.

As one moves away from the center of distribution in central and eastern Asia, the number of species declines. In southern Asia, notably India, there are five or possibly six cranes. Two of them nest on that subcontinent—the resident sarus and a much rarer black-necked crane are restricted to montane uplands.

Four crane species are found south of Africa's Sahara Desert. Two of them, the crowned cranes, inhabit open savannas around water sources from Ethiopia and northern Kenya into southern and southwestern Africa, and a band of them, wedged between equatorial forests and searing deserts, extends across the Sahel into western Africa. A third species, the blue or Stanley crane, lives in dwindling numbers in high grasslands away from water in South Africa. The fourth, the wattled crane, Africa's most endangered species, is concentrated in shallow wetlands in south-central Africa, notably Zambia. No cranes have reached Madagascar, Malaysia, Polynesia, or New Zealand, but Australia has two species.

North America is also home for two species, whooping crane and sandhill crane, of which there are six subspecies (two are considered to be endangered, see Appendix 1). One of them, the Cuban sandhill crane, which inhabits western Cuba and the Isle of Pines, is the only crane represented in the West Indies and the entire span of Central and South America. Perhaps two hundred Cuban sandhills exist.[6]

Interest in Whooping Cranes

Two important books about the whooping crane have been published. A monograph titled *The Whooping Crane* (1952), by National Audubon Society biologist Robert Porter Allen, represented a pioneer study of the bird's numbers, distribution, and natural history. In 1966, nature writer Faith McNulty came out with *The Whooping Crane: The Bird That Defies Extinction*, an update of efforts to conserve whooping cranes and a tribute to the research, industry, and dedication of Bob Allen, who had died suddenly three years earlier.

Allen visited museums and archives throughout Canada and the United States in his efforts to identify the original distribution and abundance of whooping cranes in North America. He tramped through Blackjack Peninsula salt marshes in Aransas County and Calhoun County, Texas, studying winter cranes. He examined all aspects of whooper biology, but in the collection and analysis of data this remarkable birdman never lost respect for his quarry's beauty, grace, and noble bearing. Allen grew to be a crane zealot. He dedicated himself to its well-being as he slogged through wetland habitats or talked with hunters and local residents. He picked up popular knowledge and absorbed regional impressions about cranes. His book *On the Trail of Vanishing Birds* attests to Allen's affection for endangered whoopers and shows his desire to discover the secret of their survival—breeding grounds hidden in Canada's northland. He led the first team to nest sites in Wood Buffalo National Park.

McNulty picked up the banner that Allen had unfurled. She described the context in which he and other crane experts worked, documenting the regional politics and personal foibles and intrigues of people charged with the care of the few remaining birds. Especially touching is her treatment of misfortunes besetting a handful of captive cranes that showed interest in breeding. It seems that the birds themselves were prepared to procreate but human bumbling and bickering frustrated many of such impulses.[7]

It is important to keep in mind that the whooping crane itself has demonstrated an ability and a will to survive. As numbers ebbed away in the 1930s and 1940s, a tiny cadre of experienced adults continued to nest successfully. Slowly, numbers grew as these mature cranes tugged rust-colored youngsters along an air trail to Texas. In a few years, twin chicks accompanied assiduous parents; in other years, none survived long enough to be counted on Gulf coast territories. But adult survivors kept a grasp on life. Even in captivity, cranes attempting to nest in cramped and unsuitable quarters mocked reports that their numbers had fallen too low for any hope of recovery.

Perhaps not as aggressive as other cranes, whoopers are wary. In the old days, hunters found them difficult targets. They seemed always to have a quality of alert-

John James Audubon's dramatic portrait of a whooping crane drawn at New Orleans, Louisiana, in April contrasts with mentions of this bird in his writings. Robert P. Allen lamented the apparent confusion that Audubon made between the two North American species, particularly as the bird artist traveled so widely in the South from 1810 to 1837.

ness and suspicion, as if the birds sensed where potential danger lurked and how to avoid it. Grudgingly, professional waterbird shooters respected them, knowing it was so much harder to bag "big whites" than more numerous, brown sandhill cranes.

On the other hand, over time, whoopers have accommodated themselves to humans in situations that result in no confrontations. Today, for example, they pay relatively little attention to tour boats on the Texas Gulf Intracoastal Waterway, which bisects the Aransas National Wildlife Refuge. Although wary, birds know that such boats and their occupants present no direct threat.

Whooping cranes have responded magnificently to our efforts to protect and conserve them. We have established sanctuaries, prohibited hunting, and interested and educated the general public in helping them survive. Much of this progress must be credited to biologist Bob Allen, who was determined to give the whooping crane every chance. He promoted his birds constantly in an effort to generate lasting interest and goodwill. Faith McNulty has taken a similar position. She has focused attention on captive whoopers, emphasizing those qualities that gave character to individual birds.

Since the 1960s, interest in whoopers and our commitment to save them have expanded. Private, state, federal, and international cooperation between the United States, Canada, and currently Mexico has proved that political borders need not be barriers to crane management and population recovery. The U.S. *Whooping Crane Recovery Plan* (1980, revised 1986), authorized under the 1973 Endangered Species Act as amended, which remains the capstone for saving this nation's threatened and endangered plants and animals, addressed those actions that experts deemed vital for "down listing" the species. The *Plan* aims to establish procedures and guidelines that will assist in population recovery in the foreseeable future. Recovery team members represent public and private organizations and come from a number of geographic regions in which whoopers occur or in which they are likely to be affected. In December 1987, Canada published its own *Recovery Plan*. Both nations have entered into cooperative agreements and seek to combine efforts to preserve the whooping crane, and both have representatives on their respective recovery teams.

Increasing numbers of people know more about our endangered cranes than ever before, and they are prepared to support sophisticated strategies aimed at preserving them. Along the whooper pathway in the United States, there are thirteen state agencies and three regional Fish and Wildlife Service offices, which cooperate in monitoring migrants every spring and fall. A federal center in Grand Island, Nebraska, acts as a clearinghouse for information, alerting local personnel to sightings and notifying authorities about possible diseases or contaminants along the birds' route. Likewise, Canadian Wildlife Service biologists cooperate with authorities in Alberta and Saskatchewan to check on whooper movements in Canada. In this way, details of the whereabouts of a family or small flock are relayed up and down the crane flyway. Hunters also receive reports about imminent arrivals and learn to avoid these special birds.

Over the past few years, a national whooping crane coordinator, U.S. Fish and Wildlife biologist James C. Lewis, with an equivalent colleague in Canada's Wildlife Service, F. Graham Cooch, has dealt with all aspects of human interactions with cranes. They act as troubleshooters, liaison between international, federal, and state or provincial agencies, and have a firm grasp on all policy decisions about preservation and population rehabilitation. Both of them are members of the two recovery teams.

Data about whooper life history and behavior have grown exponentially. Lewis has been at the forefront, acting as general editor for a number of publications stemming from workshops begun in the 1970s. Such proceedings, of which there have been four in the United States and four additional international workshops, one of which was convened in Baraboo, Wisconsin, in 1975, keep researchers, authorities, organizations, and interested individuals abreast of up-to-date details on the status of programs involving both sandhills and whoopers. International conferences on cranes, such as the second, the 1980 symposium in Sapporo, Japan, spearheaded by George Archibald, chairman of the Crane Working Group of the International Council for Bird Preservation, and sponsored by the Wild Bird Society of Japan and the International Waterfowl Research Bureau, have drawn together crane experts worldwide. Crane enthusiasts share expertise and, equally important, establish friendships that contribute to breakthroughs in programs for rearing and breeding cranes and in setting aside sanctuaries. The Whooping Crane Conservation Association, a group of 550 or so committed whooper enthusiasts, has voiced its range of concerns for almost thirty years, and a quarterly newsletter, *Grus Americana,* alerts readers and a broader public about the species' status and numerical trends.[8]

This book recognizes an enormous outlay of money, time, and effort that has been directed toward saving the world's crane species, especially whooping cranes. They are fascinating birds that travel with economy and precision; they demonstrate attachments for one another and for their young. These tall, elegant birds surprise us by turning up or moving on when we least expect. They seek out food in various places and in different ways, walking in oak mottes after acorns, picking crawfish from entrances of flooded burrows or gulping balls of massed ants from inundated pastures, or catching fish or flicking over dried cowchips in order to grab insects beneath. It is abundantly clear to those who watch and wonder that cranes are not machines driven by blind unwitting instinct. Whoopers are individuals, and people involved with them can readily identify traits that distinguish one bird from another. Some are noticeably wary, assertive, or aggressive; others are dependable as parents; almost all are faithful to nest sites and winter habitats, even sometimes using identical stopping points year after year in journeying between Canada and the United States. Each whooper has a peculiar temperament—a way of presenting itself to others of its kind. That distinctiveness attracts our attention, admiration, and respect.

This book examines three distinct initiatives in whooping crane conservation: protection of the Canada-U.S. flock, captive breeding, and experiments to establish a new population in the wild. The first section of the book examines the relict population of wild cranes who migrate from breeding grounds in the Canadian Northwest Territories to Aransas National Wildlife Refuge on the Texas Gulf coast. This flock is the lynchpin for survival. The official federal *Recovery Plan* aims for a minimum of forty nesting pairs in this population by the year 2020; in 1987 there were thirty-three.[9]

A second path to follow in crane recovery leads to raising whooping cranes in captivity. About thirty years ago a careful assessment was made of the species' reproductive behavior and longevity. This book picks up the theme of propagation, which McNulty's work initiated, and primarily looks at the involvement of the federal government in captive breeding.

The third aspect of whooper survival centers on establishment of additional wild populations. The 1986 U.S. *Recovery Plan* anticipates that by the year 2020 a minimum of twenty-five nesting pairs will exist at two locations, in addition to that occupied by whoopers who migrate between south-central Texas and northern Canada. First experiments to establish a second wild flock began at Grays Lake National Wildlife Refuge in southeastern Idaho.

Field naturalists have generated knowledge and understanding about whooping cranes. Committed, patient observers have learned important information about this bird's life cycle and behavior. They admire the bird's intelligence and character, and the following pages reveal how they and others have sought to engage it on its own terms.

When you do spot a whooping crane you wonder how you could mistake him for anything else or anything else for him. He looks like a great, flightless, prehistoric bird, prancing about over the mud flats. His stride, the length and thickness of his neck, and the long, sloping back with its dangling plumes over the tail are completely characteristic.

ROBERT P. ALLEN
On the Trail of Vanishing Birds, p. 41

1. Aransas Cranes

The route which we followed heralds the coastal region of Texas. There are immense prairies, sometimes swampy, without any gradient. Here and there are agglomerations of associated bushes which the creoles generally call *mogotes* [hummocks]. In the springtime, particularly in the rainy season, one travels entire leagues over ground covered with from one to two feet of water. The region then abounds in water hens, various species of ducks, cranes, egrets, and several other birds of the web-footed and wading families. Deer and wild horses are very common there, but what surprised us most was encountering a large number of foxes chasing the birds. Some wolves hidden in the undergrowth were also exercising their cunning. They could be recognized from a distance, for they were followed by birds of prey who flew to wait for their spoils, and the other birds fled at their presence. . . .

Once enclosed in these bays one cannot leave when one chooses. . . .

In the afternoon we . . . went towards a sort of island or strip of land situated inside the bar. From a distance one could sight uneven heights, covered with verdure, yet when one lands everything is reduced to some not very tall dunes where grasses are growing. In the cavities carved in the sand among the dunes one finds fresh water, where we renewed our half-exhausted supply. We then crossed over the northern point of the bar, where the Carancahuases are often found camped to catch turtles when the bays have not sufficiently furnished them with fish. On the beach we found a great many shells and a large quantity of aquatic birds. During the night we heard, from every direction, the cries of the packs of coyotes who come to the coasts seeking subsistence. . . .

On the beach which forms the northeastern coast of the bar we encountered the tracks of horses, some wolves, a large number of coyotes, and, on the sand, the prints of a large species of cat. At night those cats pursue the ducks, gray pelicans, and egrets to such an extent that those birds cannot be approached to hunt them, something which is never observed in the wilds where they are not pursued by animals of prey. (JEAN LOUIS BERLANDIER, *Journey to Mexico* [7–18 March, 1829], II, 393)

Extracts from the journal of Berlandier, a Swiss-trained botanist with Mexico's Boundary Survey, are a vignette of the Texas coastal region and its various mammals and birds. The remote area inhabited by today's whooping cranes is west of a sand dune barrier dividing shallow estuarine waters from the Gulf of Mexico. People felt isolated, even trapped in this bay-studded region, threaded by a few tracks with San Antonio's missions.

In sailing ship days, travelers often waited impatiently around a handful of jetties marking this central coast until a wind shift allowed vessels to steer through a maze of shallows and oyster reefs toward the open ocean. In 1829, Berlandier's vessel, out of Copano landing, stood off the Aransas Bar (present-day Port Aransas) for almost a week. This delay allowed him to explore outer beaches, on which he came across tracks of all kinds of animals, plus a Karankawa Indian encampment. Then, with westerly breezes, his boat was able to ease through shallow surf toward New Orleans. Running this sandbar was dangerous. On his return a few weeks later, his ship ran aground but managed to sail on. In port, mosquitoes zeroed in, causing horses and riders to press for higher ground and rude comforts in the presidio of La Bahía, today's Goliad, almost forty miles inland.[1]

Yet, life on this so-called Coastal Bend was not all a struggle that pitted humans against nature and its strange, dangerous-looking wolves, alligators, snakes, or vultures. Colors of flowers, aromatic shrubs, bird songs, tilt of sky-shearing hawks, and deliberate, graceful steps of deer, mustang, or crane—nature's wonders—raised people's spirits and curiosity. Newcomers found a landscape flung wide with waving grasses that carried the gaze to an open horizon's clouds. Travelers sought shade and shelter in copses, or "mottes," of oaks and mesquite in which wild honey bees and variously hued birds built nests. This coastal wilderness attracted and fascinated settlers who loved to fish, hunt, track game, and learn about habits of mammals and birds, including potentially useful wild horse and cattle herds, whose tracks crisscrossed the San Antonio River valley.

A few years after Berlandier's visit, a veteran of the Texas Revolution, John Crittenden Duval, encountered Texas Rangers at Copano landing. The men "had not seen a morsel of bread" in six months of frontier duty, reported Duval, who noted how healthy they looked after subsisting "solely upon beef and the game they killed." On a track to Goliad, Duval spied droves of wary mustangs and had "two or three hundred" deer in view at a time. Like the Texas Rangers, he had no difficulty obtaining fresh meat.[2]

Sea edges attracted American settlement. Historian Hobart Huson recounts how maritime folk chose to live around local bays and barrier islands as they retired from schooners plying the central Gulf ports of Galveston, Brazoria, and Indianola. This last settlement, founded in the 1840s on Matagorda Bay's west shore, north and east of San Antonio Bay and home for whooping cranes, grew to rival Galveston until two severe storms devastated the community. Indianola was ruined and abandoned in 1886.

By mid-century settlers had begun to ranch livestock on unfenced peninsulas, and they established bay ports, such as Rockport and Fulton, for shipping cattle and canning beef. As Longhorn cattle began to be trailed northward in increasing numbers after the Civil War, many packery owners turned to processing local cattle for hides and tallow and put up cans of turtle meat and soup. One long-time Indianola resident recounted how "large sea turtles were caught by means of huge nets in which they became entangled, [then] brought ashore and placed in a deep pool of water prepared for them: near a canning factory." She noted how these three- or four-hundred-pound reptiles came up "and put their heads out of the water to blow." Their flesh was very tasty.[3]

Indianola had two or three turtle canneries. Fulton, near Rockport on Aransas Bay just south of Blackjack Peninsula cranelands, had another. In 1890, this facility processed almost nine hundred green turtles, accounting for 40 percent of the entire state catch exceeding half a million pounds in weight. Turtle men in Aransas Bay used special nets to snag these huge reptiles as they swam along the channel network in summer months. They soon depleted the fishery.[4]

In spring, before turtling, fishermen and other local residents shot waterbirds, especially colonies of nesting herons and terns, in order to supply millinery houses with ornamental feathers. The same hurricane that destroyed Indianola capsized a schooner outfitted for plume hunting. The vessel, plus three hundred dollars' worth of guns and ammunition and six hundred bird skins, was a total loss.[5]

In winter, men supplied local communities with waterfowl. They glutted Indianola's market, for example, "with all kinds of game, and the air creaked under the weight of millions of wild fowls." Dealers sent oxen-drawn wagons into San Antonio and neighboring communities laden with waterfowl and fish products.

Texas was the outpost in the Southwest for traffic in waterbirds, which stretched down the Atlantic seaboard from New England to Florida and spread around the Gulf to Texas. Approximately sixty bird species, mainly waterfowl, gulls, terns, herons, and shorebirds, made up the bulk of supplies for millinery and avian meat markets. When coastal railroads opened up Rockport, for example, sport hunters took tolls on ducks and geese. Weekend visitors "sometimes killed 700 ducks and bragged about it," reported one ardent San Antonio–based nimrod. "Gum Hollow" near Gregory grew into "probably the most famous duck shooting resort in the world." Gunners around Aransas Pass found that sharks snapped up wounded ducks around that Gulf outlet.

About the turn of the century, bird authority Florence Merriam Bailey talked with millinery agents around Corpus Christi. One man exaggerated that he could skin six hundred birds a day. Another confided that he had shot a thousand birds, mostly terns and shorebirds, in a week.[6]

By 1900, plume hunters had been busy along the central coast for ten or fifteen years and had virtually cleaned out nesting waterbirds, including pelicans. Agents paid as much as $1.15 for a snowy egret skin, twenty cents for terns, and twelve cents apiece for other birds. One man used an old cannery on Padre Island's north tip for skinning them and shipped out feathers in wooden packing cases six feet by five feet using Mallory Line steamers linking Galveston with New York. Residents used reusable brass shells loaded with no. 8 shot to secure specimens, even packing shells with water to kill but not mangle hummingbirds.[7]

Cranes made up a small part of this commerce in meat and feathers. People liked to eat them but regarded them as shy and elusive. An English professional hunter, using the name "Captain Flack," recalled how difficult it was to bag large, white whooping cranes. In fifteen years of hunting in Texas, Flack claimed to have shot only one or perhaps two so-called bugle cranes per year compared with ten or more smaller, brown sandhill cranes and hundreds or sometimes thousands of geese.

Both sandhill and whooping cranes were very alert and kept "jealously to the open prairies," reported Flack, who understood the habits of all kinds of animals from large, shambling bears to tiny, porcelain-appearing shorebirds. Gregarious sandhill cranes, like geese, could be approached on horseback, he advised. One circled a flock out in the open, gradually diminishing its radius until cranes huddled together and came within range. Then, suddenly reining in his mount, a hunter fired into tightly bunched birds.

Flack admitted that it was not possible to bag whooping cranes in this way. The "great white whooping crane, with black tips to his wings, a patch of red velvety hair upon his head," said Flack admiringly, "is difficult to approach, as he is shy, and stands fully five feet high." The bird can see over great distances. Only by "a long and cautious crawl" might a hunter hope to secure a big crane, concluded Flack, but, in his mind, such a prize hardly justified the effort; the Englishman grumbled, "He is not very good to eat."[8]

George J. Durham, another British immigrant, concurred with Flack's judgment about crane wariness but disagreed as to its value for the palate. In an article printed in the *Texas Almanac* for 1868, this Austin-based sportsman considered the "noble and majestic" cranes to be superior food. He placed both species on his game list, saying that they were "granivorous" in their winter range in Texas and fed on prairies, "upon which they become quite fat in the spring," as well as in cultivated fields. Sandhill cranes, smaller, more "homely" garbed than snowy whooping cranes, were "far more numerous." The two cranes occupied "the place formerly held in Europe by the bustard," speculated Durham. Bustards are other large, edible terrestrial denizens of open, exposed, and gently rolling country, and are also taken, like cranes, to which they are related, for meat and feathers.[9]

Sandhill cranes received lengthy discussion in another *Texas Almanac* (for 1881) because, although they were abundant, city markets never received many of them. "They seem to be always on the watch, and to know precisely how far one's shooting-irons will carry," complained the writer. An admittedly unsporting remedy was to find the pond or lake where sandhills roosted. Taking whatever cover existed, a hunter remained completely immobile as birds dropped in at sunset; he waited for cranes to step into shallow water and begin

to sleep. Jerking up his gun, he fired one barrel into the massed ranks and another as they strained upward in panic-stricken flight. As the uproar ceased, all the slayer had to do was "wade in and drag out." Wounded birds were dangerous. Should a crane's beak "happen to pop a fellow in the eye, that eye is gone," the author warned. It was also important to remember that killing such waterbirds in their sleeping quarters could be practiced one time in a season, "as all the geese and cranes in the neighborhood at once take the hint, and give that pond a wide berth."[10]

Crane Numbers

Although never as abundant as its sandhill cousin, the whooping crane was relatively common, at least along the Texas central and lower coastal reaches in the 1870s and 1880s, when reports noted its presence. Ornithologist George B. Sennett collected bird specimens in winter and early spring 1877. "I frequently saw these noble birds of the prairies feeding in the lagoons, as we went down the coast, and in the wet places about Brownsville, up to about April 1st," he recalled. "They were always in pairs, and, as usual, very shy." Sennett made additional observations in 1878 and saw big white cranes on "grass-and-mud-flats near the head of Padre Island during late March."[11]

Another careful birdman, Henry P. Attwater, who visited Texas in 1883 to collect natural history specimens, glimpsed whooping cranes at "Graytown Lagoon" (a present-day ghost town in Bexar County, below the confluence of the Medina and San Antonio rivers) and again in 1884. Five years later, Attwater moved from Canada to San Antonio; he later resided in Rockport and Houston. Around San Antonio, he characterized whoopers as regular migrants in the 1880s, reporting that visiting ornithologist Henry Dresser had also observed them near the Alamo City in 1863. But they had become rare. The existence of several specimens in the city's stuffed bird collections partially explained its status: there were bragging rights to killing whooping cranes. The birds were large, handsome, and shy, alluring prizes for both trophy and pot hunters.[12]

Reports of crane kills increased dramatically from the Civil War to the early 1920s. Crane authority Robert Porter Allen reckoned that during this period exploration and settlement westward cut into whooping crane habitat and numbers. Reports suggested that cranes were unwilling to tolerate disturbance, disappearing as people moved in. Farmers reclaimed wetland breeding sites in central Illinois, Iowa, Minnesota, and north-

A pair of whoopers explore a shallow inlet. Photograph from Bruce Coleman, Inc.

BELOW: This sign below the observation tower overlooking Mustang Lake on Aransas NWR provides information about the winter territories of whooping cranes. In recent years, subadult whoopers have foraged in this area. Usually, the group of younger birds does not feed near the territorial pair. "Ms. Nyarling" of Wood Buffalo NP passed her first winter in this Mustang Lake territory. Photograph from Bruce Coleman, Inc.

EACH WHOOPING CRANE FAMILY OCCUPIES A LARGE AREA OR TERRITORY DURING THEIR STAY ON THE REFUGE. THE FAMILY DEFENDS THIS HOME GROUND FROM THE INTRUSION OF OTHER WHOOPING CRANES. THE EXPANSE OF GRASSY FLATS SEEN FROM THIS TOWER IS USUALLY PART OF THE TERRITORY OF JUST ONE FAMILY OF CRANES.

HERE IN PEACEFUL ISOLATION, THEY HUNT FOR THEIR FAVORITE FOODS... BLUE CRABS, MARINE WORMS, CLAMS AND OTHER SMALL MARINE CREATURES. IN ADDITION, THEY MAKE FREQUENT FLIGHTS INLAND TO SEEK SNAILS, INSECTS, ACORNS AND PLANT TUBERS.

ADULT   YOUNG

(SHOWN LIFE SIZE)

Whooping cranes have established territories on Lamar Peninsula on the western edge of St. Charles Bay. Photograph by author.

eastern North Dakota, and, as the species appeared doomed, hunters and collectors searched for specimens and eggs. The whooping crane was a bird for which professional hunters would not guarantee to deliver skins or eggs within a designated time, making it even more valuable. Specimens fetched higher prices than eskimo curlews, ivory-billed woodpeckers, or trumpeter swans.[13]

By carefully sifting published records and museum collections, Allen concluded that *Grus americana* was never as widely distributed or as abundant as the sand-hill crane. Allen reckoned that, before 1870, when humanly induced declines began to threaten its survival, the entire continental population totaled no more than 1,300–1,400 individuals.[14]

Before 1870, only 16 whooping cranes are listed on a "kill record" for North America, but, in the following half century until 1924, no fewer than 267 whoopers are known to have died. Most of them were shot during migration in the 1890s (67 birds), 1900s (59 birds), and 1910s (55 birds). Kills in Texas totaled 40 birds, or 12 percent of the known number taken between 1885 and 1948. This state ranks behind Nebraska (45 deaths) and ahead of third-place Louisiana (37) in mortality statistics.[15]

These three U.S. states have dominated the story of whooping crane decline. Annual reports from Nebraska's Platte River, beginning about 1912 and running for twenty years, suggested that the whooping cranes were not in serious jeopardy. Observers reported several score at various spring staging points in that river valley, so that some experts calculated that overall numbers were higher than winter counts suggested. They reckoned that there must be other wintering grounds holding more than the fading remnant that passed the coldest months on lowlands in coastal Louisiana and Texas.

Whooping cranes both wintered and nested in Louisiana. Allen marshaled evidence suggesting that they were still abundant in five coastal parishes in the early 1880s, before rice farming expanded into their wetland stronghold. He estimated that aboriginal habitat could have supported as many as 2,500 birds, more than his estimate for North America. But by 1918, due to cultivation and overhunting, all whoopers had vanished from tall grass prairies. In that year Alcie Daigle shot twelve at his rice thresher near Sweet Lake.

Small numbers continued to winter in sea rim and brackish marshes closer to the open Gulf until the early 1920s, when muskrat trappers shot them out. A few resident birds, including a dozen or so whooping cranes on White Lake, adapted to areas of panicum grass wetland,

clung to survival.[16]

Allen discounted reports of a large aboriginal whooping crane population in the United States. Most, he arged, were fanciful or based on misidentification. For instance, he paid scant attention to John James Audubon's encounters with whoopers because the great bird artist confused crane species. Allen regarded botanist Thomas Nuttall's oft-quoted description of migration along the Mississippi Valley as highly colored. Nuttall wrote about thousands of whooping cranes passing overhead for most of one December night in 1811, giving "some idea . . . of the immensity of numbers." This unsubstantiated account, wrote Allen, contributed to a myth of whooper abundance, and it most certainly referred to sandhills. "It is contrary to everything we know about *Grus americana*," he concluded.[17]

This crane authority read and distrusted similar accounts of large numbers of whooping cranes, including references to Texas. Other reports, like one in 1845 made by U.S. Army Inspector General George A. McCall, did provide reliable information about the species. McCall observed a pair at Arroyo Hondo, above San Antonio, and observed additional pairs and parties of three or four near Corpus Christi. Whoopers were "never in large flocks, nor in company with *G. Canadensis*, although the latter were innumerable," wrote McCall. Whooping cranes, he noted correctly, preferred wet places, such as ponds, river banks, or edges along salt-water bays. Sandhills spread out across prairies away from open water. There was no doubt, according to McCall, that the latter were more numerous by far. In New Mexico, he traveled across a fifty-mile stretch between Albuquerque and Socorro, which was literally "covered" with sandhill cranes, who foraged in grain-fields quite close to houses. This officer made no mention of any whooping cranes in New Mexico.[18]

Whooping cranes frequented a band of salt marshes and coastal prairies reaching all the way from southwestern Louisiana to Brownsville, Texas, and probably occurred south into northeastern Mexico's Tamaulipas Province. They were not evenly distributed in these Gulf coast marshlands, however. Allen did not believe, for example, that the marsh and bay zone from the Sabine River to the River Brazos estuary supported many white cranes, although he noted (without comment) birdman Henry Nehrling's claim in the early 1880s that the whooping crane was "exceedingly abundant" in grasslands around Houston.

Interior-facing flats along Matagorda Island, including mainland edges around Matagorda Bay, Espiritu

Santo Bay, and San Antonio Bay, south to present-day Rockport and Corpus Christi were much more important winter habitats. In addition, Laguna Larga, Baffin Bay, and northern Mustang Island were excellent cranelands. The Rio Grande was also a good place. Whooping cranes occupied its open, remote delta from at least 1863 through 1924. Eighteen specimens were shot there between February 1889 and January 1893.[19]

Whooping cranes also wintered with sandhills on interior uplands in both Texas and Mexico. Allen traced back about forty whooper specimens to Mexico, many coming from its grass-filled plateau. Other birds used grasslands around San Angelo, Texas, and also, as we have seen, around San Antonio, Texas. In 1767, French naval officer Pierre Maria François Piagès visited Texas and Mexico. His comments about cranes deserve mention because so many similar reports whet curiosity yet frustrate clear comprehension of species or numbers.

Piagès saw irrigated fields around San Antonio's missions "filled with a large number of cranes" and near Laredo glimpsed a Christmas sky "filled with an immense quantity of cranes" circling over beautiful country planted in cornfields. We do not know whether any were whooping cranes, although the Frenchman probably recognized them as cranes because they resembled Europe's migratory common cranes. A little over a century later, Attwater reported both North American species in the same area close to San Antonio.[20]

Cranes lent a special quality to wild Texas. In February 1836, William F. Gray traversed rolling prairies toward the coast: "The country everywhere presents the appearance of a cultivated region, only wanting a few good farm houses on the beautiful eminences that everywhere present themselves to form a splendid picture of rural beauty and fertility. Immense flocks of geese and cranes were feeding on the prairies, and some ducks in the ponds." Such flocks of wild birds reassured this influential politician about the goodness of frontier Texas. Such fowl added beauty and freshness to a bountiful land, enhancing its attractiveness and possibilities for settlement. Near the coast, they inspired interest in an otherwise open, exposed, and homogeneous landscape. They still do. Coming upon snow geese or sandhill cranes adds vibrancy and scale to flat terrain.[21]

A final example from literature about coastal Texas involves an experience of U.S. Boundary Commissioner John Russell Bartlett, whom President Zachary Taylor appointed in 1850. In early January 1853, after completing his boundary survey, Bartlett sailed north from Corpus Christi toward Pass Carvallo, exit from Matagorda

Bay to the Gulf of Mexico. As his steamer churned slowly down a narrow channel into Aransas Bay, Bartlett observed that sandbars on both sides "were covered with myriads of waterfowl, including cranes, swans, herons, ibises, geese, ducks, curlews, plover, sand-pipers, etc. The large cranes and swans stood in lines extending for miles, appearing like a light sandy beach or white cliff; and it was impossible to dispel the illusion, until the vast flock, with a simultaneous scream that could be heard for miles, rose from their resting place." Bartlett complained that shallow water prevented him from shooting at myriads of ducks and geese that thundered away from his vessel's path. "With a light skiff, and a few bushes or a bunch of grass, a gunner would have good sport as no other portion of the world can surpass," he chuckled.[22]

What were "large cranes" representing a "white cliff"? White pelicans perhaps. These big, pale birds winter in coastal bays, but "screaming" must have come from snow geese or possibly from tundra or trumpeter swans, both common species in the 1800s. However, could "large cranes" have been whooping cranes bugling defiantly at the boat? Such a tantalizing description makes this determination impossible, but, given white coloration and nomenclature, one can speculate that at least some birds were whoopers. Bob Allen, who was familiar with similar accounts, invariably warned about reading too much into such passages. He preferred to make a case, and a conservative one, that focused on relative scarcity, not abundance, of whooping cranes.

When we turn to *The Bird Life of Texas,* a monumental, two-volume work by noted ornithologist Harry Oberholser (1870–1963), we discover that a good deal of agreement exists between Oberholser and Allen about whooping crane distribution and numbers. Oberholser's major book, published posthumously, presents a shortened version of a manuscript on which he labored for many years. Both this lengthier manuscript and *The Bird Life of Texas* contain important information about cranes.

The whooping crane, according to Oberholser, was "a fairly common, not rare, winter resident . . . in the coast region of southeastern and central southern Texas." It migrated through eastern and middle sections and was "formerly a casually breeding bird in the middle zone of the coast region." How "common" was it, and how "casually" did it nest? Allen drew upon reputable ornithologists to paint his picture of spotty distribution and relatively low numbers. Oberholser, another meticulous worker, agreed substantially but not com-

A whooping crane pair showing off their telltale shape, color, and alert behavior on Aransas NWR. Photograph from Cass Germany Photography.

pletely with this interpretation. Like Allen, he examined records from coastal counties. Highest crane numbers occurred in the Coastal Bend and lower Rio Grande Valley. There were anomalies.

Oberholser quotes from observers who were impressed by whooper abundance. One of them was Wisconsin-born bird collector and traveler Henry Nehrling, who compiled bird lists for different localities. Nehrling characterized whooping cranes as "exceedingly abundant" on tall grass prairies around Houston in winter 1880–81. Another reporter, J. D. Mitchell, declared them as "common in winter about 1905" in Wharton and Jackson counties, north of what is now the Aransas National Wildlife Refuge. John K. Strecker, another authority on natural history, regarded the whooper as "formerly an abundant transient" in McLennan County on the main track for present migratory cranes. George Benners in a serialized essay in *Ornithologist and Oologist* (1887) agreed. Like Strecker, Benners reported whooping cranes on the Texas Blackland Prairie and "saw immense flocks" forty or fifty miles or so south of McLennan County "on the praries [*sic*] in

Williamson County." He also met up with birds, "but always out of gunshot," farther south in Comal County, where the Blackland narrows.[23]

These cranes were probably migrants moving with sandhills across a swath of interior grassland being planted intensively in corn and cotton. They remind us of Frederick Law Olmsted's surprise on a similar prairie just south of Austin. Heading toward San Marcos in January 1854, this New Englander came across what he took to be "sheep." The animals grew clearer as his party approached:

> "Yes, sheep," said one. "Decidedly not sheep," said the other. Suddenly, one of the objects raises a long neck and head. "Llamas—or alpacas." "More like birds, I think." Then all the objects raise heads, and begin to walk away, upon two legs. "What! ostriches? Yes, ostriches, or something unknown to my eye." We were now within four or five hundred yards of them. Suddenly, they raised wings, stretched out their necks, and ran over the prairie, but presently left ground, and flew away. They were very large white birds, with black-edged wings, and very long necks and legs. They must have been a species of crane, very much magnified by a refraction of the atmosphere.

Later, on Salado Creek near San Antonio, Olmsted saw a second flock of "immense white cranes (I suppose *grus Americana*)" and found them very shy. He failed to bag one even with a Sharp's rifle.[24]

The Laguna Larga, on the Kleberg County King Ranch north of Baffin Bay, was another favorite wintering area for whooping cranes. Oberholser and Allen documented as many as sixteen birds present in this area from about 1915 until spring 1937, when two individuals, having wintered on the King Ranch, left and never returned. There was a report of seven in February 1947; a single, presumably from Aransas, passed time on that ranch in 1958.

In January 1933, Oberholser flushed four cinnamon-dashed young whoopers from a lake set back in chaparral on the Kenedy County Yturria Ranch, south of the King Ranch. This most unusual sighting of unaccompanied young feeding in such dense habitat caused him to inquire about other birds. Ranch hands estimated that at least thirty whoopers existed on 20,000 acres. Allen characterized this coastal zone near Laguna Madre as being generally too arid for cranes, with its water table inland lowered by overgrazing.

Breeding records for whooping cranes in Texas are sparse. Allen speculated that nesting may have occurred at one time in the Rio Grande delta. Local inhabitants told visitor Henry Dresser, who found nine or ten birds there in June 1863, that cranes did in fact nest there. Subsequent visitors, however, never found any, although about 100 miles farther north, King Ranch owner Richard Kleberg believed that whooping cranes may well have nested as recently as fifty or sixty years ago. Allen concluded that, just as birds occasionally summer on the Aransas Refuge, the "minor mystery" of nesting reports from such places as the King Ranch probably involved cranes that failed to migrate due to illness, injury, or old age. He doubted whether they nested in Texas.[25]

Oberholser, however, cited four possible breeding records. Three of them from the extreme southern tip of Wharton County (1867, 1869, 1878) included a nest and young. An additional one is mentioned from Eagle Lake, Colorado County, in June 1889. The latter record may in fact refer to Eagle Lake, Iowa, where a similar account of a nest and eggs is repeated in Bent's *Life Histories* using almost identical language. The only verified breeding record in Texas involves two captive birds who nested at the Aransas Refuge (1949 and 1950) and succeeded in producing a chick, the famous Rusty.

While authenticity of nesting is cloudy, trajectory of winter visitation in Texas is clear. By 1900, whooping cranes were in deep trouble. The species disappeared from upper coast wetlands (in Jefferson and Chambers counties) after 1923, although two sightings took place in the 1930s. It vanished from habitat along the lower coast at about the same time. Only the Coastal Bend Blackjack Peninsula was left as the whooping crane's winter home in Texas.

While there is no need to revise Allen's basic picture about winter distribution from Louisiana down through Texas, it is useful to comment on his estimate of 1,300–1,400 whoopers in North America. Federal ornithologist Richard Banks had drawn attention to a lapse in Allen's calculations, which show not the population in any one year, but rather the cumulative total over a 78-year period without adjustments for recruitment. Using Allen's data, a new total of 500–700 birds emerges for 1870, about half Allen's estimate.

Another way of grasping past numbers is to backtrack from a known starting point using annual percentage losses. Again calling on Allen's figures, Banks has shown an average decline of 5 percent between 1912 and 1917, rising to 10 percent from 1917 to 1922, then falling dramatically from 1922 to 1927. With 1912 as a starting point, and assuming 5 percent annual decline, he projects population increases backward in time to arrive at 683 live whoopers in 1870. A 7 percent decline changes totals markedly, yielding 1,509 cranes in 1870 or 2,968 for 1860. Obviously, an endless series of curves can be made from varying decline rates; larger annual percentage losses give higher original numbers. Frankly, we do not know what these loss rates were, just as present increases (in excess of 20 percent in recent seasons) make it hard to predict future populations.[26]

Aransas Refuge

On 31 December 1937, Franklin D. Roosevelt signed Executive Order No. 7784I declaring 47,215 acres of Blackjack Peninsula in Aransas, Calhoun, and Refugio counties, Texas, a wildlife preserve. This presidential decree saved the whooping crane. At that time only two small flocks survived. One was a migratory flock of about fourteen white-plumaged birds, which wintered on this new federal "Aransas Migratory Waterfowl Refuge," as it was called. Another dozen or so cranes inhabited isolated, unprotected marshlands around White Lake, Louisiana, about 285 miles north of Aransas.[27]

Louisiana's whooper flock was abruptly halved by a tropical storm sweeping across exposed coastal habitat in August 1940. High winds and water drove out resident cranes, scattering them, and within a few seasons six survivors disappeared one by one, until a single white crane haunted its ancestral domain. Officials captured this bird, nicknamed Mac, and released it at the Aransas Refuge in March 1950. Within six months, solitary Mac died, a pathetic note in whooping crane survival.[28]

It took about ten months to appoint and install the first Aransas Refuge manager, James Osborne Stevenson. Taking control on Monday, 3 October 1938, Stevenson ordered a crew of CCC and WPA workers to make the huge preserve both habitable and accessible to people. He wanted to make Aransas known to a larger world, and he was eager to get a feel for the place himself.[29]

Before his swearing-in, Stevenson accompanied staff member Arthur R. Custer and CCC foreman Leslie E. Beaty ten miles down San Antonio Bay's west shore from Austwell to Jones Lake to survey this vast estate. The three men found that Jones Lake, today a spot for alligators, was dry. Two peregrine falcons hung over its bed, indicating that migration was in full swing. During his first week Stevenson noted other signs of the season: flocks of barn swallows, scissor-tailed flycatchers, and cowbirds crowded the air between Austwell and refuge headquarters; on 5 October five ospreys flew over.

Two weeks later, as a signal for a new hunting season, duck blinds went up in both San Antonio Bay and St. Charles Bay next to the refuge. On 20 October, CCC workers reported sandhill cranes flying near their camp on San Antonio Bay's west shore (close to the present picnic grove), and the next day forty brown sandhills had two white cranes for company near Mustang Slough. Stevenson was delighted: the *real* birds had begun to move in.

By 6 November, ten whooping cranes, including a rusty chick, foraged on salt grass flats south of Mustang Slough.[30] A couple of weeks later, Stevenson waded across Mustang Lake, close to the present visitor tower, to make color movies of his charges. The tally climbed to ten whooping cranes with four juveniles along the Blackjack Peninsula; an additional four birds lived on the barrier chain.[31]

Other species drew manager Stevenson's attention as he began to compile a bird list. On 2 November, Stevenson noted two thousand Franklin's gulls wheeling over the CCC bayside camp. Three days later, fifteen prairie chickens, an increasingly rare and presently endangered gamebird, turned up on Salt Creek near the head of St. Charles Bay. On that day, a flock of twenty-five European starlings, then unusual, now abundant, appeared off the refuge at Tivoli, a few miles northwest of Austwell.

In July 1939, Aransas manager Stevenson filed his first annual report. In addition to fourteen whooping cranes that wintered on tidal flats around Sundown Bay and Mustang Lake, several hundred sandhills had made frequent use of interior prairies. The growing Aransas Refuge bird list stood at 187 species, with pintail, wigeon, and gadwall being the most common winter ducks. Only mottled ducks nested. There were 16 species of shorebirds, including a record for the rare hudsonian godwit (13 May 1939). Attwater's prairie chicken appeared to be declining; Stevenson thought they moved into refuge uplands but didn't stay. He was pleased, however, with numbers of white-tailed deer (about 4,000), javelina (100), and wild turkeys (about 500), noting that armadillos were also fairly common. He and his staff trapped and destroyed indigenous coyotes and bobcats.[32]

The federal establishment received civilization's trappings, including mulberry, American plum, and tamarisk trees planted around headquarters. Civilian Conservation Corps workers put in patrol tracks, cleared fire breaks, established boundary markers, and built a shell-based road leading seven miles to Austwell. An unusual ten inches of winter rain stymied their operations, but by late January 1939, thirteen months after President

Table 1. Wild Whooping Crane Populations, 1938/39–1988/89

Winter	WOOD BUFFALO–ARANSAS			LOUISIANA	ROCKY MOUNTAIN			Total
	Adult	Young	Subtotal	Subtotal	Adult	Young	Subtotal	
1938/39	14	4	18	11				29
1939/40	15	7	22	13				35
1940/41	21	5	26	6				32
1941/42	14	2	16	6				22
1942/43	15	4	19	5				24
1943/44	16	5	21	4				25
1944/45	15	3	18	3				21
1945/46	18	4	22	2				24
1946/47	22	3	25	2				27
1947/48	25	6	31	1				32
1948/49	27	3	30	1				31
1949/50	30	4	34	*				34
1950/51	26	5	31					31
1951/52	20	5	25					25
1952/53	19	2	21					21
1953/54	21	3	24					24
1954/55	21	0	21					21
1955/56	20	8	28					28
1956/57	22	2	24					24
1957/58	22	4	26					26
1958/59	23	9	32					32
1959/60	31	2	33					33
1960/61	30	6	36					36
1961/62	34	5	39					39
1962/63	32	0	32					32
1963/64	26	7	33					33
1964/65	32	10	42					42
1965/66	36	8	44					44
1966/67	38	5	43					43
1967/68	39	9	48					48
1968/69	44	6	50					50
1969/70	48	8	56					56
1970/71	51	6	57					57
1971/72	54	5	59					59
1972/73	46	5	51					51
1973/74	47	2	49					49
1974/75	47	2	49					49
1975/76	49	8	57		0	4	4	61
1976/77	57	12	69		3	3	6	75
1977/78	61	11[a]	72		6	2	8	80
1978/79	68	6	74		6	3	9	83
1979/80	70	6	76		8	7	15	91
1980/81	72	6	78		15	5	20	98
1981/82	71	2	73		13	0	13	86
1982/83	67	6	73		10	4	14	87
1983/84	68	7	75		13	17	30	105
1984/85	71	15[b]	86		21	12	33**	119
1985/86	81[c]	16	97		27	4	31**	128
1986/87	90	21[d]	111		24	2	26**	137
1987/88	107	25[e]	132		19	1	20**	152
1988/89	119	19	138		14	2	16**	154

SOURCE: Mark S. Boyce, "Time-Series Analysis and Forecasting of the Aransas/Wood Buffalo Whooping Crane Population," in *Proceedings 1985 Crane Workshop*, ed. James C. Lewis, p. 3; U.S. Fish and Wildlife Service, *Whooping Crane Recovery Plan*, 1986, and news release, 15 September 1988; Tom Stehn, personal communication, December 1988.

[a] One juvenile wintered in some unknown location.
[b] One juvenile (Blue–White) wintered at El Campo, Texas.
[c] Two subadults wintered near Freeport, Texas.
[d] One juvenile wintered near Hydro, Oklahoma, then near Victoria, Texas, the following winter.
[e] One juvenile wintered in the Texas Panhandle.
* Extinct; final bird captured and released on Aransas NWR, Texas.
** Estimates.

Roosevelt's executive order, several miles of telephone wires strung on poles shipped from Idaho and sunk five feet into sandy substrate connected CCC camp workers with refuge headquarters and an outside world.[33]

With basic utilities in place, Stevenson tackled another problem: tallying numbers of alien mammals and birds that attorney Leroy G. Denman of the San Antonio Loan and Trust Company had liberated on Blackjack Peninsula after the company had assumed operation of the St. Charles Ranch, as the area was called, in 1923. Although huge expanses of marsh, prairie, and oak woodland looked primeval and entirely wild, the refuge landscape had been considerably transformed by human activities.

Denman reported in a letter to Stevenson that he had freed hogs, deer, pheasants, quail, and wild turkeys behind a tall game-proof fence marking Blackjack Peninsula's north end. Between November 1930 and June 1933, for example, Denman released 11 European boars, purchased from four U.S. zoos, to forage in ridges and swales. These bred with existing wild "rooter" hogs, and their offspring proved impossible to extirpate. Denman shot or trapped at least 2,500 hogs between October 1936 and November 1938. Stevenson eradicated an additional 861 during his first nine months as manager. Today, refuge staff don't hesitate to shoot these "earth ploughs" whenever they come upon them, but feral hogs continue to roam.[34]

In the early 1930s Denman also turned loose more than one hundred deer (possibly five times that many), mostly exotic fallow deer. He also freed about 250 California quail, plus several hundred ring-necked pheasants and wild turkeys. Although a native, wild turkeys had disappeared, so importation of 318 birds between 1931 and 1933 enabled a native species to reoccupy the Blackjack region—at that time, a huge game ranch.

Fallow deer never prospered. There were about twenty or thirty animals when federal biologists made their survey before purchasing St. Charles Ranch. Refuge employees removed odd deer until 1941. Other nonnatives also died out. California quail disappeared quickly, and four hundred or so ring-necked pheasants were gone in a few years. Fifty mule deer brought in from Salt Lake City, Utah, began to die within a few months, and all had expired by 1939.[35]

White-tailed deer, on the other hand, thrived. People had shot out native specimens, but Denman's reintroductions between 1925 and 1937 began to multiply, particularly after the land came under federal protection. About 13,500 whitetails trapped on the Aransas Refuge

from 1940 to 1966 served as seed stock for recovery programs in other parts of Texas, particularly in Hill Country and Piney Woods counties. Even with trapping, growth of deer numbers enabled U.S. Fish and Wildlife Service staff to authorize a bow hunt in 1966, extending it to firearms in 1968. One year later they opened a public hunt for feral hogs on Aransas.

Wild turkeys enjoyed similar success. When Denman took charge of ranch operations, wild turkeys had been extirpated. He set about reestablishing this proud species. Most came from King Ranch lands and have remained a feature of Aransas oak-motte grassland, although numbers fluctuate markedly.[36]

Stevenson supervised management of both birds and mammals, but he never lost sight of whooping cranes as a centerpiece for the 74-square-mile preserve. In his three-year tenure, manager Stevenson recorded a slight crane increase, then a setback. In fall 1938, first year of official records, eighteen birds showed up. Numbers climbed to twenty-six, including five chicks in fall 1940; then a year later they dropped to sixteen with only two young. Stevenson wondered whether this first increase was due to an influx from Louisiana. But with numbers so low and fluctuating, it seemed that the crane's tenuous hold on existence was about to give way.[37]

Stevenson carefully observed whoopers, which old-time area ranchers assured him had wintered in "hundreds" sixty or seventy years earlier. He knew that cranes preferred salt marsh habitat—hence the Mexican name "Viejo del Agua" (Old Man of the Water)— whereas refuge sandhills lived more in the grasslands. He noted that parents kept a protective eye on their young; they didn't bunch together like the brown cranes but spread out in "small groups." Nevertheless, when families did come together and gather around artesian wells in order to drink fresh water, they displayed little animosity.

Stevenson observed courtship, including dancing, in April when his white birds seemed eager to be on their way. As one pair engaged in nuptial displays, their offspring stood by like an "unwanted wallflower," he noted. In 1941, a family summered on Aransas. The adults danced until late June and one of them drove off the juvenile, which rejoined them in August. The manager was disappointed when they failed to nest. He wondered what had happened to "thousands and thousands" who had flown back to Canada and prairie states and danced in similar fashion. He pondered the fate of other whoopers that once wintered in northern Mexico. Persecution, he knew, had played havoc with the

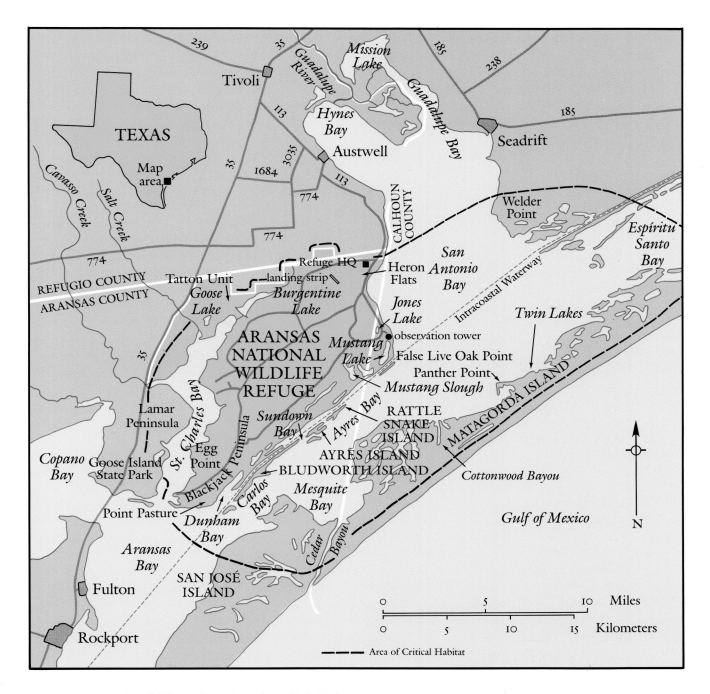

Aransas National Wildlife Refuge (based on U.S. Fish
and Wildlife Service, *Whooping Crane Recovery Plan*,
1986; idem., *Endangered and Threatened Wildlife and
Plants, January 1, 1986; Federal Register,* 15 May 1978)

species.[38]

Manager Stevenson's chief concern was to protect this pitiful remnant of whoopers. A new Gulf Intracoastal Waterway sliced away prime habitat, giving access to boatmen who could practice target shooting at cranes, unused to humans in their midst. Oil and gas exploration caused disturbances and threatened to pollute marshland. A new well blew out in January 1941 with an explosion "that could be heard in Austwell," but, luckily, workers shut it off. To exacerbate disturbances, U.S. Army Air Corps personnel decided to build "bombing and machine-gun ranges" on nearby Matagorda Island.

Stevenson doubted whether the white cranes could sustain such pressures in this last stronghold, and he predicted that they would be shot out or driven from Blackjack. With so few birds, a "little pot shooting here and there," he complained, would undo any number of regulations, laws, or international treaties. Learning of Stevenson's anxiety, a local rancher attempted to reassure him, reporting that he and his family had never shot for the table "more than one every week or so." Stevenson was aghast; "the last faint hope of saving the crane," he concluded, lay in public education and learning more about the bird's life history.

Earl Craven, Stevenson's successor who managed Aransas from 1942 to 1945, also worked to make the bird better known. In six years (fall 1939–spring 1945), twenty-six young cranes followed their parents to Aransas, and none, as far as was known, had died there. The birds had proven adaptable, declared Craven, growing accustomed to airplanes and to other war-related activities in their surroundings. They seemed able to look after themselves by foraging both on shore flats and in interior uplands. "It is unfortunate that the protection afforded the whoopers by the Aransas Refuge is so limited," Craven concluded, noting that migratory flights "half way across the continent" complicated tasks of ensuring their safety. He urged that effective protection be extended to other stopping places and that the plight of whoopers be more widely recognized.[39]

Robert Porter Allen

Bob Allen proved a godsend to whooping crane conservation. Pennsylvania born, Allen was instilled with an early love for outdoor life after reading Ernest Thompson Seton's *Two Little Savages*. With strong interests in birds and conservation, he began work in 1930 for the National Audubon Society. Allen was soon promoted from book sorter to field ornithologist. The National Audubon Society pressed ahead with a program for

sanctuary acquisition and, in 1934, made Allen head of this new division. He first visited Aransas in this capacity in June 1939, when he and John H. Baker, National Audubon Society director, came to Texas and considered extra protection for breeding waterbird colonies near the Aransas Refuge. The following April, Allen returned to Aransas for three months of field work. He grew familiar with an array of islets, bays, and tidal marshes and noted many of 285 bird species that Stevenson had identified. Allen added the varied bunting and other species to the Aransas Refuge list.[40]

It was not whooping cranes but beautifully dressed, odd-looking roseate spoonbills that drew this thirty-five-year-old biologist to coastal Texas. Setting up a trailer on Rattlesnake Point close to the newly dug barge waterway, Bob Allen studied nesting behavior of the rare spoonbill, which was slowly making a comeback after plume hunters had decimated it. Audubon Society staff were anxious to assist this recovery and asked Allen to divide research time between spoonbill colonies in Florida and Texas. His *The Roseate Spoonbill*, National Audubon Research Report No. 2 (1942), published directly before his whooping crane study (Research Report No. 3), remains an important contribution in field biology.

After World War II, Allen returned to Aransas to work on the whooping crane. Under a cooperative agreement between the U.S. Fish and Wildlife Service and the Audubon Society, Bob Allen pioneered studies of this species. He loved the bugle bird, passing the best part of three years (1947–1949) committed wholeheartedly to unlocking the secrets of its existence. In addition to research at Aransas, Allen traveled over twenty thousand miles by plane and an extra six thousand miles by jeep looking for whooper nests in northern Canada. "His sense of the romance of the whooping cranes proved unquenchable," McNulty wrote. In Allen, the whooping crane met its greatest enthusiast.[41]

In the opening to "Migration" in his 246-page monograph, *The Whooping Crane*, Robert Porter Allen looks upon a crane in flight as "an experience packed with beauty and drama." The reader can almost feel Allen's heart begin to race as he suddenly comes upon a trio of cranes. "Their heads come up and the shrill, bugle-like notes, *Ker-loo! Ker-lee-oo!* send a shiver along the length of your spine," he says, as satin-plumaged giants run a few steps and lift off, skimming away with characteristically shallow wingbeats. Allen was able to communicate genuine affection for his birds, and his writings stirred up public interest, conveying precious biological and behavioral information. Subsequent data have built upon Allen's broad foundation.

Allen forged a unique bond with whoopers, piecing together details about how the few wary survivors endured flood and tempest in their Texas marshlands. He studied cranes carefully, checking movements, exploring territories, and working as close to wild birds as possible. Allen committed himself to understanding this elegant, rare, and mysterious species. He immersed himself in its life.

Earlier, during studies of the roseate spoonbill, Allen had exercised patience, picking out subtleties that the biologist was able to apply to cranes. On one day, for example, he witnessed a spoonbill "mass ascent" as three hundred pairs of pink-and-carmine waterbirds lifted upward in nuptial display. Allen was both stunned and humbled: "It was as if a creature of such extraordinary beauty was more perfectly guarded than most wild things from the prying eyes of casual, disinterested Man," he declared. Allen knew he was an interloper; and but for his sense of responsibility to family and to Audubon Society employer, this fieldman would have stepped "quietly away replete with unspoken and somewhat mystic wisdom, perhaps, but no wiser by a whit in matters of Science."

Allen never shut off that ability to perceive "mystic wisdom." He let it flow into him as he stood quietly, almost reverently, before whooping cranes, but Bob Allen was just as ready to cultivate art as to practice science. He regarded the whooping crane as more than a trophy to be grasped, measured, analyzed, and reduced by science; it was a mystery, a being to be appreciated and accepted, not explained. This sense of wonder deepened his contacts with wild things.[42]

When Allen entered the picture in late fall 1946, the whooping crane's hold on life was growing more and more precarious. Louisiana's cranes were almost finished; those in Texas hovered about the twenty or so mark. Allen's research helped end this slippage, particularly in respect to habitat preservation and hunting. It was essential, he knew, to terminate illegal hunting. Accordingly, Allen worked hard to educate people who might be tempted to shoot cranes out of ignorance or perversity. He demanded effective protection for wintering cranes, already helped by their Aransas sanctuary, and for the breeding cohort, which meant discovering where in Canada the white cranes nested. Nobody knew.

Allen pushed for new preserves, fully aware that a late hurricane or oil spill could quickly finish off the small flock in its Texas home. Sympathy for the species was

his motto; each single crane was important. Ingredients that fostered greater appreciation—awareness, interest, delight, knowledge—were the cement that this conservationist used in order to solidify the whooper's hold on existence.

As a scientist, Allen helped create a unique opportunity to expand crane research while simultaneously, as an artist, he built up public awareness. With such a scarcity of wild cranes, Allen followed his dictum in making every whooper count. He coordinated efforts to place together those few captive-held birds in hopes that they might breed. Audubon Park in New Orleans and the Aransas Refuge itself were important in early experiments to breed whooping cranes in captivity; and McNulty tells how Allen and the Audubon Society helped to create the conditions for crane matchmaking. Her book credits Allen for establishing contacts and initiating a dialogue between conservation-minded people that resulted eventually in the first whooper chick, Rusty, being born on the Aransas NWR.

Bob Allen took time off from field research to assist with captive whoopers. His first attempt matched Pete, blind in the left eye, captured in 1936, and owned by the Gottenburg Gun Club, Nebraska, with Josephine, a female from White Lake, Louisiana, held captive in Audubon Park Zoo, New Orleans. Allen monitored the transfer of this pair from New Orleans to Aransas in 1948, observed their unsuccessful nesting in May 1949, and witnessed Pete's untimely death in July. Convinced that whooping cranes could breed successfully in captivity, Allen helped capture a wild bird, so-called Crip, who had been injured on the refuge and could no longer fly.

Within a short time of being placed together, Josephine and Crip developed signs of bonding, and the new pair gave Allen the opportunity of a lifetime—observing the nest cycle at close quarters. Since 1922, when Fred Bradshaw had pilfered the last known eggs from a whooper nest in Muddy Lake, Saskatchewan, no one had seen whooping crane nests or eggs. As a log reveals, Allen and colleagues followed the intricate courtship and nesting process on Aransas with curiosity and a sense of awe.[43]

Rusty and the 1950s

MAY 26, 1950

5:45 a.m.   Day opens with Jo setting deep on nest and Crip standing sleepily beside her (and chick?). There was a heavy rain 3:30–3:40 a.m., now wind is gentle from east. Sky partly cloudy.

Hock-deep in bay waters, these adult-plumaged whoopers are well able to spot approaching predators as they rest, dig clams from the substrate, or feed on other saltwater delicacies. Photograph from Entheos.

6:00   Crip asleep or dozing with head tucked in under back feathers. Jo slumped on nest as if weary (her pellet dish is empty but 'coons probably cleaned it out). No way of checking conditions of youngster from here at present but they'll have to feed "it" pretty soon, I should think.

6:15   No change.

6:18   Crip wakes up, flaps wings and then returns head to sleeping position.

6:23   Crip preening now, Jo still deep on nest. No sign of chick.

6:27   Crip stretches & moves to S (left). Jo up and Crip hurries at once to nest.

6:20   Crip "fussing" with contents of nest (chick?). Jo watching & slowly probing around rim.

6:30   She moves off, very slowly, N. then Crip follows (and "it"?)

6:34   THERE HE IS! Tiny and red as the devil, trotting along in the wake of his proud papa. Sometimes he runs between Crip's feet so that the big fellow must back up very cautiously. Both adults are extremely attentive and it sure makes a beautiful picture . . .

1:35   The male, Crip, covered quite a wide area in foraging while Rusty evidently remained with Jo. Crip now with them again.

1:49   Jo wandered off to feed herself—some distance away leaving Rusty with Crip. Now she suddenly walks back to them, sounding a little query of sound towards them when close by.

2:51   Same routine, with Rusty evidently taking it easy. Adults quietly attentive.

3:20   All afternoon the parents have been busily feeding themselves at every opportunity.

3:28   Both adults feeding—one N and one S of position of young. Young must have peeped as both birds called (goose honk) and hurried to Rusty. Rusty trotted out of a spartina patch in full view. Gosh but "he's" red. And tiny! When they had reassured themselves they went on feeding, but closer . . .

[MAY 27]

[1:50]   Birds' behavior little changed from this morning. Jo seen to have Rusty in tow while Crip preens. Through the glasses the family seems to be on a continuation of the Nest Slough which can be detected from the tower only by vegetation—salt grass bounded on either side by a sea oxeye band. From the tower they are now in line with the 2nd Island of T. slough as shown on above sketch . . .

2:16   Two-(twin) motor plane flew rather low over. No attention paid by either parent! Weather looks like "local showers" later.

2:19   Jo, who has been feeding, head down in a low area, now walks across country as though coming to tower— no feed here—she'd refused last batch of pellets and it was left at hq. Reached Tower slough & paralleling shore (in grass), comes south.

2:25   Crip up, apparently following Rusty around. Jo gives a high whooper call, raises wings and hot-foots it back toward Crip, half flying first 1/3 way. She was on Tower slough shore about opposite lower of 3 islands. Slows down as she nears Crip. Within 6′ of Crip stops, he raises wings and flaps as tho exercising, turns back on [sic] and begins preening.

2:30   No sun now. Both birds preen. All's quiet in Whooperville—close sta. at 2:38. JAH . . .

MAY 28

12:15 p.m.   JAH drove to tower, having seen parents beyond mott enrough [en route(?)]. Returned down road & watched few min. They worked slowly toward NE of mott. Can't see well through window. Rusty must be there! They walk slowly—but he wasn't! Watching for some distance while they waded up a small slough leading N. of E side of mott. Close & full view—no Rusty! Closed Sta. 12:42.

1:58   Opened Sta. (R.P.A.). Pair together. Caracara on ground 200 ft. SE. No evidence of location of Rusty at the moment.

2:10   Both birds walking NW. Rusty with 'em?

2:15   They kept on to Tower Slough so must have parked Rusty back yonder . . .

3:05   Pair still far to NW. Has something happened to Rusty?

3:10   Pair walk back, quite leisurely, to bay side of slough.

3:20   Moving toward bay slowly. No indication yet of presence of young.

3:39   Both walking faster now, east.

3:40   Crip on ahead with something dangling from tip of bill. Maybe Rusty is there! Jo still foraging off to west. *NO.* Crip moves on. Still looks bad.

3:50   Both adults walking together N. toward shore of bay in distance. Bad! . . .

4:35   Bob Allen and Julian [Howard] enter enclosure to determine if young still exists. Crip sees them and stands alert. Jo soon alerts, but resumes feeding . . .

6:07 (B.A.)   Covered area without any sign of chick. Walked route from nest site in northerly direction along which pair had evidently led chick during its first 3 days of life. No sign of Rusty. The pair continued to stand at ease on the far side of Tower Slough, unconcerned at our presence. No calls. As we departed area both danced, typical nuptial dance, Jo briefly, Crip with some enthusiasm . . .

MAY 29

7:30 a.m.   Both birds at tower, on corn. As I drove up they danced for about half a minute. They walked to pool and drank. A deer walks by, close to them. They scarcely look at it. It's all over. ("Aransas Log: Nesting of Josephine and Crip," Aransas Refuge, Files)

The birth of Rusty showed that Aransas could support nesting cranes. A 150-acre pen, constructed on the area of Heron Flats, east of headquarters, proved a good site (except for unrestricted entry of both mammal and avian predators that ultimately undid the crane's hard work). Most important, Rusty was a public relations windfall. The story of whoopers nesting at Aransas drew press coverage from all over the world and turned a spotlight on these special birds. *Life* magazine carried photos of Jo and Crip. People flocked to the Texas sanctuary for a glimpse of showy cranes, only to find their nest site off limits. Failing to gain access, visitors and reporters satisfied their curiosity by picking up information and tidbits about crane life and lore.[44]

Rusty disappeared, taken by predators, but his message reverberated around North America, and Bob Allen made sure that people understood that the whooper was neither a "tired" species nor one unfit for "civilized" society. Human interest, knowledge, and understanding, judiciously applied to crane welfare, paid dividends and made people think more optimistically about such glorious creatures.[45]

The 1950s, however, were not especially kind to whooping cranes. Mac, the sole survivor from White Lake, Louisiana, chased down by helicopter and given the pilot's first name, arrived in Aransas on 12 March 1950, after an all-night drive from the place of capture. This was about a month before Josephine and Crip built their nest. Wild cranes attacked Mac when staff released him near a territory on East Shore, leaving the aged and wing-clipped whooper confused and wounded. After resuscitating the bird, refuge staff selected Burgentine Lake, an impoundment at the head of St. Charles Bay away from other crane territories as Mac's new home. Time, energy, and money expended in capturing and transporting this last wild Louisiana-

born crane went for nought. When personnel set out to relocate the Cajun-born whooper to an area frequented by wintering migrants, they found only a fresh carcass. Attention to activities of Crip and Josephine, who had begun to incubate her egg on 22 April about six miles away from Mac's haunts, made this last captured of the nonmigratory wild cranes a bit player who was largely ignored in the drama that spelled hope then tragedy in crane reproduction.[46]

The loss of Rusty in 1950 was compounded the following year, when, after a period of drought, Crip and Josephine's nest was flooded. Elaborate precautions against further predation, including a smaller pen, new wire mesh, and poisoning indigenous raccoons, could not anticipate the vagaries of weather. Unsuccessful, the captive pair was summarily returned to New Orleans when zoo director George Douglass presented himself to the Aransas manager in December 1951 and announced that he had come to claim "his" birds.

Nineteen fifty-one also proved a bad year for wild whooping cranes; three died on or near Aransas. One whooper, failing to migrate, summered on Sundown Bay and apparently died of natural causes. Refuge workers came upon its decomposed body in September. Two other birds died from gunshot wounds. On 3 November 1951, observers found one of these, an adult, dragging an injured leg. They captured the emaciated crane near a freshwater source just over a week later, but it died. The body of a second whooper, whose foot had been blasted off, was retrieved from the west side of St. Charles Bay in mid-December. It, too, was emaciated and had probably starved to death. Total numbers fell to twenty-five individuals—six fewer than the previous fall.[47]

At the end of that decade, the crane population stood at thirty-three, only eight more than in 1951; thirty young had been counted on Aransas during this period, but most, it appeared, had not survived. In fact, a low of twenty-one birds (bringing no young) turned up in 1954. Irresponsible shooting and hardships imposed by prolonged drought combined to make survival of the species a matter for continued speculation.

Allen was fairly sure that numbers would show an upturn if only illegal hunting could be stamped out. He reported that, between 1950 and 1952, twenty-four birds had disappeared, or almost half the number that had died since records began in 1938 and double the previous fourteen-year average. One way to tackle illegal shooting was to redouble education. Nine million children enrolled in Audubon junior classes represented an investment for the future, thought Allen; as adults many would retain an interest in and affection for birds. He addressed his long-term message to schools, but immediate results came from a "whooper watch" that he helped to organize in the Plains states from Canada to Texas. People began to report and check sightings. More and more interested observers looked out for the migratory whoopers and contacted local newspapers urging respect for passing birds. This publicity portrayed the whooping crane as underdog. Whoopers were a beat away from extinction's brink and needed assistance, most especially as they passed along their flyway to winter quarters.[48]

On 17 October 1954, refuge employee Leslie E. Beaty witnessed what he claimed to be an actual arrival of whooping cranes. "Weary behavior" of three adults on Mustang Lake, where an observation tower was under construction, made him conclude that they had completed a long journey. An additional two pairs turned up later that day. But that year no young arrived. The new 47 1/2-foot-high wooden overlook at the head of Mustang Lake enabled visitors to glimpse a whooper pair, but observers noted no territorial activity, speculating that absence of young may have broken down traditional boundaries, or that a scarcity of rain and the low tides were forcing birds together, especially around freshwater ponds.[49]

Away from Aransas in 1954, stirrings among crane enthusiasts centered on the accidental discovery of nesting grounds in Canada's remote, untraveled Wood Buffalo National Park in Northwest Territories. This important event marked a conservation turning point. At long last, Canadian Wildlife Service experts were able to check on breeding success and monitor more closely the 2,500-mile-long flight track to the federal preserve near Austwell, Texas. Allen and colleagues in Canada were jubilant. The discovery of crane nests led to ground surveys and fostered cooperation at the international level to create safe passage for the whoopers.

Whooping cranes continued to require assistance in Aransas. Commercial fishermen teamed with sportsmen's groups to oppose "Project Photoflash" proposed by U.S. Air Force authorities in 1955. Project planners wanted to drop bombs from high altitudes over San Antonio Bay and film detonations. Opposition to this project reached high government levels when Canadian officials expressed concern to U.S. State Department representatives about the impending military activities, arguing that they would likely jeopardize the whooping cranes. Intergovernmental agreement shelved the proj-

ect, but Matagorda Island, winter home to a number of cranes, remained a bombing range on which live ammunition was deployed.[50]

In the 1950s, a combination of natural and induced events threw the whooper program into disarray but in the end served to head it in new directions. Droughty weather concentrated birds around choice feeding spots and also forced them into longer forays both on and beyond Aransas. A bill to enlarge this sanctuary in order to accommodate crane wanderings and provide space for future population increase died in Congress in late 1957. There was not enough political support, it seemed, to set aside extra habitat on barrier islands. An oil slick and another bird's death on Aransas in July 1957 added to a sense of gloom and frustration.

Uncertainties about the adequacies of winter space led to discussions of establishing a captive flock. The cause of aviculturalists and others interested in actually rearing cranes in order to save the species had received a filip when Josephine and Crip hatched out two eggs in 1956; one chick lived for forty-five days before dying from aspergillosis, a respiratory ailment. In 1957, the famous whoopers reared two young in Audubon Park.

This success spurred efforts to find a mate for a single bird, Rosie, who had hit a high wire and was picked up injured near Lampasas, Texas, in May 1956 and subsequently transported to the San Antonio Zoo. United States Fish and Wildlife Service officials reluctantly agreed to a proposal to capture a wild crane summering on Aransas as her mate. Employees chased and tackled their quarry rendered flightless due to a summer molt. After a few hours, however, the new captive collapsed and died from stress and exhaustion. Postmortem examination proved it to be a female! Fish and Wildlife Service officials were dismayed, and Audubonists were furious, complaining that such a madcap escapade in the full July heat was poorly planned and irresponsible. Efforts to bring wild birds together with the handful of crippled whoopers in zoos were put on hold.[51]

As if to challenge once more the belief that wild whoopers were finished, and that captive rearing provided the best hopes for survival, whoopers convoyed a record nine young (four sets of twins) from Canada to Texas in fall 1958. The population in Aransas rose to thirty-two birds.

Food Handouts in the 1960s

A decade's remorseless drought broke in grand style in 1959. Precipitation continued above normal and turned into a flood in September 1961 when Hurricane Carla

A crane family aloft over Aransas NWR with the young
bird following its parents. Photograph from Photo Researchers, Inc.

deluged Blackjack Peninsula, silting up several prime feeding areas for whoopers. Too much water in tidal marshes seemed to be as hard on cranes as too little. Interpreting unusual restlessness and movement as a sign that abnormally high water levels had made food unavailable, refuge staff began to set out grain.

Cranes readily took the free handouts. This decision to augment food supplies agreed with Allen's thinking and helped offset what he perceived as the service's lack of commitment to cranes and its general inattention. The new feeding program, he imagined, reflected perhaps a change of heart. Ironically, it began just when Bob Allen and Audubon Society director John Baker were retiring from full-time participation in conservation.[52]

Allen had based his suggestion for food supplements on ecological studies of blue crabs—key items for cranes. He recognized that at certain times, during midwinter especially, numbers of crabs and other marine invertebrates fell in response to low temperatures or persistent offshore winds that pushed water off the tidal flats. To compensate, whoopers foraged for other items over a wider area, including oak scrublands, where they were vulnerable to predators and to the guns of hunters. Handouts could keep the birds on the refuge under the watchful eyes of personnel.

In that first year, refuge authorities concluded that crabs and similar marine organisms were in short supply or were unobtainable because of flooding and they began to open bags of grain in crane territories along East Shore Road. Some bags were thrown from an airplane, and the manager reported white birds "rushing to the air dropped wheat." Whoopers learned quickly, and they continued to receive a variety of grains through the rest of the 1960s.[53]

In 1969, refuge manager Robert H. Shields and maintenance foreman Earl L. Benham published details about extra foods. They justified this "hands on" stance because of an apparent dearth of marine organisms and decided that handouts were useful in enticing birds away from dangerous situations, especially close to the busy Gulf Intracoastal Waterway. Such concerns reflected heavier than usual human activities near the refuge, for super-power jockeying affected even Aransas. The Cuban missile crisis intensified military training in the area, particularly on nearby Matagorda Island.[54]

In 1964, workers planted a 97-acre field with tidbits for whooping cranes. They had cleared an area beside East Shore Road close to several crane territories. Desultory efforts at growing crops in earlier years served to attract deer, javelina, hogs, and raccoons but no cranes,

so an eight-foot-high chain-link fence encircled the new field. This structure excluded deer and cattle; electrified wires stopped raccoons from climbing into the compound.

Crops, however, proved difficult to grow. A substrate of fine sand supported dense stands of shrubby live oak. Refuge staff bulldozed and burned this vegetation, then applied fertilizer to the poorly developed organic horizon, disked the field into strips, and intercropped beet, corn, and wheat between grass. They waited until September to plant nutritious foodstuffs in order to provide an autumn feast for whooping cranes. Large numbers of geese and up to nine hundred sandhill cranes visited the big enclosure; it was not until 17 November 1964 that observers glimpsed a whooping crane pair in the field. A total of ten white cranes foraged together at one time there—taking green wheat, hegari (sorghum), and corn. They didn't touch beets. As stocks dwindled, employees opened sacks of wheat and spread out up to one hundred bushels over thirty acres. Cranes fed on this extra grain from February 1965 onward.[55]

In fall 1965, thirty-six returning whoopers (plus 8 young) found two plots awaiting them. The original 97-acre field grew peanuts, sorghum, chufa, peas, and sweet potatoes; a mile to the north, a second field was planted in wheat, rye grass, peas, and clover. The staff, now turned farmers, tried to protect their hard work by placing propane-activated scare guns in both enclosures in order to ward off sandhills and geese until all the whooping cranes showed up. When they did arrive, the whoopers were unappreciative. Only one bird fed in the original field, amid flocks of sandhill cranes and geese. Observers concluded that white cranes preferred marshland foods except when loose grain was available, at which time whoopers readily flew in for a free meal.[56]

The following year, whoopers developed a taste for hegari and fieldpeas. As many as fifteen individual birds used the two fields, but three thousand sandhill cranes devoured most of the standing crop. At the end of November, wheat and milo were spread out at seven- to ten-day intervals and promptly attracted whoopers.

By April 1967, a record 1,330 whooper-use days was estimated for the planted enclosures, most between January and April. Personnel felt, however, that the high effort and cost of sowing feed did not really pay off; growing plants benefited geese, sandhill cranes, and other species more than whoopers. The big cranes still responded to grains spread in fields, particularly in coldest months, but not to planted crops.

In August 1967, Aransas workers planted again, sowing 50 acres of one field in corn and hegari, and the second in black-eyed cowpeas. Hurricane Beulah washed out the tender plants, flooded enclosures, and undid all their hard work. But, again, spread corn and milo attracted wintering whoopers. "As many as 34 cranes at one time were observed feeding on the seed during latter 1967," noted Shields and Benham.[57]

Crowding in the two enclosures worried refuge authorities. Like the twelve Louisiana cranes shot at Alcie Daigle's rice thresher near Louisiana's Sweet Lake, whoopers appeared just as gregarious and focused on spread grains. Such a concentration, people reckoned, was becoming unhealthy; it promoted "domestication within the wild flock." Associations between cranes and waterfowl in such spaces, where birds trampled seeds and muddied the ground with droppings, also increased chances for an outbreak of disease.

Management, it seemed, had succeeded beyond expectations by pulling thirty-four of forty-seven wild cranes off territories on tidal marshes. The key to this crane "round up" lay in spilling grains not in growing crops. The lesson was clear: in a crisis situation, such as a chemical spill along the public waterway, whooping cranes could be held along the marsh edge or attracted to the refuge interior by corn, sorghum, or wheat stored near the headquarters and scattered in safe areas. With the right stimulus whooping cranes would behave like big white Leghorn chickens!

Shields and Benham agreed with Allen that there were times when cranes "may need supplemental food while on their wintering area." But they concluded that such handouts "should be employed only during those years and at precise times of food scarcity." What constituted scarcity? Allen had pointed to blue crab declines but noted that a switch to acorns or crawfish in freshwater ponds might carry birds through. What was needed was a more precise understanding of patterns of feeding and of food availability. Nobody had delved into whooper life history since Robert P. Allen had studied winter food habits in the late 1940s. Another biologist, David Blankinship, working like his predecessor for the National Audubon Society, picked up where Allen had left off. His investigations dominated research on Aransas in the 1970s.[58]

Consolidation in the 1970s

During the 1970s crane numbers grew. The wild population increased by 33 percent from fifty-seven birds in fall 1970, to seventy-six ten years later. This increase,

however, was neither continuous nor gradual. In fact the number of cranes fell during the first half of the decade, dropping to a low of forty-nine, before rebounding as a result of two bumper seasons: forty-nine white birds returned towing eight young in 1975, and in 1976 all fifty-seven survivors flew back to Texas again, accompanied by a record twelve chicks. Water conditions on Canada's nesting grounds were excellent and favored chick survival. At Aransas, staff set fire to parts of the interior uplands to open up areas in which cranes could forage; and they continued to spread out grain. Whoopers prospered; numbers reached seventy and have remained above that mark ever since.[59]

Three events in Aransas characterize this era of consolidation. First, a land-use plan established priorities for manipulating refuge habitat. Second, behavior research sponsored by the National Audubon Society shed new light upon crane biology, including territoriality and food preferences. Biologist David Blankinship carefully observed and noted crane activities. Third, new acreages became available for cranes as federal land was turned over to the Fish and Wildlife Service on nearby Matagorda Island.

In 1970, Aransas staff took stock of refuge policy. In their opinion, a generous schedule for grazing livestock, under which 2,500 or more head of cattle roamed widely, had brought about overgrazing and excessive trampling. Certain areas, specifically tidal flats, should be retired from pasturing cattle, they argued, and fees per head should be raised on the remainder. Within eighteen months, cattle numbers had dropped by almost two-thirds. Aransas Refuge was also partitioned into units, one of which was a 14,128-acre "Whooping Crane Management Unit."

This unit encompassed prime crane habitat along Blackjack Peninsula's east shore and included a marine impoundment and the two fields previously sown with crane foods. The objective was to manage both peninsula marshes and interior uplands, especially those pastures closest to wetlands, for the whoopers. Thick woody vegetation was burned off to enable cranes to forage widely. Grains planted in the big fields near the marshland edge, plus a marine impoundment that staff constructed nearby and into which they pumped a concentrated mix of natural aquatic foods, showed the lengths to which workers were prepared to go in order to manage habitat intensively. Previous anxieties about attracting, and crowding cranes and making them dependent, were subordinated to the desire to make sure that the wild flock would return to Canada's nesting grounds in prime health.

Cattle were excluded from this special crane unit because they grazed heavily, disturbed vegetation, caved in warrens used by crabs and crayfish, muddied or stirred up pools and sloughs, and required the presence of cattle hands working from horseback or jeep. People in and near the marshes disturbed the white cranes.

Livestock continued to graze a backland 21,000-acre "Indigenous Species Unit," divided into nine pastures in which grazing was rotated and brush mowed to favor white-tailed deer. Habitat for native mammals existed in the "Wildlife Interpretation Unit," consisting of 8,700 acres along the west shore of San Antonio Bay, including the headquarters complex. This was, and still is, the portion of Aransas that most visitors experience. Workers built a tour loop, intersected by trails and overlooks, and kept out cattle. Mowing created grassy openings amidst thickets to provide visitors with glimpses of deer, javelina, and wild turkeys, and perhaps an armadillo digging for bugs in the sandy soil.[60]

In 1970, for the second consecutive year, a saltwater impoundment inland from Sundown Bay and served by a 36-inch pipeline was filled up. The purpose was to pump brackish water into a shallow 60-acre pond located in the crane unit and trap a "soup" of crabs, fish, and shrimp for whooping cranes. Staff began the project in October 1969 and spent three months filling the impoundment but waited in vain for whoopers to use it. Grain scattered around the edges eventually attracted birds, but they seemed reluctant to explore the deeper crab-filled waters. After a drawdown in March, however, thirty whooping cranes began to feed in this pond. Birds picked over a veritable smorgasbord almost daily until they set out for Canada a month later. "On one occasion 48 of the 56 cranes were observed in the impoundment," noted manager Gordon Hansen.

Undeterred by such obvious crowding, staff reactivated the feeding pond in mid-October 1970. Initially, they found it difficult to fill as bay tides were exceptionally low, but, after water levels had risen, pumping was more effective and soon filled it up. Whoopers, however, failed to use the pool, preferring to snag morsels in the marshes. In subsequent years, although dikes and a pump remained intact, observers reckoned that an abundance of natural foods made the facility redundant, and it was reserved for emergency use only.[61]

Although they ended the impoundment, workers continued to dispense grains and grew crops in some years. The semi-official Whooping Crane Advisory Group supported and encouraged the practice of food supple-

ments. However, refuge personnel knew how costly and time consuming it was, especially planting crops, and, although they made strenuous efforts to return the flock to Canada in excellent health, other waterbirds, notably geese, ducks, and sandhill cranes, usually got the bulk of the food.

Other things than increased costs in time and money contributed to a gradual reduction in handouts. The bumper acorn crop in 1972 attracted whooping cranes into uplands and helped reinforce a program of burning thickets to make acorns and other food items more accessible. Prescribed burning also offered a much more inexpensive method to develop extra habitat and, therefore, allowed staff to rely less on crops.[62]

As the 1970s progressed, U.S. Fish and Wildlife workers burned more and more of the crane unit. In 1976, for example, they torched more than 2,000 acres, and about thirty birds responded to a 300-acre burn in a south section of Blackjack Peninsula. In early December 1977, staff noted twenty-four whoopers stalking across an area they had set on fire a month or so earlier. This practice of fall burning invariably drew in cranes to gobble up acorns in blackened areas.[63]

In his 1980 annual report, manager Frank Johnson noted that "prescribed burning continues to be the most desirable method, both from an economic and ecologic viewpoint, of maintaining Peninsula grasslands in an open or at least savannah-like condition." In that year, he and others set fire to more than 3,000 acres on south and east segments. Experience suggested that winter burns every three years or so in any one section encouraged a prairie-type response consisting of tall grasses—bluestems, Indian grass, switch grass—mixed with croton, goldenrod, and other forbs, and legumes, such as partridge pea and wild indigo. Wildlife profited from this native plant association, and live oak, while suppressed, grew acorns useful to cranes. The two fields were burned, not cultivated, in 1980.[64]

Another reason for terminating the feeding project included David Blankinship's assessment that plenty of natural foods existed out in the marshes. This Rockport-based researcher began a new study of whooping cranes in November 1970. The wild population had more than doubled in the thirty years since Allen's initial studies, although shell dredging, oil and gas production, and tourist and commercial use of the Gulf Intracoastal Waterway had expanded enormously in and around Aransas. Blankinship set about rechecking Allen's findings and examined the impacts of human activities on the winter needs of cranes. He constructed eight stations to sample food organisms, also testing for possible contamination.

Hurricane Celia whirled by on 3 August 1970, producing 130-mph winds in Corpus Christi and a tidal surge of about nine feet, which destroyed the impoundment on Aransas. This tropical depression carried in sparse amounts of rain, so that when the whoopers flew in, they faced lower than normal bay levels and high salinity, which had depressed the blue crab population in the tidal flats. Hungry whooping cranes shifted from the marshes to shallow bays where Blankinship observed them feeding on five species of clam. On 10 September the following year, however, Hurricane Fern flooded Aransas as it hit the coast a few miles south in Rockport. This storm lowered salinity levels and enabled large numbers of crabs to scuttle throughout the marshes. This wet weather cycle persisted throughout 1972 and once more crabs became a staple food for cranes.

In fall 1972, good habitat conditions provided little solace when thirteen whooping cranes failed to return from Canada. Blankinship flew down the coast into Mexico in search of missing birds, but he found none. This loss was especially galling because that summer Canadian biologists had spotted sixteen nests with thirty-one eggs, but only five chicks made it through to Texas. This small group of surviving chicks and the failure of thirteen older whoopers to return reduced the overall population to fifty-one birds, eight short of the previous spring. Experts speculated that heavy storms had killed migrating subadults as they headed north but had left a core of breeders intact. To depress the 1972 situation further, an adult with a chick disappeared in November, barely two weeks after arriving. Another adult disappeared and was presumed dead in February 1973. Its mate and chick consorted with another crane; the birds paired and chased off the youngster. Observers were relieved to note, however, that the lone chick was quite capable of fending for itself, watching it "catch 9 blue crabs in about 10 minutes." This youngster teamed up with two other birds, and it was one of the last whooping cranes to head north at the end of April.[65]

Blankinship continued to record details, noting that some birds inhabited wetlands on Welder Point, north of the refuge across San Antonio Bay. He also checked reports of stray whoopers along the lower coast, and even as far away as El Paso, but found nothing.[66]

Two aspects—territoriality and food habits—drew most of this biologist's attention. He observed that several pairs or family groups shared territories or at least tolerated other cranes on areas that they normally occupied along the mainland shore. Crowding did not appear to explain this unexpected activity, as his calculations of territory size in 1971–72 agreed with Allen's—each pair or family occupied roughly 420 acres. Some birds appeared simply more tolerant than others. When defensive actions were called for, larger males usually took the lead. Females associated more with their chicks, who begged for food with continuous high-pitched squeaks, or "peeps." Such pestering did not always sit well with some fathers, noted Blankinship, who saw one male grab his youngster by the upper neck, bringing a temporary halt to its supplications.

Blue crabs made up the bulk of crane food in early winters of 1973 and 1974. As bay levels dropped, birds waded out to dig for clams. Blankinship observed that bivalves appeared important during periods of low water when back marshes were drier and at times of high salinity when blue crab numbers fell (as, for example, in winter 1970–71). Both clams and smaller crabs were swallowed whole, although whoopers often carried larger crabs to a convenient spot and hacked them apart, sometimes leaving the claws.[67]

Cranes were able to gobble down clams at better than one per minute, reported Blankinship, who timed such feeding activities. This was a remarkable rate when one considers that clams inhabit underwater burrows in bay sands and require digging out. Often a crane must thrust its head entirely underwater for many seconds, probing and pulling the clams up to swallow whole with a slight backward tilt of the head. Crustaceans, including fiddler crabs and mud shrimp, also figured significantly in bayside diets.

On tidal flats, red-colored wolfberries (*Lycium carolinianum*) grow abundantly in fall and cranes feed heavily on them. Inland, acorns, freshwater crayfish, and, occasionally, snakes provide sustenance. Blankinship did not find fish important. Allen had noted that whooping cranes took a "good many," and he identified three species, black chubb, striped mullet, and sheepshead minnow; but he, too, did not think them critical. Cranes, he wrote, "will stride through a school of mullet in the water almost up to their bellies to reach a shallow area where decapods [crabs and shrimp] are readily captured." Like his predecessor, Blankinship concluded that whooping cranes drew heavily on five or six items; blue crabs and clams headed this list, while eels (omitted by Allen) and reptiles appeared to be more chance prey.[68]

MATAGORDA

From mainland point,
                    compass
        fix and
boat

hits that pencil
line of grass
        dunes,
            yucca, some
mesquite,
        grounding
            you in
                solitude

where bugle
birds winter as
        wetland
sheep.

    No English
blackface, no Saint
Kilda browns,

but flying weatherbacks
who teach red
young

to graze the flats
and search out
        clams

til they turn salt
white and
head for spring,

    the airscape
left open and
bare.

Matagorda Island

Our skiff slices across San Antonio Bay toward Matagorda Island, last barrier of sand before the open Gulf. At Christmas time, this nursery for marine life has playthings strewn all over its surface: hundreds of squat ducks, tiny pinhead grebes, and rubber-necked cormorants. Black cormorants are a long snake that dissolves upward as score after score lumber into the air. White and brown pelicans glance lugubriously at our racing boat as they flap heavily overhead. A tern splinters the thick surface in a shiver of feathers and is gone, as buoys, platforms, and other debris of technology flash past.

Landfall is Panther Point, a fishhook-shaped promontory home for a crane family. We ground in an isolated spot for winter cranes, where sea and land have made an uneasy truce. The Panther Point trio loafs on the bay's fringe, fluffing out feathers as a warm sun melts a rime of ice in the cordgrass. The chick, like its parents, is unbanded. It leans forward, ready to fly, relaxes, then scrambles after its parents who beat away with wingtips virtually touching pellucid waters. We have come too close. The youngster glides momentarily after every eight or ten wingbeats until all three cranes land a half mile away toward the northern end of their large territory.

At such a distance whooping cranes stand out clearly on tidal marshes. Apart from a few yucca and mesquite only the backdrop of grass-covered dunes gives scale and perspective to Matagorda's emptiness. In this landscape, egrets, pelicans, and cranes are giants.

North of the Panther Point family we discover two subadults feeding on wolfberries. One wears Yellow–Blue/white spiral leg bands while its consort has none. The banded crane wintered here with its parents in 1984 and has found its way home. (Tom Stehn uses capital letters in referring to colors on the larger 80-mm bands and does not capitalize colors of stripes on smaller 40-mm bands. Hence, the name of this subadult male is abbreviated Y–Bwsp, referring to a large yellow band on his left leg and a large blue band threaded by a downward white line on his right; *B* at the beginning of a name or standing alone always stands for blue, while *b* in the middle always stands for black.)

Near Twin Lakes, there is another trio whose chick has red/blue–Orange bands; they stalk shimmering marshes. Wanting to see if the adults bear leg bands, refuge biologist Tom Stehn trudges after the retreating birds. The first six feet of tidal edge is massed with decayed vegetation piled up by a recent norther. Here and

A juvenile whooper, 76-7, in flight over Bosque del Apache NWR. Photograph by Rod C. Drewien.

there a jelly fish is stranded in sea oxeye. A few red wolf-berries serve as morsels for cranes and waterfowl. The high, deliberate step of a crane makes it surefooted in this tangle.

Twin Lakes is alive. A bittern jumps up from thick cordgrass, while a tricolored heron scurries along a narrow lead, surprising crabs. Things are in constant motion. Rafts of wigeon, pintail, and gadwall upend in the shallows. Bufflehead ducks whir past, black-and-white males busily tracing wide air circles before crashing heavily into the lagoon. A dozen avocets, loafing with heads tucked into their backs, begin to stretch, preparing to sieve for food. Goose and distant gull calls erase silence. Marsh-burnt greens, browns, and yellows glimmer in growing day.

Tom slogs back satisfied that one adult wears above his foot a narrow silver-colored identity tag stamped with numbers. This crane has lost its big color bands, which made it easier to identify, so that watchers were speculating that it is a new bird. The puzzle is solved; this is the habitual pair.

After swinging away from the direction of the old bombing range back to Panther Point and skimming off southward, we spot another whooping crane pair on a slough bank where other white species congregate in a waterbird frieze. There are three species of egrets—some keening forward, others with necks raised or heads bent—all still, intent on spearing food. Suddenly, four white pelicans clatter up and break the frozen scene. Egrets follow, but cranes remain, standing impassively 250 yards behind the bird flock that was feasting in this marsh.

A third crane family, consisting of a chick (Orange–Yellow), a male (Red–red/white), and female (nil–high silver), calls loudly and chooses to walk away, not fly, as we bounce up Cottonwood Bayou. One bird picks up its mate's call so quickly that the low-high combination sounds as if bugled by one bird. This is a well-known pair, being in one sense sentries on the Gulf. Cottonwood Bayou, Panther Point, and other barrier island territories represent the most easterly outposts for wild whooping cranes.

A choppy surface bangs the skiff as we cross back to False Live Oak Point on the Aransas Refuge for calmer waters in the protected Intracoastal Waterway. Cormorants have vanished, but flocks of gun-shy scaup replace them and whirl up quickly as our craft surges by.

Matagorda Island cranes roam enormous territories by mainland standards. As the total increases, there is a tendency to crowd together, slicing into older home areas. Even so, Matagorda's solitude offers ample space for cranes. It is hard to understand why more birds do not inhabit barrier islands. Expansion on them is slow. Whooping cranes occupying these remote marshes do not face disturbance as do birds along the Intracoastal close to the mainland shore. They are sentinels on the edge of a continent: cranes that few people know.

Officially designating space for whooping cranes has been debated among federal agencies and between U.S. and Texas authorities for the past twenty years or so. Recently, with Nature Conservancy assistance, Matagorda Island's southern end, directly opposite the Aransas refuge mainland, has been set aside for cranes. There are two reasons for this push for land acquisition. First, whoopers gravitate naturally into relatively secluded reaches of sand barrier marshes and have done so under adverse conditions, including disturbance, noise, and risks associated with military maneuvers. As Canada-U.S. totals increase, more and more marsh spaces will be required for these winter residents who spill over from their traditional core along Blackjack Peninsula.

Second, Matagorda Island offers insurance against chemicals emptied into the Gulf Intracoastal Waterway. If such an accident occurs, cranes immediately adjacent to that water would take the brunt of poisons. More-distant members of the Aransas flock, such as the approximately thirty-five to forty who live beside the ribbon of dune comprising Matagorda and San José islands next to the ocean, stand a better chance, although they are never more than three or four miles away from barges chugging across San Antonio Bay.

Most of these remote Texas barrier islands were, and still are, undeveloped marsh and grazing lands. Matagorda Island is a low, exposed, sand-built island, thirty-five miles long and in some places barely a mile wide. Meandering Cedar Bayou is its southern boundary. Pass Cavallo, a second major ship channel between Texas bays and the Gulf of Mexico, separates the northern end of Matagorda Island from a similarly narrow-necked mainland peninsula. Whoopers frequent western bay-facing wetlands on both Matagorda and San José and set up territories in a mosaic of sinuous sloughs,

lagoons, oxbows, and leads of brackish water that snake into a twenty-foot-high backbone of beach ridges. Thousands of gulls, terns, shorebirds, and waterfowl remain for days or weeks, and island marshes provide habitat for endangered or rare species, such as brown pelicans, reddish egrets, and roseate spoonbills. In fall, peregrine falcons navigate by following the crescent-shaped sea beach as they migrate toward Mexico. These speedy predators twist and turn among flocks of sandpipers and toy with other migrants until they find one to feast on, perhaps a grosbeak or kestrel, knocked down by murderous talons.[69]

Ownership of Matagorda Island has been in federal, state, and, until recently, private hands. In November 1940, the U.S. government used its powers of eminent domain to purchase through condemnation about 19,000 acres of privately owned property. The federal government also leased about 16,500 acres of state land and more than 11,000 acres in the south belonging to Toddie Lee Wynne, a Dallas-based oilman. Under federal control, much of Matagorda Island became a military range upon which a small air base was built. The Air Training Command of the U.S. Army Air Corps operated this facility through November 1945, causing Aransas Refuge manager James Stevenson to grumble about noise and disturbance. His Aransas report noted in October 1941 that "aeroplanes [are] in constant flight over Austwell and cadets diving planes at geese have driven them silly."[70]

The military range was deactivated after World War II but reconstituted in 1949 when the U.S. Air Force Strategic Air Command took over. During the war in southeast Asia, Matagorda Island was the only "live" practice range in America, proving especially attractive because its marsh terrain replicated parts of Vietnam. The Air Force invested at least $5.5 million in improvements and housed dozens of workers on the island's north end.

In the mid 1960s, Texas began to push for more authority over portions of Matagorda Island leased out to the Air Force. Initial efforts to open up state marshlands for recreational use failed, but the military decreased its activities and ceased bombing runs in winter months when whoopers were around. As a result of a memorandum of agreement with the U.S. Air Force "allowing certain management activities for whooping cranes" on the Air Force range, signed in November 1971 and put into operation in 1973, half of Matagorda Island came under the jurisdiction of Aransas NWR. A year later, military authorities made public a decision to close down facilities, paving the way for the U.S. Department of Interior to take control.[71]

Whooper protection lay behind the military's decision to transfer authority to the U.S. Fish and Wildlife Service. The state of Texas, however, continued to press for recreational access. Land Commissioner Bob Armstrong argued that Matagorda Island should become a state park while accommodating needs of whooping cranes. The U.S. Air Force gave the General Services Administration responsibility for final disposition and both the Department of Interior and the state of Texas applied for ownership. Texas Attorney General John Hill took steps to cancel the federal lease over state lands—baylands used by cranes—and pressed the case for state ownership.

In 1977, a tentative settlement offered two-thirds of federal lands to Texas, retaining one-third adjacent to the Aransas Refuge. Governor Dolph Brisco rejected GSA's offer, and negotiations continued until January 1981, when Interior Secretary James G. Watt indicated more flexibility about turning over federal lands to states. This included a portion of Matagorda used by whooping cranes, which fell under the jurisdiction of Aransas Refuge.[72]

Environmental groups challenged Watt. They were unhappy to see nationally owned lands turned over to Texas Parks and Wildlife whose record, they claimed, was uneven in conserving and managing its own state lands effectively. Only by substantially agreeing with Interior Department strategy to subordinate activities on Matagorda to the needs of rare and endangered wildlife did state wildlife authorities dampen increasing criticism.

Under terms of the agreement between the Department of Interior and the state of Texas signed by James Watt in December 1982, a cooperative management plan was established whereby through an easement Texas Parks and Wildlife combined 19,000 acres of federal lands with 24,893 acres of state lands as a "Matagorda Island State Park and Wildlife Management Area." The U.S. Fish and Wildlife Service exchanged a similar conservation easement with the state. This elaborate decision solved tensions that had spanned three U.S. presidencies. The critical factor was that state lands used by whooping cranes fell under the National Wildlife Refuge Administration Act.[73]

Other than the Wynne Ranch on Matagorda's southern tip, there has been no private, commercial, or industrial development on the island. Matagorda will not become another "Coney Island," as some feared. Recreational facilities exist on the northern end of the island, away from prime whooper marshes, and most of the Gulf beach remains in a primitive, undeveloped state. Moreover, through the auspices of the Nature Conservancy, critical habitat on the Wynne Ranch across from Aransas has been turned over to the U.S. Fish and Wildlife Service. In 1986, the Conservancy signed a purchase agreement for this 11,502-acre ranch and, as part of the Aransas Refuge, the Fish and Wildlife Service has made payments to the Wynne family.

As whooping crane numbers grow, Matagorda Island will become a larger stronghold. Today, about a quarter of the flock forage in these marshlands and there is every reason to expect that state-owned habitat will be occupied and that potential conflicts between cranes and recreationists can be resolved.[74]

In April 1987, Texas authorities requested the Fish and Wildlife Service to consider interim state management of the Wynne Ranch. Texas has proposed to purchase this wetland area, although in 1988 federal authorities made a substantial payment toward the estimated $13 million cost for this new section of the Aransas Refuge. An additional 734 acres on the Lamar Peninsula is also scheduled as refuge property.[75]

ARANSAS NORTHER

October rain
is sharp glass,
  blasted in tumult.

  Gulls scrabble
sand, terns hunker
tormented,
   songbirds wrack.

The shout
that all whirling things
start up. Wind

whips leaves,
    zings
  wires. Palms
lash the air,
needing legs.

This sky hurl breathes
  cranes, whose gutteral
chevrons will
sound

the change . . . to wintertime.

2. The 1980s

Whooping cranes took forever to get here this fall. With only 27 cranes counted on a November 10th aerial census, this was the second slowest migration on record in the last 30 years! Then the cranes fell out of the sky, riding north winds associated with the first arctic cold fronts that reached Texas November 11 and 13. An aerial census on November 18th counted 65 adults and 19 chicks. An additional family was confirmed the following day, bringing the total to 67 + 20 = 87. The 20 chicks is a record! Three unbanded chicks reached Aransas. Since the Canadians only knew of two, this proved that 21 chicks had fledged from 29 nests. Only one pair expected to bring a banded chick turned up without their juvenile. . . . The whooping crane population at the end of 1986 stood at 89 adults and 20 chicks for a total of 109 cranes. On January 30, 1987, chick WBW–0 (1986) was confirmed present with sandhills near Hydro, Oklahoma. This was the one chick banded by the Canadians that had failed to show up on the wintering grounds. It is the 21st chick that fledged in 1986 and crane number 110 in the Wood Buffalo/Aransas flock. (Aransas National Wildlife Refuge, Annual Narrative Report, Calendar Year 1986, pp. 42, 43, 47)

In 1980, manager Frank Johnson wrote optimistically about saying "our goodbyes in late April to 76 adult-plumaged birds, hoping to see them return 80-strong in the fall." His buoyancy seemed justified. That summer the Canadian Wildlife Service counted nineteen nests and spotted sixteen chicks. The record eighty mark seemed a sure bet. Then the situation took a more ominous turn. By banding time in August the tally was down to six young and, although two unbanded youngsters made it through to Aransas, two of the newly banded birds failed to show up. The final count was a disappointing seventy-eight cranes (72 adults and 6 young).

This tone of expectation and optimism followed by exasperation at less-than-hoped-for numbers springs out of refuge reports time after time from earliest years.

The manager and staff monitor cranes closely, watch them spiral upward into spring skies, and wait. Unusual reports are generally bad—a bird crippled after hitting a power line or incapacitated by disease—but as June and July come and go, they listen for information about nests in Canada and the count of cinnamon-colored young that experts band. The people far away in Aransas calculate new numbers, speculate about how many cranes will arrive, check and recheck reports of white birds heading southward, and drive out to the marshes, waiting for their tired charges to swing down over peninsula live oaks into winter territories.

With an increase of two birds in 1980, the trend was in the right direction, but progress was painfully slow. Big jumps in 1975 and 1976 by eight and twelve birds, respectively, had raised expectations of similar or greater progress in the 1980s. This hoped-for leap did not occur in 1980, or in the next year, or in the one after that. In fact, the total of wild cranes flying between the United States and Canada fell to seventy-three birds in 1981 and 1982. Nineteen eighty-four finally brought an end to this decline with an increase of eleven whoopers. Growth continued in 1985 and in the summer of 1986, when a record eighteen young birds were banded (from a total of 21 chicks), the population topped the long-sought-after one hundred mark. That fall, Johnson was elated as numbers on the Aransas flyway topped the record (96) for the previous spring and continued to climb. Birds piled into the refuge after dawdling in warm weather far to the north. In fall 1986, migration was unusually late; cranes lingered in nesting grounds well into November, then pushed hard for Texas as winter's impending onset impelled them southward.

Manager Frank Johnson died suddenly in December 1986, but he knew that a record number of birds had reached Aransas. During his term as the eleventh manager of the Texas refuge, the whooping crane population had more than doubled. In 1973, Johnson's first year, forty-seven white birds and two young showed up. In 1986, his last year, ninety white birds plus twenty-one young flew south. In this thirteen-year tenure, longest for any manager, Frank Johnson created opportunities both for cranes and for people fascinated by them. He assisted staff and researchers, welcomed the public, and cemented support for whoopers in local communities, such as Austwell, Tivoli, and Rockport.

In the 1970s and 1980s, a great deal of new data from banding and experimental tracking were generated. But Johnson was not enthusiastic about fitting colored leg bands or radios to the whoopers; he preferred to see them left alone or, rather, approached with regard for their own ways and agendas. Johnson chose to assist the flock in less direct ways, by managing habitat and affording protection. While he did not oppose collecting data from banding or radiotelemetry, he gave Aransas biologists full rein to explore the lives of wild cranes by encouraging his staff to get into the field. Frank Johnson was above all a great facilitator. Experienced in the ways of government, knowing how to tackle problems and crises associated with animal comings and goings, hunting on the refuge, and running a 50,000-acre preserve, he remained humorously unruffled and upbeat. Wild cranes received essential help from this most thoughtful, urbane manager, and in return they gave him great satisfaction and joy.

In his 1980 survey of other animals in trouble, manager Johnson painted a mixed picture. The American alligator had a poor nesting season due to dry conditions. Its population of about 150, however, appeared stable and was relatively secure within refuge borders, although some harassment occurred on more inaccessible Matagorda Island.

Numbers of marine turtles washing up on that island's Gulf beach fluctuated. Between July 1978 and December 1980, fifty-six turtles, mostly loggerheads with a few Kemp's ridleys, turned up dead or moribund along a 26-mile stretch south of Pass Cavallo. October, June, and March (in that order) were the months for the most beachings. People speculated about the mortality, presuming that shrimp trawls snagged and drowned migrating turtles. Fishermen also cut them from nets and left them to die. Most cadavers were immature animals. There was no evidence of breeding on Matagorda, although some old-timers remembered huge reptiles lumbering up the beaches to dig nests.[1]

Johnson reported that brown pelicans had a "splendid year" in 1980. Seventy-six young fledged from rookeries along the Coastal Bend, including twenty-two from Carroll Island next to the Aransas Refuge. This increase reversed declines of the late 1960s and early 1970s when virtually all nests failed due to effects from pesticides.

During the same period bald eagles stopped nesting on the refuge and became only irregular visitors. Illegal shooting, disturbance, and pesticide residues factored into their plight. The last eagle nest was reported in 1971, although twenty-six records of breeding in six different sites go back to 1937. Between four and ten eagles often wintered on Aransas in earlier years.

The decline of the bald eagle was widespread. Numbers fell in Texas until only half a dozen pairs bred in the early 1970s. Survivors constructed bulky nests in riparian woodlands on the coastal prairie. Although no nests were on the refuge after 1971, two or three pairs existed within thirty miles of it and almost all nests are located between Rockport and Houston. Bald eagle numbers have begun to build back. In 1985 and 1986, biologists recorded seventeen active nests in the state, but our national symbol has not yet returned to breed on Aransas.[2]

Like whooping cranes, Attwater's prairie chickens have received enormous attention and time from refuge personnel. During the 1940s a few birds lingered on grassy openings within Aransas National Wildlife Refuge. A high of nine was counted in fall 1942, and additional pairs or single birds appeared for two or three years after that until the species disappeared. On 29 December 1965, a single bird near an interior pond was the first recorded since 1946.

In 1967, the Meredith Tatton family donated 7,568 acres of grassland northwest of the refuge. A small flock of twenty-five to thirty-five Attwater's prairie chickens roamed this area, creating new opportunities for protection. Enthusiasts appointed a subcommittee consisting of the refuge manager, two biologists, and range specialists to prepare a management plan for Aransas' new Tatton Unit. The objective was to build up bird numbers whose stronghold lay farther inland. Two thousand acres of open coastal grasslands seemed to be good habitat, so experts planned a number of measures, including grazing schedules, food plots, and control of predators, but not all were implemented.

Chicken management on the Tatton Unit has continued to pose a challenge. In consultation with range experts, refuge staff have tried to make this grassland increasingly attractive. They have mowed certain areas and placed mounds of shells in order to create "booming" sites on which breeding males congregate in order to court females. They have moved cattle on and off certain pastures to maximize a variety of grasses and cover. They have also tried to eradicate weeds, specifically spiny aster and groundsel, which invade habitat.

Success has been hard to measure. One good sign occurred in 1976 when observers noted "booming." As many as twenty-five male prairie chickens stomped and strutted in early spring, and, as weather conditions remained warm and dry, the staff hoped the birds had a good nesting year. A total of forty-eight males returned to the communal booming grounds in 1977, leading to estimates of an overall population of ninety six. That year, however, April and May proved wet and nest success was low.[3]

But workers took heart. Efforts to improve habitat seemed to be paying off and they turned more attention to prescribed burning. The 1976 report noted that the "future of burning in the refuge's grassland management program seems to have secured approval at last," after years of vegetation control by grazing livestock, cutting, and spraying. In that year more than 2,000 acres were scorched, including 343 acres on the Tatton Unit.[4]

Fire management is an issue about which people disagree. Setting fires was and is a dangerous, seemingly "unnatural" thing to do on open land. To burn successfully and safely, conditions must be dry with no wind shifts expected, and a crew must be prepared to act quickly if flames jump boundaries and run out of control. Due to risks, Aransas staffers have hesitated to torch large acreages, preferring to control woody plants by cutting. Some people point to dangers from fires that can race unchecked and engulf neighboring rangelands. Others note, however, how burns eliminate parasites and weeds and that a variety of grasses and forbs draw upon nutrients freed up by fires. Grasses regenerate in greater profusion after such burns, they argue. Reliance on more frequent use of fire has proved important for both prairie chickens and whooping cranes.

In March 1979, refuge biologist Steve Labuda, observing twenty-five cocks and three hens, calculated that fifty to sixty chickens existed on Aransas. In June, he came across a brood of six quail-sized young. The following year, the population approximated seventy-six birds and dry conditions favored nest success. In 1981, 1,200 acres of the Tatton Unit went up in flames and staff burned an additional 5,800 acres on the refuge. Prairie chickens turned up in two burned areas, but groundsel resprouted and drought caused a probable decline in population.

This downward trend has persisted. In 1982, about eighteen birds lived on the Aransas Tatton Unit—half of a thirteen-year average. Gamebird experts consider this coastal lowland to be marginal habitat: it is too wet and flood prone, and such plants as spiny aster and shrubby groundsels have spread markedly. Grazing, fallows, and burning have not always benefited prairie chickens. In 1985, sixteen birds (down from 24) were counted, in 1986 the number increased marginally to twenty-two, but in 1987 it fell to an estimated ten chickens and remains low.[5]

After 1980–81, for four successive years, numbers of whooping cranes at Aransas hovered in the seventies. Drier-than-usual summers in Canada did not favor the survival of young, and two additional events also led people to speculate about additional factors limiting population buildup. The first one involved radio-banding chicks.

Back in 1977, Canadian Wildlife Service researchers began concerted efforts to capture cranes every year in order to place colored leg bands on well-grown but still flightless young. They usually fix a colored plastic band to each leg above the tibia-tarsal joint and refer to each bird by its color combination; Blue–White, for example, is a whooper carrying a large (80-mm wide) blue band on its left leg and a large white one on its right. The objective of this banding is to permit researchers to follow an individual's activities as it grows and matures. This practice has generated new, important biological data about crane behavior.

In 1981, Canadian biologists placed miniature radio transmitters on a number of chicks. Six of the ten whoopers banded in the summer of 1983 carried radios. An airplane check in late August turned up only seven birds from a total of thirteen that had been counted, and only two radio-tagged birds were still alive. Wolves, it appeared, had seized the other four. Some people suspected that this instrumentation was making young cranes more vulnerable to predation. A data check revealed that, while cranes with colored plastic bands did not have unusually high mortality, between 1981 and 1983 twelve of fifteen chicks fitted with radios died or disappeared, whereas four of five banded but not instrumented survived (through to 1986). A difference of 20 percent survival versus 80 percent, albeit with low overall numbers, was cause for concern.[6]

Summer 1983 was the first in which Canadian Wildlife Service spotters Ernie Kuyt and Paul Goossen came upon a color-marked breeding pair. A 1977 female (Red–Green) and a 1979 male (Blue/white/Blue–green/red)

Red/white/Red—Orange and its unbanded consort stand alertly in shallow bay water at Aransas. Photograph by John Jefferson.

nested unsuccessfully; they failed to establish a territory on Aransas that fall and tolerated the presence of younger subadults. Two teams tracked radioed birds from Aransas to Canada in spring 1984, noting the activities of a chick turned loose by its parents in Saskatchewan and the movements of two subadults into Wood Buffalo. A record twenty-nine nests were counted and thirteen of nineteen chicks were banded. But no birds received radios, and biologists limited observations to those survivors still carrying operational transmitters.[7]

A second factor limiting population buildup involved disease. Two young cranes died on the Aransas Refuge in January 1983, an unfortunate but not unique event. The first casualty was a radio-tagged chick whose partial remains were found on Matagorda Island. Transmitter signals led refuge employees to a pile of feathers, which gave no clues as to why the bird died.

The other crane, white/red—Green, a young female from Sundown Bay on the refuge mainland, also carrying a radio, was a more clear-cut case. Howard E. Hunt, a graduate researcher from Texas A&M University studying crane use on the Aransas uplands, was surprised when this lone youngster visited backlands on four separate occasions toward the end of January. Unaccompanied, the chick paced about looking for acorns. As curious observers approached, it flew only a short distance, settled, then proceeded to forage some more.

On 2 February 1983, the young female chick's body lay on the uplands; teeth marks indicated that a coyote had grabbed it by the neck. Tests suggested that avian tuberculosis had struck white/red–Green, apparently causing it to wander away or be rejected by usually protective parents. Other young cranes have died or disappeared in winter in Aransas, but none has been monitored as closely, nor has an affliction been as clearly established as for the 1982-born female. People have watched for such telltale signs of illness ever since.

During the winter of 1983–84, veteran crane pilot Bob Tanner completed twenty-five years of aerial surveys by flying twenty-nine weekly sorties. His Cessna 150 spun over the flats on transects that made it possible to pinpoint the locations of cranes and determine band colors. The 1983–84 winter population numbered twenty-seven pairs, fourteen subadult or immature birds, and seven cinnamon-flecked young. Twenty-seven, or forty percent of the flock, bore color bands.[8]

The Big Leap Forward

Nineteen eighty-four proved a banner year and set the tone for the remainder of the decade. A total of eighty-six birds flew into Texas; fifteen chicks wintered on the refuge, although two of them, one on Lamar Peninsula and another on Welder Point, were technically beyond its boundaries. Five youngsters remained with their parents on Matagorda Island, another five stayed on the mainland, and the balance lived on the nearby barrier of San José. One chick, the notable Blue-White, passed the entire winter with sandhill cranes on grain fields near El Campo, Texas.

Refuge staff were jubilant, but their joy subsided after two radio-carrying subadults died. One of them (a 1982 Green–white/red female named Sass) was picked up on Bludworth Island on November 15, suspected victim of a great horned owl. The second, a 1983 bird, vanished. "It was last located on the refuge on November 21. Its fate remained a mystery, but is presumed dead," stated a report laconically.[9]

At the beginning of 1985, 150 whooping cranes were known to be in existence: eighty-four in the Canada-U.S. flock; thirty-one in the Rocky Mountain group; thirty-two in captivity at Patuxent near Laurel, Mary-

land; two in the San Antonio Zoo; and a single bird housed at the International Crane Foundation in Baraboo, Wisconsin.

At Aransas, most cranes (41) wintered in areas next to the mainland; Matagorda Island had twenty-one, and San José Island carried a dozen. An additional six whoopers frequented marshes around Welder Point, north of Aransas, and a family used an area across St. Charles Bay on Lamar Peninsula, almost within hailing distance of the refuge's southwest perimeter.[10]

By the end of March three families and three pairs among eighty-four wintering cranes had set out for Canada. Between the first and ninth of April, an additional forty cranes flew north. Among these the "Brady Bunch," two widowed adults (each with a chick) who had associated together in winter quarters, took advantage of strong southeast breezes and clear skies. Just before 10:00 A.M. on 3 April, the two adults and two well-grown young lifted off Dunham Bay, spiraled upward, and headed on a 330-degree bearing—directly for Wood Buffalo National Park, more than two thousand miles away.

By 17 April 1985, only two whooping cranes lingered. One of them, a banded young female, circled up five hundred feet over Matagorda, found headwinds, and put down again. By 1 May, a single whooper hung on—eighty-three others had migrated, strung out and moving at different speeds in various groups and age-classes, along a track to birthplaces in the hidden, cool marsh country of North America's northland. Established pairs needed to procreate and nourish a new generation, teaching their young the ways of cranes and leading them to a sunken coast that would blossom white with cranes in another six months.[11]

That summer, Canadian Wildlife Service biologists Ernie Kuyt and Paul Goossen recorded twenty-eight nests. They switched eggs to certain nonproductive pairs to increase hatching and were pleased to count twenty chicks (another 21 youngsters hatched out in Idaho and Maryland from eggs flown from Canada). By mid-August 1985 experts banded sixteen survivors, marveling at how healthy and robust they were. Each bird averaged in excess of ten pounds. These Canadian Wildlife Service experts identified sixty-nine cranes, that is, eighty-two percent of the Aransas winter flock. Air surveys recorded thirteen subadults, including errant yearling Blue–White, now back close to his parents' summer territory.[12]

The Wynne Ranch foreman reported the first whooper on Matagorda Island on the afternoon of 2

October, leading some to speculate whether this earliest record had ever left the coast at all. A lone unbanded bird had remained on Matagorda throughout May, perhaps it had stayed all summer without being reported; there was an unconfirmed sighting of a crane over Baffin Bay south of Corpus Christi on 13 May.

Later that October, carried southward by strong northwest winds linked with Hurricane Juan, additional whooping cranes spun into Aransas. As the storm tracked inland east of Texas, winds swung from the east, then north, and whoopers rode them. On 18–19 September, seventy-nine whoopers were noted in Wood Buffalo; two months later a record ninety-four cranes had reached their winter sanctuary, including all sixteen banded chicks.[13]

Although the Aransas management received reports of additional cranes—one turned up in late January 1986—weekly census flights never duplicated the record ninety-four set on 18 November 1985. At year-end, biologists estimated that there were twenty-nine mated pairs, twenty subadults, and sixteen chicks. Paired birds remained generally on territories. Subadults roamed about a good deal, sometimes visiting refuge uplands, even straying over to Matagorda Island or Welder Point and back to the mainland.

Identity bands on forty-two of ninety-four birds helped researchers monitor specific cranes. Marked subadults shifted about; two flew from Matagorda to San José, for example, then fed on the mainland interior, returned to San José, and were spotted on Matagorda again. Another two birds confined activities to Matagorda Island but moved farther north than cranes had ever been seen before. Cranes also turned up for the first time near the head of St. Charles Bay and reports from Copano Bay west of Rockport and from Burgentine Lake, Mac's original refuge home, suggested exploration of new areas.[14]

Speculation arose about why some whooping cranes were more mobile than others, why they tended to congregate in specific places, and why they associated with each other. Color bands, if read correctly, began to supply answers to some of these questions and provided greater details for the biographies of specific birds. Some individuals posed complications, however, as crane spotters realized that at least ten of them had lost one or even both of the colored leg bands, making identifications a matter for conjecture.

The peak population for the entire Canada-U.S. wild flock in late winter 1985–86 was ninety-seven, although, as noted, no count above ninety-four was made on

Aransas in one day (one chick [Blue–White] and one subadult [Blue/white spiral–Blue/white spiral] wintered off the refuge). One banded bird (from 1984) disappeared in late November 1985; thus, there were ninety-six cranes to start out from Texas in spring 1986. About fourteen headed out early, prior to a census flight on 25 March 1986. By 1 April, only forty-six whoopers remained, enabling refuge biologist Tom Stehn to calculate that 52 percent had set out in late March. All whoopers had departed by 28 April.[15]

In 1986, Canadian Wildlife Service biologists pinpointed twenty-seven of twenty-nine whooping crane nests and drew off fifteen eggs for placement in Grays Lake, Idaho, and four for Patuxent; six eggs that were to be transferred turned out to be infertile or contained dead embryos. The biologists retrieved the body of a nine-year-old male near his nest, apparently the victim of a heart attack, but, overall, May and June proved a bumper season. Cranes hatched twenty-six chicks and fledged twenty-one, of which a helicopter team banded eighteen—both fledging and banding numbers were new records.[16]

A Biologist's Day

14 NOVEMBER 1986

At 5:30 A.M. in a cold drizzle, Tom Stehn leaves his home in Aransas Pass. Twenty-nine miles north, he turns off Highway 35 into the Tatton Unit, Aransas Refuge's west extension, which is a popular roosting ground for cranes and geese. The biologist keeps track of both crane and waterfowl numbers on the refuge, continuing a tradition that goes back forty-nine years. Estimates of waterfowl populations on the Central Flyway include numbers and distributions of different duck and geese species wintering on the Texas Gulf coast. Today's count will go in the annual report and become a piece of a larger picture. Aransas is not just for whooping cranes.

Nothing stirs around Goose Lake, although vague forms of waterfowl cover much of its dark surface. Suddenly, geese punch a blackened land's silence. Voices quaver in the biting north wind as a waterfowl army lifts from its roost and beats upward into pale light where hundreds of white snow geese are distinguishable in lines of darker Canadas.

Sandhills soon join the flight, tracking away from Salt Creek. Pintail, wigeon, and gadwall remain, guzzling water plants. Upward of five hundred black-bellied plovers explore mudflats and are joined by a few dunlin, dowitchers, and bleached avocets along the lake's gale-whisked sides. On its woody shore, titmice, kinglets, and even a Carolina chickadee, unusual for Aransas, scold a sharp-shinned hawk in a mesquite thicket. While smaller birds mob this accipiter, a merlin spins unnoticed from a nearby snag.

Stehn sees the bird hunter and keeps a lookout for its larger endangered look-alike peregrine falcon. He also records the large congregation of plovers, which usually spread out in ones and twos on open beaches or interior flats. Fellow experts send requests for sightings of particular species; this season it's for banded piping plovers, another bird in trouble. One or two have been reported on the Gulf beach near Port Aransas, but none on the refuge.

By 9:30 Stehn has completed another twenty miles to headquarters, pausing to examine four hundred or more sandhills head high in uncut milo. After coffee, phone calls, and office routines, he heads toward whooping crane territories that line the Gulf Intracoastal Waterway. His FWS truck tows an olive green boat. Monitoring crane arrivals and initial jostling for territorial space is best done by boat.

Migration is late. In fact, fall 1986 is the second slowest year ever. By this time in 1985, more than ninety whooping cranes had taken up residence. So far Stehn has tallied merely twenty-four birds. Near the boat ramp, he spots Mustang Lake's pair with a rust-colored chick carrying orange and white leg bands. Surely, other cranes must be nearing Aransas. Yesterday's fierce norther may well have carried them a final one- or two-hundred-mile leg to winter homes.

At 11:00 A.M. Stehn is speeding along the Gulf Intracoastal Waterway. He stands up now and then to peer expectantly toward a distant tree line marking the marsh's upland edge. Suddenly, three white-colored birds show up near the waterway. Stehn throttles back, swings his flat-bottomed skiff to the bank, and, crouching low, scrambles forward and chucks an anchor ashore. He grabs a telescope; it is important to read color bands correctly.

The crane trio walks away without concern. The pair, red/white–nil and his unbanded mate, are a few paces from White/black/White–Blue/yellow/Blue, a year old crane who passed her first winter on Matagorda Island's Cottonwood Bayou. A duo and a single together suggests that they have flown in recently, probably with yesterday's norther, and are now settling down. The pair calls loudly and WbW–ByB sets off across the bay. Immediately, a white pelican tucks in behind and fol-

lows for a short distance. As the pelican drops away, the subadult swings toward the mainland. Within minutes she is on the same marsh about three hundred yards from the territory-claiming pair.

Both adults walk slowly but deliberately toward this interloper, foraging as they approach. As distance closes, they call another warning. The subadult leaves. Spiraling upward in a stiff wind, the whooper beats northward following the waterway until a tiny crane speck disappears among a flock of nearby gulls trailing a barge. The break has been made.

While following this interaction, Stehn sees a new family close to Mustang Slough. Hurriedly, he retraces his course, grounds his craft in shallows, hits better water in a lead, and glides in. Whoopers call suspiciously. Slowly the boat moves up a narrowing channel and bumps into cordgrass.

The family's chick is unusually large and handsome. It raises its head and looks intently in Stehn's direction. Reading bands is tricky. The chick bears Yellow and Orange, although the chart shows yellow over blue on the left leg; possibly the blue has slipped inside the yellow band. Both parents are unbanded. As Stehn watches, the family strides off haughtily, quickly turning into white forms shimmering in haze.

When concentrating on new cranes, Stehn must ignore other birds. A single male mallard—unusual for Aransas—flushes with mottled ducks. Stehn remembers that a dozen black-crowned night herons also flapped heavily away from his churning boat. New bufflehead scuttered around meanders. Under an uncluttered circle of sky, a jigsaw puzzle of land and water sprawls open and flat. Fresh water from last night's rains gurgles into this marine nursery.

Back in the Gulf Intracoastal Waterway, Stehn spies another crane family on Rattlesnake Island, an old marsh covered heavily with spoil. He reads the young female's orange–red/blue bands before it flies away. On the mainland another two adults and a chick wade in Sundown Bay, and still another stands in open water several hundred yards farther south. Sundown Bay is an important habitat for whooping cranes, who probe for clams in its muddy substrate while commanding unobstructed views of anything that approaches. Tom detects white and orange leg bands on the distant chick. But the closer one stalks inland, giving no chance for identification.

Near the far end of Sundown Bay, biologist Stehn's boat roils a mixture of mud and water, causing the motor to chatter. He tries to close in on two new

A banded whooper holds a fish at Aransas NWR. The second large white bird is a white ibis. Photograph by John Jefferson.

cranes. One of them loafs, standing on one leg for fifteen minutes before letting the other down to give Stehn a clear look at its green band. The second crane, White–Green, a chick from last year, stalks about. She returns to her immobile partner, Green–Green. The newcomers are young cranes from territories close by who have migrated back to the same marsh to which their parents led them the previous winter.

Against distant upland, another family moves about but is too far away to identify. Stehn charges back into deeper water and a mile south spots a crane pair close to the ship channel. By pulling up, Stehn determines that both birds wear no bands. Suddenly, they scramble away as another lone crane swings in low and menacingly. It is chasing them from its territory. Stehn is not sure which family this bird represents, possibly so-called Lobstick cranes from Canada's summer home on Lobstick Creek; if so, this male is enlarging his territory. The remaining adult, presumably the female with a young crane, calls from a thickly vegetated place about three hundred yards away. Her mate starts to walk back from where he drove off two subadults.

It is nearly 4:00 P.M. Tom Stehn has been checking whooping cranes for five hours. He comes about and heads back ten or so miles toward vehicle and towing equipment. Tomorrow, he will check cranes in Dunham Bay, where there is at least one family and probably others.

On the voyage back, he passes a threesome that had hurried from Rattlesnake Island. They have moved a few hundred yards to usual haunts on Ayres Island. This time, two additional whooping cranes, Red/white/Red—Orange and White—Red/white/Red, wade in open water within seventy yards or so of territory holders. Such close proximity surprises Stehn, who throttles back to watch the five birds.

The tranquil scene erupts as the family charges the two trespassers. Gaining on them, one crane pecks hard at an intruder, one of which is last year's chick. The subadults fly off and land but not far enough away to satisfy last year's parents, who renew their chase. This time, the two young make a longer flight. They alight a mile or so south and are undisturbed.

Stehn doesn't know how long these two young cranes have been feeding close to Ayres Island but such encroachment pushed tolerance beyond limit. Presence of boat traffic may also affect crane responses to each other and perhaps the male has been disturbed often and arrival of competitors, even RwR—O, his own older young, caused him to attack. Or maybe the parents recognized the immature and were initially tolerant but, like this morning's instance of territory holders bugling to WbW—ByB, this Ayres Island family issued an identical message, albeit more forcefully. Their older offspring will have to go somewhere else.

Bottle-nosed dolphins surface in the wake of Stehn's craft. Several small parties swim north in the late afternoon. As Tom drives past the tour route picnic area, dozens of turkey vultures also glide north, heading for safe perches in live oaks.

In this rapidly darkening day, whooping cranes are also preparing to sleep by standing in open water. There are now at least thirty-eight on Blackjack Peninsula, and undoubtedly more. Others are going to roost on Matagorda Island and San José Island. Usual sparring is taking place as families, pairs, and nonbreeding birds are swinging in for their winter sojourn. Aransas cranes are coming home.

Tom Stehn had good reason to take careful note of crane arrivals and distribution. From late August through October 1986, an outbreak of "red tide" along the Texas coast threatened to compromise the summer's good fortune by wrecking an important component of winter food on Aransas. Red seawater stained by billions upon billions of tiny, single-celled organisms known as dinoflagellates streaked a 200-mile stretch from Mexico to the Colorado River estuary, north of the federal preserve. Millions of dead fish poisoned by toxins released from "blooms" of these microorganisms littered beaches or floated in bays. The size of this kill (estimates ran in excess of 20 million fish) astonished biologists, who had not witnessed a similar-sized disaster in Texas for fifty years. Reports of dead fish, including mullet and eels, both taken by whoopers, came from Aransas Bay.[17]

It was not a possible dearth of fish foods that concerned Stehn and colleagues but rather impacts of the red tide on shellfish. State officials closed oyster beds to harvesting because these filter feeders and similar clams and mussels concentrate toxins and may poison people who consume them. Red tide toxins do not kill oysters or clams and will be diluted and flushed away after the outbreak subsides. But this cleansing process happens over several weeks or months, depending on the severity of contamination; therefore, refuge staff were concerned that whoopers would grow ill after feeding on infected clams.

Fortunately, in fall 1986, tardy whoopers found conditions more to their liking. By mid-November, the red tide had largely subsided as rainfall and lowered sea temperatures decreased blooms. Earlier tests on oysters close to the refuge's mainland shore showed no toxins, and experts concluded that clams dug out by cranes were also clean, although samples of water and oysters collected by state authorities near Welder Point showed "moderate" toxin levels, certainly unfit for humans. Several whooping cranes wintered in the Welder Point area and Stehn judged that they had been exposed to contaminated clams although none showed any ill effects.

Red tide is a new threat for Aransas. Staff in Texas and in the National Wildlife Health Laboratory in Madison, Wisconsin, take this health hazard seriously and have devised procedures for reporting, monitoring, and, if the threat is clearly established, hazing cranes from clamming areas.[18]

In fall 1986 the poison issue was not limited to red tide. On 19 November, crane watcher Stehn noted a whooper family inside a long, oblong-shaped impoundment located on the Gulf Intracoastal Waterway's east bank. These spoil areas are filled with materials dredged up to ease passage of fully laden barges. Nobody had

AUSTWELL

Snow cranes stand out
in Austwell field, like
two pale posts in

furrowed mile. Errant pair
draw cousins to their
side, whose winter flocks

fill this space. Tramps stride,
deaf to white bugles
from Aransas marsh. For

tilled horizon they steer,
glean sandhill food, love
corn, and shun

tidal flats, where one hundred
brothers welcome prodigals
home. These are turncoats,

white grain-picker cranes, who
live with brown flocks and share
the same brown land.

reported cranes in such areas before.

Stehn watched a crane family on Rattlesnake Island for more than an hour. The cranes plucked red wolfberries from low shrubs dotting sandy areas. In subsequent days he observed other cranes feeding in spoil areas, mostly on wolfberries. Knowing that dredged substrate contained levels of nickel, arsenic, and mercury in excess of EPA standards, Stehn collected berry samples. Tests on them were negative; the wolfberries in spoil impoundments were uncontaminated.[19]

Aransas' wolfberry crop ripens from mid-November through early December and whoopers devour the tasty red fruits on tidal flats and upland edges. Stehn and other watchers noted initially in fall 1986 that the big cranes visited interior places. As many as ten birds grouped together on Blackjack Peninsula's south end on at least two occasions in December. But there seemed to be little to eat. The acorn crop had failed, and, except for a few beetles and grasshoppers, pickings appeared to be slim, at least to human eyes. As if to confirm this, observers noted that whoopers did more walking than feeding and use of this refuge interior tapered off quickly. Scarcity of foods may have caused some birds to shift to spoil areas, which, like interior pastures, are largely undefended.

Charter aircraft troubles precluded detailed tabulation of whooping crane arrivals from late November through December. But a U.S. Fish and Wildlife airplane discovered a third unbanded chick, bringing to twenty the total number of youngsters on Aransas. One young pair nesting for the first time and using San José Island were without their chick, a female the Canadian Wildlife Service biologists had banded and judged a late hatchling smaller than average. Biologists concluded that the chick had probably not survived to migrate. On 30 January 1987, however, this chick, White/black/White—orange (1986), was sighted with sandhill cranes near Hydro, Oklahoma. Somehow, perhaps in a storm or disturbance, normally strong bonds between parents and young had been severed, but the young female managed to reach grain fields along the Red River on the Texas-Oklahoma border.

The peak population for winter 1986–87 was twenty-one chicks plus eighty-nine adults, giving a total of 110 wild cranes. Stehn wrote happily that "record highs were set for most adults, most chicks, and total number." More than half (62) inhabited marshes along the Aransas mainland, while about one-quarter (26) wintered on Matagorda Island; almost 10 percent (12) lived on San José Island, and 8 percent (9) occupied Welder

Point.

By 19 April 1987 most of the Aransas flock, minus a banded chick that disappeared and was presumed dead on its parent's territory on Sundown Bay, had departed. With "red tide" and hazards of potential spills and contaminants in food behind them, crane experts watched expectantly for results from the 1987 nesting season.[20]

Errant Cranes

Records suggest that fewer than two chicks in a hundred fail to reach Aransas by becoming separated from their parents while tracking from Wood Buffalo. This rare event and the fact that strays appear in unexpected places and that some do survive draw considerable comment. Some cranewatchers speculate whether such whooper wanderers are pioneering new routes or winter homes, thereby expanding range.

An early record of a wandering juvenile occurred on southeast Missouri's Mingo NWR in December 1958. This bird remained until December 17, then vanished. A color-banded whooper, nil–Red (1977), appeared with three sandhill cranes near Meade, Kansas, from 3 to 9 April 1978. The band identification made it evident that this crane had not wintered on Aransas but at some unreported location. That fall nil–Red did appear on Aransas but did not live long enough to reach maturity.[21]

Blue–White

To date, the most complete and detailed record of a stray whooping crane involves a male chick, Blue–White (1984), who was observed 65 miles northeast of Aransas close to El Campo in Wharton County, Texas, near the end of December 1984. Blue–White's parents claimed a territory on the refuge peninsula's South Sundown Island and had arrived without their chick. Concern about an upcoming sandhill crane hunting season in coastal counties, including Wharton, spurred federal and state wildlife authorities, in liaison with the Canadian whooping crane coordinator and National Audubon Society representatives, to establish procedures for monitoring and protecting Blue–White. Fortunately, landowners cooperated by excluding hunters from most of a 2-mile-long by 1-mile-wide area of coastal lowland that Blue–White had picked out as his winter range. He usually left his wetland roost at about 7:00 A.M., fed in milo, soybean, or ploughed rice fields during the morning, sometimes loafed with sandhill crane neighbors, then foraged again before flying back to a sleeping site shortly after 6:00 P.M. Blue–White selected a variety of night roosts, including flooded rice fields and a pond backed by heavy vegetation.

Officials stationed a dawn-to-dusk watch near Blue–White during the sandhill crane hunt, which lasted from 12 January through 19 February 1985. "Babysitting" tapered off as the crane's movements grew regular, and instead he was checked three times per day. There were anxious moments, however. On the evening before sandhill hunting began, a winter storm swept across Central Texas into Wharton County. Blue–White promptly disappeared but turned up again two days later as the freezing rain and low temperatures eased.

Transmission wires and supports for a communications tower slanted across Blue–White's home area and experts feared for his safety as the youngster headed off to roost in fading light. In mid-January 1985, U.S. FWS whooping crane coordinator Jim Lewis informed Texas Parks and Wildlife personnel that three sandhill cranes on nearby Attwater's Prairie Chicken NWR were suspected of contracting botulism. Risks appeared all around.

Understandably, monitors expressed relief when Blue–White migrated on 17 March 1985. Canadian Wildlife Service researchers caught a glimpse of him on 8 June close to his natal area in Wood Buffalo NP. Blue–White had found his way back to a summer home.[22]

On 28 October 1985, Blue–White was in a flock of seven whooping cranes in South Dakota, heading toward Texas. Instead of pushing for Aransas, Blue–White and one of the flock's females, Blue/white spiral–Blue/white spiral, named after a downcurved white streak in a broad blue band on both legs, showed up on Christmas Day forty miles east of El Campo and almost one hundred miles up the coast from Aransas. The two whoopers established themselves beside another federal sanctuary, the 24,500-acre San Bernard NWR, ten miles southwest of Freeport, Texas.

The errant couple passed seventy-five days in croplands and coastal marshes in Brazoria County. Refuge staff and volunteer birders teamed up to check regularly on their whereabouts. They observed that the birds associated freely with sandhills, foraging for waste grain with them, but as supplies dwindled, the duo acted like Aransas cranes, feeding in marshes close to the ocean.

By the end of January 1986, B–W and Bwsp–Bwsp switched into freshwater habitat along San Bernard River but also fed in brackish tidal flats. They selected a small marsh near the river and ceased to make the four- or five-mile flight to croplands that carried them over a high power line.

In early March, however, both cranes began to visit nearby fields in which chemically treated corn had been

This tallest feathered denizen of North America's wetlands shows off its characteristic white plumage and imperious bearing as a shrill bugle sounds across an Idaho marsh. Photograph from Entheos.

planted. Personnel hazed them off this contaminated food source on five separate occasions. As he did so on 30 March, assistant manager Mike Lange noticed that they appeared reluctant to leave the grainfields, but the next day he found the duo on their tidal marsh preening busily. The whoopers continued arranging plumage for almost an hour, then they flew into a clear sky. Strong tail winds pushed B–W and Bwsp–Bwsp quickly out of sight.[23]

Nobody reported them around the San Bernard or along the migration corridor. In midsummer, on an air survey, Canadian Wildlife Service biologists found Bwsp–Bwsp close to her birthplace in Wood Buffalo, Canada. That fall, Lange and associates continued to hold out hope that B–W would continue his errant ways and pass a third consecutive winter away from Aransas. They half expected a breakout to Brazoria County, the first major move toward whooper reoccupation of suitable habitat on the Texas coast.

In October 1986, a phone call to Aransas claimed that six whoopers were heading south near Conroe, northeast of Houston. It was Blue–White leading a posse, joked manager Frank Johnson, who was used to such false alarms.

Little information about B–W had filtered down to Texas. On 29 November, just after sunset, two cranes flew into Salt Creek close to the north boundary of Aransas NWR. The pair startled staffer Barry Jones, who had watched a single whooper fly in twenty or so minutes earlier. The single bird had used Salt Creek and nearby Goose Lake for several weeks, so seeing three whoopers in such a spot was puzzling.

Three mornings later, on 1 December 1986, Tom Stehn checked cranes leaving Salt Creek roost. At 8:30 A.M. he spotted a pair who made a short flight from soggy ground to dry pasture before departing with some six hundred sandhill cranes toward milo fields. One of them carried a blue band on its left leg and a white on its right; its companion was unbanded. A wanderer had come home. Blue–White had taken almost two and a half years to reach Aransas, and, although technically within the refuge, he and his new companion did not take up tidal flat life until January 1987.

Blue–White joined up finally with other subadults. Stehn saw him in late January within a mile of his parents' territory; his companion was close by. Bwsp–Bwsp, his previous winter associate, passed a more solitary existence on northern sections of Matagorda Island; she had lost one of her bands. Without identity markers, Stehn and others could not tell either the age or sex

of B–W's new companion, although they presumed it was a female. Dominant B–W showed hostility toward female Yellow–Red, the third whooper on Salt Creek, and kept close to his associate. Eventually, Y–R moved off croplands into refuge marshes, leaving the pair feeding together on milo.[24]

In mid-March 1987, near Dunham Point, ten whoopers were feeding, demonstrating none of the aggression that marks disputes about territory. One of them was Blue–White, a tall male who walked beside a smaller, unbanded crane, presumably his intended mate. He caught a crab, pulled it apart, swallowed and drank, briefly tilting his head upward. Subadult cranes stalked backward and forward close to each other. They kept in discernible pairs, especially bold Blue–White, who danced momentarily in front of his companion by jumping upward and spreading his wings. He was an Aransas crane, living on marine foods not waste milo or corn, which had nourished him in previous winters. Blue–White was preparing to migrate from the Blackjacks.

In spring 1987, Canadian Wildlife Service biologist Ernie Kuyt found Blue–White's nest containing a single egg. However, the new pair failed to raise a chick and on 10 November around 9:40 A.M., a tour boat operator glimpsed what appeared to be the pair's return to Aransas. Two whoopers set down on the tip of Blackjack Peninsula near Yellow–Red, with whom they had consorted briefly near Goose Lake the previous fall. Stehn was glad to lift the "errant" tab beside Blue–White's name.

The unusually tall crane has become a respectable member of the Aransas flock, occupying a winter territory along the eastern side of St. Charles Bay close to Egg Point. The pair nested successfully in their short season and guided a banded youngster to the Aransas territory in December 1988.

Stehn has continued to be puzzled by other wandering cranes. So-called Oklahoma, or WbW-o (1986), spent her winter of 1986–87 in southern Oklahoma, then flew to Nebraska's Platte River, an important sandhill crane staging area, only to head off before early whoopers passed en route to Canada's nesting grounds that spring. In summer 1987, WbW-o showed up in Wood Buffalo, then flew north to near Yellowknife.

That summer, her parents raised their second chick but flew in to Matagorda Island without it. Curiously, this new bird, yellow/black–Yellow/black/Yellow like WbW-o, had become separated and was spotted near Amarillo, Texas, that November, while his sister moved much closer to Aransas. The young female WbW-o remained with sandhill cranes near Edna, Texas, about fifty miles north of the refuge closer to the area in which Blue–White had foraged during his first winter. Other chicks have picked up Blue–White's vagabond ways![25]

In spring 1988, Oklahoma flew back north again and was seen close to her first winter home near Hydro, Oklahoma. Her younger brother y/b–YbY turned up in early April near Panhandle, Texas, after moving at least one hundred miles southeast into the Brazos River drainage. Hard weather around Amarillo had caused him to push to southeast of Lubbock and he had disappeared for three months.

Winter Territories and Pair Formation

During the 1980s, researchers began to investigate social relationships among Aransas cranes, concentrating specifically on how birds establish and defend winter territories. Drawing upon banding data, biologists followed activities and movements of specific individuals. They observed parents guiding chicks to winter territories, juveniles seeking companionship with other subadults and, over the seasons, pairing off, nesting in Canada, and returning to newly staked-out territories in Texas.

The practice of banding and weighing cranes before they could fly began in Canada a dozen years ago. Various combinations of colored markers in different widths on the upper legs of each crane gave researchers opportunities to identify birds. Blood taken from the wing (now replaced by other techniques) during banding has also provided information about the sex of birds. With such visual and biological keys people set about watching whooper movements and interactions, just as Allen had done earlier but without such identifiable tags.

In Aransas, Mary Anne Bishop, a graduate student at Texas A&M University, sponsored by the National Audubon Society, studied subadult whooping cranes for five winters from 1978 through 1983, the final three in the field. She noted that most subadults spend at least half of the daylight hours procuring food. They accelerate feeding rates toward dusk before going to roost in shallow lakes or bays. Bishop determined that about 35 percent of a day is devoted to preening and other forms of body maintenance, and an additional 6 percent is given over to "alert behavior," that is, looking out for potential threats or predators.[26]

This amount of watchfulness is multiplied four or five times by members of the experimental cross-fostered flock on winter grounds in New Mexico. Whooping cranes feed there on grain crops along the Rio Grande

and must guard against predatory coyotes, who make use of woody cover and even standing corn or barley to work close to geese or cranes. They will attack whoopers if they can. Cranes know this and devote much more time to being alert than on Aransas tidal marshes where cover is scant and access by terrestrial predators more limited. When they visit interior uplands, however, Aransas birds are very alert and are much more difficult to approach.

In winter studies Bishop noted several differences between the behavior of paired cranes and that of single adults or subadults. Adult pairs occupy the same territories from year to year, spending most time within boundaries that they establish and defend; pairs may leave chosen areas for a few hours over one or several days in order to feed at unusual food concentrations where subadults are also found. Territory size varies among pairs, as does the tolerance they show toward neighbors or younger cranes who fly into their domains. There are pairs, for instance, who permit subadult groups inside their territories. Also, Blankinship made note of "sharing" between pairs in his studies. Other crane pairs, however, are quick to detect encroachment and chase off trespassers.

Bishop reported that subadult presence invariably elicits some response from territory owners. Often adults will guard call as if to identify and give warning to potential or actual trespassers. One bird, usually the male, or sometimes both adults may attack by flying at intruders, pursuing, even pecking them in the air. Trespassers invariably leave, often hurriedly, giving ground to the owners, who preen, shake their wings, bow, or posture after these skirmishes. Subadults are always submissive to adult pairs in contests over winter space and tend to frequent undefended areas. Such sites, on lower Sundown Bay and along western shores of Dunham Bay, for example, are used throughout winter months from season to season, until, with gradual population buildup, a new whooper pair stakes a claim and challenges the flocks of unpaired individuals.

One interesting aspect of this selection process is tied to bonds of kinship. Bishop recorded that subadults gravitate toward those territories to which parents guided them their first winter. They may try to "squeeze" into a zone or edge between older, traditional use areas only to be ejected by the rightful owners. Some older birds, however, appear to tolerate these flocks more than others, at least for a time. They probably recognize their older offspring and may permit a degree of association. Temperament and personality, which are most

Whooping crane dipping down over a slough at the south end of Sundown Bay, Aransas NWR. Photograph by John Jefferson.

noticeable in older, more dominant males, appear to play a considerable role in the frequency and degree of tolerance that birds show one another.[27]

Male nil–White is an experienced and successful parent noted by observers for bold, authoritarian behavior in his territory on lower Sundown Bay. On any winter day you can find him assuredly guarding mate and chick in cordgrass or wading along a slough, raising his periscopelike neck abruptly then lowering it again for fifteen seconds or so as he pokes for food in a shallow lead.

On one early afternoon in November 1986, an osprey flaps above nil–White and family. It feints, rears up, and slams into their feeding slough, emerging with a silver fish. Clutching its wriggling prize, the fish hawk labors like a torpedo bomber toward east shore oaks, sits on a snag, and rearranges its catch crossways. Except for an odd squint downward, the dappled predator ignores its meal and, slinging the fish tightly under its belly, heads inland.

Ten minutes later, nil–White's family follows an identical path. Gaining altitude in swirling wind, they cross the shore road and flap over oak thickets. The chick's wings are as long and broad as the adults' and show conspicuous black terminal patches. Overall, it appears whiter in the air than on the ground as it flaps, glides, and flaps again in synchrony with its parents' wingbeats. Abruptly, the three white cranes angle down, lower their legs, and land out of sight.

An hour later, the whoopers swing back, and, as he sweeps past another pair, male nil–White bugles, then all three land gently in a large pool. Both adults carefully survey their locale before beginning to preen. Their chick adopts a hunched, submissive posture. It shakes its head repeatedly and arranges feathers, working its bill through them, nibbling from belly to tail. The trio stand in a line, each about six feet from another, facing into wind, tidying their plumage, slicking the backs of their heads along scapulars. Then, in synchrony, each one raises a right foot, shakes off water, and tucks it into body plumage.

After preening steadily, the cinnamon-colored youngster buries its bill into back feathers and sleeps. The female pulls her head and neck close to her body, relaxes, occasionally twisting back to arrange more feathers. She also sleeps.

At the head of the line nil–White relaxes, then grows taut as a vehicle passes within three hundred yards. Finally, he too slips bill into mantle and remains motionless; his tertial plumes flutter like a sailboat's telltales in a stiff breeze. He was banded as a chick in 1978 in his home territory along Canada's Klewi River in Wood Buffalo National Park, barely three hundred miles south of the Arctic Circle. Temporary captors placed a Red/white/Red band on his left leg and a broad White one on his right leg. His left band has dropped away, leaving only the White, hence his name, nil–White. The chick is orange–Red, a female replacing last year's sister, White–Green, who has teamed up with another juvenile from last year a few hundred yards away. The parent cranes have conveyed three female chicks in succession to North Sundown Island, the pair's fall territory close to that in which nil–White passed his first winter. Growing more dominant, this male whooper claimed and enlarged his present space when another pair failed to return.

Raising his head, nil–White steps away from his family and spies something in the water. With long bounding strides he sets off in pursuit, twisting and turning to keep pace with whatever is in the shallows. His poised bill fails to strike.

These antics arouse the others. Angling black primaries downward, his mate bugles loudly. Immediately, nil–White ceases his run, answers with upraised bill, and strides off solemnly along the lake margin. Mate and chick follow. Moving into open water, he leans forward in a usual stiff-necked flight posture. The female refuses to leave. She preens again, but her mate growls in a low throaty mutter until finally she takes wing. The chick responds within a split second. Nil–White flies behind his two charges across open water. He shepherds them onto a tidal flat a few hundred yards away from the Blackjack mainland—safer ground but well within his territory.

Nil–White exercises natural authority over his chosen area; next year orange–Red will have to avoid this area, just as her older sister, White–Green, does now. The sibling before her, Bwsp–Bwsp, shifted up the coast with Blue–White after her first season in Texas but now lives on Matagorda Island. Seasoned campaigner nil–White does not tolerate transgressors. On the other hand, a pair on Dunham Bay, several miles south, demonstrate unusual patience toward crane visitors. Often this couple feeds in its territory within a few yards of six or even ten subadults and only occasionally shows hostility.

Farther north in 1986–87, the Mustang Lake family, close to the observation tower, rarely acted aggressively toward three immature whoopers who took to feeding along the south boundary of its large territory. This family's decision to switch to an unoccupied marsh near

Heron Flats Trail, from which visitors obtained spectacularly close views for several weeks in December and January, led observers to speculate whether these aging birds preferred to fly several miles away from their regular area rather than challenge trespassing cranes or moved to that unusual site in search of food. Two of the intruding subadults had wintered initially on territories not far from Mustang Lake.[28]

Other crane pairs are more like nil–White, unwilling to share space, and they include the male of the so-called Brady bunch, named after the TV show because the male flew into Aransas with a chick but no mate and took up with a widowed female and her chick. Brady-male has since paired off again (but not with Brady-female) and lives on Dunham Bay. On one occasion (in mid-March 1987) his new chick was standing close to another youngster as two families foraged together by the Gulf Intracoastal Waterway. Suddenly, Brady-male charged at an adult trespasser, who lunged away, swung into the air, and landed fifty yards away. This distance was not enough. The aggressor ran again, causing the intruder to jump aloft and swing back to its family. Brady-male flew in low and hard and actually passed under his victim's upward leap. He landed, paused, then turned on the strange adult and chick, who flapped away in panic. Then he stopped, turned and glared, presumably at the trespassing male, original object of his fury, and headed for him again. The slender whooper slipped aside like a matador, gave ground, and rejoined his companions. Thirty yards now separated the two families. This distance seemed to satisfy Brady-male, who strode back to his mate and chick and began to preen. The other threesome trooped away. They had lived without a territory all winter. By giving some ground here, a little more there, persistence had paid off. Dunham Bay had sustained them.

An abundance of natural food, or that created artificially by setting out or growing grains, helps decrease such overt aggression and may result in temporary abandonment of territories. A prescribed burn, freeing up acorns or other palatable items, brings cranes together, in many instances away from usual haunts. Whooping crane pairs and families fly to such food sources, mingling with one another (but keeping discernibly separated) and with more loosely bonded subadults.

Although data suggest that food stocks within wetlands and bays are normally sufficient to satisfy nutritional needs, group foraging on uplands may have important dietary as well as social implications. Interior sites increase the range of food types, and while foraging in them normally isolated chicks come into contact with other yearlings.

Howard Hunt of Texas A&M University (Department of Wildlife and Fisheries) studied whooping crane use on five selected Blackjack Peninsula pastures subjected to different grazing and burning schedules. He collected fecal samples in order to determine what cranes eat. Results agreed substantially with David Blankinship's work, showing just how variable crane diets are from month to month and from one winter to another.

In 1983–84, for example, wolfberry, blue crabs, and fish were important in early winter but as months passed clams became a food staple, comprising almost two-thirds of volume in more than two-thirds of all fecal samples. Next year, snails and wolfberries predominated in late fall and early winter; then blue crabs, acorns, and fiddler crabs supplied most food from January to mid-February 1985 before the cranes shifted to clams and aquatic snails.[29]

Upland visitation, when several birds can often be seen together, also varies markedly. Some pairs will make a ten- or twelve-mile round trip from Matagorda Island to visit mainland interiors. Why they do this is not clear. Hunt linked such opportunistic coming and going to easily obtainable foods.

Hunt recommended to refuge staff that habitat diversity be maximized so that cranes may forage more widely. Early winter burns on a three- to five-year cycle maintain "openness," he argued, and enable cranes to spot any potential threats while looking for food. Burning off more and more woody vegetation, which dominates the interior portions of Blackjack Peninsula, expands the terrestrial area useful for cranes. Birds avoid areas thick with trees. By spacing and thinning out mesquite and oak mottes and by eradicating dense cattail (*Typha* sp.) stands in freshwater ponds or dugouts, managers can make habitat more attractive. Tall cranes spot potential predators a long way off across low, ancient dunes, and, while they are very alert in such localities, they are able to gain nourishment from a range of plant and animal foods.[30]

Subadult whoopers are naturally the most gregarious cohort of the species, associating together in small winter flocks of up to ten birds, most often in groups of four or six. Mary Anne Bishop studied these subadult birds and witnessed the formation of life-long pair bonds for the first time in 1981. Such pairings came about after individuals had associated together for one to three winters. She noted that, while any subadult flock might be characterized as a loose membership of individuals coming and going, definite associations existed between specific cranes. Birds tended to congregate around a food source for a few weeks or even a season, and as individuals came to know one another they began to forage and rest with certain other cranes within the larger flock. From these associations, a pair would eventually leave the flock to establish a first territory.

Subadult flocks, therefore, provide situations in which cranes meet and select a partner. Some birds paired but remained in flocks throughout most of the winter before nesting for the first time in Canada. Others established a winter territory prior to breeding. At least one successful pair, as we have seen, arrived in Aransas with a chick and never succeeded in setting up a well-defined territory. There are few hard and fast rules for cranes to follow.[31]

One rule that cranes do follow, however, is to return to the same winter territory, with the same partner, year after year. A pair or family group may leave its chosen tideland habitat from time to time as events or opportunities dictate; it also may enlarge its proprietary space if owners of adjacent territories fail to show up. But it is faithful to a specific locality. Observers like Tom Stehn identify these territories by geographic features, such as north or middle or south Sundown Bay, Egg Point, Lamar Peninsula, and so on, and can plot them on a base map. Unless one or both birds fail to return, researchers expect that cranes linked with these geographic locations are the same individuals season after season. If only one bird shows up it may fail to defend its former territory, although a male (with or without a chick) is more likely to hold on, at least for a few weeks. Biologists have noted that one female who lost her mate left her territory and associated with subadults.[32]

Aransas experts Frank Johnson and Tom Stehn combined historical data with more-recent air censuses to determine the number, location, and size of territories in Texas. They concluded that whoopers occupy merely 37 percent of the 54,600 acres of available wetland on the refuge and adjacent areas. Most of the 6,997 acres on the east shore of Blackjack Peninsula is currently in use. Birds frequent merely 3,000 of 27,000 acres (11%) on Matagorda Island, 7,600 of 15,000 acres (51%) on San José Island, and 2,000 of 5,000 acres (40%) on Welder Point across San Antonio Bay. At first glance it seems that there is ample habitat in which birds can spread out as numbers increase.

Closer examination reveals a more complex situation. Studies that track individual banded birds suggest that subadults return to locations to which their parents guided them. As they mature and pair off, these new adults, particularly males it appears, try to set up territories close to original winter homes. Allen calculated sizes for fourteen territories along the mainland edge and arrived at an average of 435 acres per territory. Twenty-five years or so later, Blankinship figured that there had been no change. He mapped ten territories and came up with an identical figure. Within a decade, however, Tom Stehn made the same calculations and discovered that territory size had fallen to about 289 acres, a decrease of 33 percent. It is clear that cranes are crowding together in spaces paralleling East Shore Road and are making do with as little as 136 acres per pair in Sundown Bay or as much as 617 acres toward the northern and southern edges of the peninsula. Some "sharing" does take place as cranes move in if owners are out of sight or at their territory's far end; therefore, precise linear boundaries are impossible to establish. But the trend is unmistakable—crane space in Aransas Refuge core is growing smaller.[33]

From 1941 to 1987, the Aransas crane population jumped from 16 to 132 birds, and, given fidelity to traditional use areas, observers conjecture about limits to progressive "crowding." Speculation on this topic goes back to second manager Earl Craven's opinion in 1946 that numbers would never be large enough for this to be a concern. Nineteen birds in eleven square miles of shore flats in 1942, for example, hardly appeared to be crowded. Happily, numbers on that key shoreline today have reached record levels (70 in winter 1987), but so far expansion outward has been relatively slow.

Crane numbers have increased and spread out on the barrier islands. Matagorda's use as a bombing range until 1973 inhibited occupation of those areas heavily used by the military north of Panther Point. A crane pair appeared at Panther in winter 1968–69, but expansion into the old military range has been slower than some biologists had anticipated. One reason is that, generally, only offspring of pairs that have already pioneered Matagorda marshes establish new territories on the islands, although in at least one instance a whooper has crossed to Matagorda from Mustang Lake, where it wintered as a chick.

Similar colonization and expansion on San José Island south of Matagorda dates back to 1971–72. Three pairs were there in 1984–85, four territories in 1985–86, and five territories in 1986–87. Recruitment has come largely from families established on the island's north end. Curiously, in 1986–87 no subadults were located on any of that barrier's wide marshlands where it would seem there is an ample habitat, but a new breeding pair, in which a four-year-old female was the youngest recorded as nesting, did pass time on the island. Stehn did not think that this pair ever set up a proper territory but led a mobile existence, frequenting the south end of Matagorda Island and even portions of the mainland.[34]

Evidence of cranes on Welder Point, a little over 8 1/2 miles north of Aransas refuge, dates back to 1941. Fearing that hunters might shoot the precious birds, refuge personnel used a helicopter to flush a family back to federal lands in 1965. Obligingly, birds flew over to Matagorda Island, then moved to Mustang Lake. A territory on Welder was occupied in 1973–74 and has remained in consistent use. In 1985–86, two pairs, one with a chick, defended areas on Welder and two additional subadults roamed other marsh lands. In 1986–87, both pairs protected a chick each and three subadults occupied nearby habitat. In 1987–88, two families and five subadults were there.[35]

While there appears to be more than enough wetland space for the minimum forty nesting pairs that the *Whooping Crane Recovery Plan* outlines for a Canada-U.S. population, experts speculate about an "implosive" tendency in the trend to pack together and slice up territory, rather than expanding outward. With record numbers of young cranes on the Texas coast after 1984, it is not yet clear how this increasing congestion, especially on the mainland, will work out. Some "breakout" appears inevitable if tensions between older mated birds in traditional spaces and younger ones wanting to find food on the tidal flats are to be resolved. One possibility is that, as subadult numbers increase, intolerance will grow, and, as siblings fail to satisfy food needs close to their parents' territories, they will be forced to forage more widely, although refuge biologist Stehn considers that there is enough food to support much higher numbers.

Banding data suggest that some birds move about quite freely. In December 1985, Stehn recorded a two-year-old from the Blackjack mainland flying to Welder Point where it consorted with a subadult from that area. On the last day of 1986 an air census turned up 109 cranes on Aransas, including two Matagorda-based subadults on the refuge mainland. One was a year-old female with two males who strayed into Mustang Bay territory; another, a 1985 male crane from Panther Point, foraged with two females, one of which was close to her parents, on the edge of North Sundown Island.

In January 1987, a subadult crane from Matagorda Is-

land turned up with sandhills near La Ward, sixty miles inland from the Gulf. When the brown cranes started north on migration in March, this 1985 subadult flew back to Matagorda Island where it mingled with a flock of other whoopers. Raised on Cottonwood Bayou where its parents had a new chick, the wandering crane, Green/white/Green–Green/white/Green, left on schedule for Canada the following month. Subadult GwG–GwG disappeared for most of the following winter. It was not spotted on Aransas after 12 November 1987 but was observed on spring migration and in Wood buffalo in 1988. Banding reveals that cranes move about the refuge, and perhaps off it as well, more than experts had thought and may appear in unexpected localities. They may always have done so, but, as cohorts from recent years mature and numbers continue to grow, such excursions will probably become more recognizable and pronounced.[36]

I have scarcely mentioned the journey from the banks of the Slave across to the Sass River. It is a route that is used in winter by beaver trappers but not traveled by anyone after they come out in April. The Grand Detour portage between the Slave and the Little Buffalo lies through one of the most beautiful wilderness areas I have ever seen. The spruce timber gives way to prairies many miles in extent from north to south, and on most of them were herds of buffalo, a magnificent sight. Coming out of one of the wet, mosquito-ridden forests we were on the shores of Long Slough, where we pitched our first camp and our packers left us. The bird life is wonderfully abundant—hermit thrushes and olive-backs singing, horned grebes and sandhill cranes calling, and ruffed grouse drumming all around us.

ROBERT PORTER ALLEN
*A Report on the Whooping Crane's
Northern Breeding Grounds, p. 26*

3. Canada and Radio Tracking

Wood Buffalo National Park

In 1945, with a growing commitment to conserve the whooper and unravel its life history, Fred G. Bard, director of the Saskatchewan Museum of Natural History, Regina, began assembling reports about flight tracks that led to possible breeding places. To assist investigations, the Canadian Wildlife Service notified waterfowl flyway biologist Robert H. Smith to keep a sharp lookout for whooping cranes on his waterfowl surveys and to assist people like Bard who were dedicated to finding the secret of their nesting grounds. Smith spent four successive summers on this extra whooping crane detail. In the first season he checked out Alberta's Athabasca River drainage; the second he watched for whoopers in the Peace River watershed and, with ornithologist Olin S. Pettingill, flew over Lake Athabasca, over Lesser Slave Lake, and into western Saskatchewan. Both surveys failed to locate nesting grounds. In June 1947, Smith teamed up with Robert P. Allen, and they flew almost six thousand miles in fifteen days, as far north as Great Slave Lake looking for whoopers before turning back to Fort Smith on 25 June. On that afternoon their Grumman *Widgeon* may have passed over the nesting area. The two men were heading back to Fort Smith along the upper sections of the Klewi and Sass rivers. Allen noted: "1:40 P.M. Rain squall. Rough going. Poor visibility all the way in. Set down on the airstrip at Fort Smith at 2:45 P.M. This ends our search." Later he was to comment ruefully, "Little did we know how very close we had come to our objective."

From 4 June to 4 August 1948, the two crane hunters flew more than fourteen hundred miles reaching west to Point Barrow, Alaska, and east to Bathurst Inlet, Northwest Territories. Again, whoopers eluded them. On 31 July, Smith and Allen landed at Yellowknife, "definitely licked!" After that failure, Smith pursued his

waterfowl surveys without whooper hunters aboard and it was during one of these flights, on 11 July 1952, southwest of Yellowknife—where he and Allen had given up in despair four years earlier—that he glimpsed a white crane on the ground. "The whooper was standing on the margin of a small pond, under some open-grown spruce," Smith recalled. "It moved a short distance as I took several passes over it at about 100 feet." It was located again the following day, and there was another one about thirty miles away. That same summer, a geologist reported a possible whooper near the Slave River between Fort Smith and Fort Resolution.

Subsequent flights failed to confirm Smith's sighting and the following year, despite searches, he saw nothing. It was helicopter pilot Don Landells and a forester companion, G. M. Wilson, flying between a wild fire near the Hay River and Fort Smith on 30 June 1954, who came upon adults and young along the Sass River within Wood Buffalo N.P. and alerted the outside world.[1]

Allen led the charge toward the hidden nesting grounds. By July 1954, the season was too advanced for a ground expedition. But the following May, after Canadian Wildlife Service biologist William A. Fuller had located seven cranes in a 500-square-mile tract comprising the Sass River and Klewi River, Allen and colleagues flew into Fort Smith and set out by boat. They headed north on the Slave River; after forty-four miles they portaged westward to the Little Buffalo River and into its tributary, the Sass River (Chepewyan name for bear). Allen's party was defeated by countless log jams on their path to crane nesting grounds and was forced to return.

A helicopter ride left the party equally frustrated after the birdmen realized that the pilot had set them down at the wrong place. A third try and thirty-one days after his ground search had begun, Allen knew he was finally closing in. On 24 June 1955, the team finally glimpsed

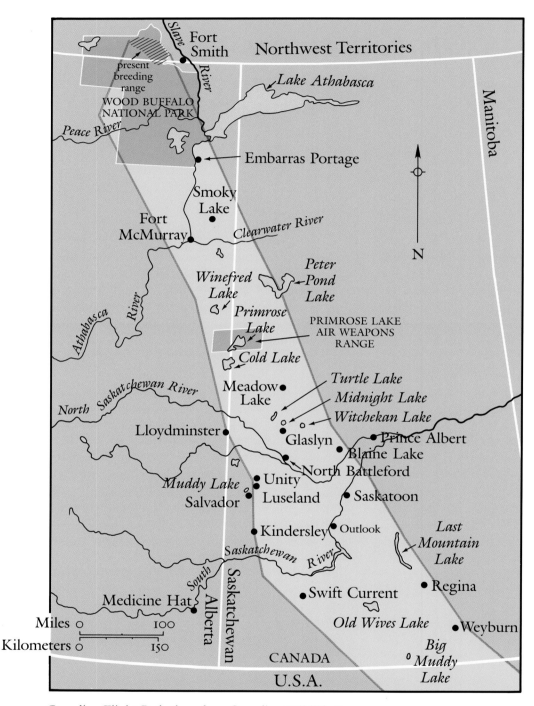

Canadian Flight Path (based on Canadian Wildlife Service. *Canadian Whooping Crane Recovery Plan*, p. 10)

whooping cranes and passed ten days exploring their wilderness home, which Allen termed a "sort of arrested subclimax," consisting of spruce forest, tamarack, and spruce bog and thickly dotted with small, shallow ponds. He surveyed the bird and pond fauna, collected water and mud samples, and noted tracks of whoopers and their young. But, after the initial encounter with the rare cranes, the quarry eluded him.[2]

Mosquitos, biting flies, thunderstorms, hail, frozen lakes, and frigid nights are common in that open, untrammelled 11-million-acre vastness in which the cranes summer. Woods and damp thickets restricted visibility often to less than 100 feet, and Allen's party endured bone-jarring stumbles over burnt logs and debris. Ponds, small lakes, and marshes laid out in huge odd-shaped curves and edges filled in spaces between woody groves. Cranes as well as humans must pick their way carefully through such tough country, especially when guiding flightless young and during molt when older birds may also be earthbound. Basic food needs are met in the marsh complexes that adjoin these major tributaries of the Little Buffalo River. Canadian Wildlife Service biologist Ernie Kuyt, who knows these places intimately after twenty years of slogging through them summer after summer and tilting by plane over the boreal forest edges in which this trellis-type network of creeks, ponds, and lakes is situated, notes that cranes inhabit smaller ponds and marshes, each of which is separated by small ridges or hummocks from which larger conifers sprout.

These alkaline water bodies sunk into an old limestone substrate are filled with cattails, sedges, and bulrushes, which cranes pull up to build large nest platforms for their eggs. Ponds are frequently shallow and filled with soft marl. The ones in which cranes nest are barely nine or ten inches deep around the actual nest platform and enable the long-legged cranes to wade easily in search of aquatic insects, fish, and snails, although little feeding is done in actual nest ponds.

After Allen's initial exploratory foray, three Canadian researchers, W. A. Fuller, N. S. Novakowski, and E. Kuyt, began in turn to assemble information about whooper breeding. Current whooper biologist Ernie Kuyt has worked with the cranes since 1966, mapping nest sites, calculating territory sizes, and monitoring bird productivity year after year. He pioneered the collection of eggs for transplant programs and headed up the team that began banding well-grown chicks.

Before Kuyt took over, only the Sass River, where Allen's group was let off, about fifty miles northwest of Fort Smith, was surveyed regularly. However, in the last twenty years or so air coverage has extended both north and south. Kuyt has checked out cranes along two adjacent water courses, the Klewi and Nyarling rivers, north of the Sass, and has discovered two additional nest areas toward the upper reaches of the Little Buffalo River in the south. He recognizes that pairs show strong homing tendencies, returning to certain marsh complexes in the different watersheds. Although they do not use the same nest, adult cranes adopt what he terms a composite nesting area (CNA), which includes the nest site and the territory or home area in which parents forage and guide their young when the latter leave the actual nest one or two days after hatching. CNAs vary in size from a hundred acres in the only Alberta nesting area, to 11,600 acres along the Nyarling River near the park's northern boundary; the mean area for each comprises about 1,800 acres.[3]

Inaccessible terrain on crane nesting grounds mandates a reliance on aerial surveys and negates regular daily observations for fully understanding territorial behavior. Kuyt, who has found nests as close together as half a mile, believes that vocalizations between pairs help define home ranges, whose geography a pair must know in great detail. Use of CNAs shifts with water conditions and food supplies. In drier years, nest success is depressed when wolves and bears gain easier access to whooper territories and pilfer eggs or kill small chicks. Drought can also lead to lightning-caused fires that consume wooded ridges. In summers when water levels are high, aquatic foods are more plentiful and terrestrial predators find it harder to penetrate crane nesting areas.

Over the years, Kuyt has discovered that certain pairs are more successful in fledging young than others; some are chronically poor breeders. For example, pair Sass-3 (named after Sass River, CNA 3) failed year after year to hatch chicks, until 1979 when both eggs hatched for the first time. Unfortunately, a wolf killed chick 7-79 just before it was able to fly. Wolves are believed to have killed nine of sixty-three well-grown and banded whoopers from 1977 to 1984. In this instance, however, researchers were able to reconstruct 7-79's tragedy from tracks seen on the bottom of a pond. The family had been wading in the shallow water body when the big canid charged, bounding through foot-deep water as the cranes flapped awkwardly away. After a chase, the wolf grabbed the youngster, and all that searchers discovered was a pile of feathers and the tip of its bill. The deceased chick's sibling, however, hatched and fledged

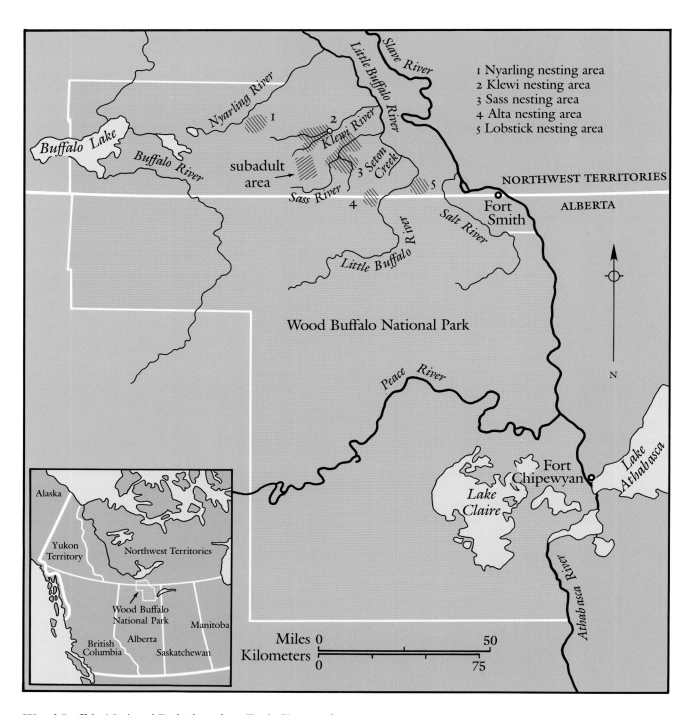

1 Nyarling nesting area
2 Klewi nesting area
3 Sass nesting area
4 Alta nesting area
5 Lobstick nesting area

Wood Buffalo National Park (based on Ernie Kuyt and
J. Paul Goossen, in *Proceedings 1985 Crane Workshop*, ed.
James C. Lewis)

from an egg planted on Grays Lake, Idaho. Kuyt adds a twist in this sad incident, suggesting that the two chicks may not have belonged to Sass-3 but to Sass-7, an adjoining pair who may have nested in Sass-3's territory before shifting to their traditional home range later in the summer.[4]

In other areas, where water levels are more dependable, certain productive, experienced pairs laid a two-egg clutch every year between 1967 and 1979 and fledged many young. Nil–White's parents, for example, raised him in 1978 Klewi River CNA 2, which has breeding sites plotted back to 1967. Nil–White has returned to the same watershed as an adult and has guided chicks to Aransas in four successive years (prior to 1988). Such consistent productivity is normal among such long-lived birds. Newly established pairs may fail to rear a chick for a year or two, but experience helps make them successful parents.

In addition to checking on traditional CNAs and monitoring productivity, Kuyt has looked for identity bands in order to plot the location of subadults who return to nonbreeding areas within Wood Buffalo National Park. Since 1977 when banded juveniles were first observed in the park, Kuyt noted that they concentrate in a stretch of marshland between the Sass and Klewi rivers. Single birds or two or three together may forage in this area, establishing informal bonds and becoming familiar with the environment as parents set up breeding duties in CNAs only a few miles away. Chicks, that is, birds less than a year old, usually follow their parents back to Wood Buffalo N.P. Those that separate earlier on spring migration and older subadults tend to return later than the more experienced adults, who arrive in the final days of April to take full advantage of this short summer season. In 1988, three families separated in faraway Aransas as the adults set off for nesting grounds without their well-developed charges. The chicks later teamed up with other subadults and headed north. Kuyt knows of only two instances, both unsuccessful, of whoopers nesting again after losing their eggs; hence, reproduction begins as soon as the ground clears of snow and ice.

Much of Ernie Kuyt's information comes from overflights of the breeding grounds after the adult cranes arrive. After pinpointing nests, ascertaining that most contain two eggs, and calculating approximate dates for hatching, Kuyt uses a helicopter to land in each territory and removes one egg from most nests. These eggs go to foster parents in Idaho or Maryland. In August, he supervises a banding team, which includes Roderick C. Drewien, who drives north from Idaho where he is employed by the Wildlife Research Institute, University of Idaho, Moscow, and is under contract to the U.S. Fish and Wildlife Service for the Whooping Crane Cross-Fostering Experiment. Kuyt, Drewien, and other team members capture and band well-grown but flightless whooper chicks. Between 1977 and 1987, Kuyt's team banded 117 crane chicks and lost two. The first probably drowned after banding, and the second succumbed probably to shock after sustaining a leg injury while being chased in a burn area strewn with blackened snags.[5]

On 21 August 1987, Kuyt's five-man Canadian and U.S. crew captured, weighed, measured, and banded twenty-one chicks, four more than they banded in 1988. As a territory is checked and a family is spotted, the helicopter swings down, drops off one to three crew members, and lifts away. The catchers race toward the chick, trying, often futilely, to keep it from entering ponds, whose marl bottoms, so-called loonshit, impede movement. After a chase of five minutes or so, the chick is subdued and the breathless team calls in biologists who band and examine the youngster. People must guard against bills and feet, which cranes can use to good effect. Generally, the entire procedure is conducted quickly in order to minimize stress on the bird and on its parents, who often remain close by. Then the helicopter spins away, directed by a spotter aircraft, toward another territory.

Needless to say, the entire operation is exhausting work; the team may grab a sandwich as the helicopter heads off to a fuel cache in the bush, then regroup, poised for another drop-off. Drewien states that working with whoopers in a place that is "more water than land" is the hardest bird-banding of all. A catcher must be prepared to flounder in pond mire, stumble on snags, get bitten by mosquitos, then face a large, angry quarry; assistants must be ready with the right bands, scales, and measuring equipment under hard-driving Kuyt, who oversees this very sensitive operation. Kuyt knows how traumatic such a procedure is for cranes and prefers to inflict stress on teammates by demanding speed and efficiency so that the chick is released quickly. The day after banding he flies over each family territory in a fixed-wing aircraft to ensure that families have been reunited.[6]

STOPPING PLACE

Birds   skim cloudbase

                                to line a

roost   hard specks

                        against overcast.

    Calling out of one

                    thousand throats

    a rumble of

                    sawcut and

        houndsbay from a   crane
        and goose show.   Noise
        billows with   spent
        day,   sharpens air
        in wingbeats, and
            spins away.
        Geese plummet.
        Shear sky like
            big leaves
        rocking to a
        cradle wetland.
        Cranes circle
            the wind,
        pinions set slant
        down with dangle
        legs to cushion stop.
    Heaven dashes earth
            and water with salt
        geese and pepper
                            cranes
        who   seeking sanctuary
        crowd this   lower
        horizon parley in
                        dappled flocks and
        come to order.
                            Silence
        steals tumult
                        from the marsh.
    Moonglow
                        lights the
    roost whose   bird kindling
    will liven the
                    morning with a thousand sparks!

Radio Tracking

Important information has been compiled in this decade from tracking cranes along migration routes between Canada and the United States. Field workers attached small radio transmitters to chicks in Wood Buffalo National Park. In a remarkable cooperative effort between Canada and the United States, air and ground trackers monitored signals emitted by these tiny instruments as the marked whoopers flew to Texas, wintered, and returned to Canada. In a few instances, people followed the same whooping crane or cranes on more than one journey, noting how many miles and what routes were covered and in what places birds fed and rested. Such telemetry has provided vital data about habitat preferences along the migration route, particularly roosting and feeding sites, and from it followers have identified locations in which cranes are likely to stop, feed, and rest.

Between 1981 and 1984 during three southbound and two northward migrations, wildlife personnel from the Canadian Wildlife Service, U.S. Fish and Wildlife Service, Texas Parks and Wildlife Department and other state agencies, plus Texas A&M University, and the National Audubon Society monitored a total of eight radio-marked whoopers. Tracking aircraft checked altitude, compass bearing, air speed, flight characteristics, and the duration of daily movements; air crews listed other bird species associating with migratory cranes. On the ground, another team of biologists examined the stopping places used by whoopers. They took food samples around roost sites, checking whether these wetlands were publicly or privately owned and if local residents were aware of the cranes and concerned for their well-being. Observers also endeavored to discover whether stopover places were likely to be altered, destroyed, or made unattractive to passing birds in the future.[7]

The project to follow individual whooping cranes began in August 1981, when a three-member team of biologists fixed tiny radios to one of the plastic colored bands placed on the legs of three still-flightless young. Weighing 2.5 ounces and attached by nuts and bolts designed to corrode and drop off the bands after a year or so, transmitters emitted signals from ground to air that could be received up to eighteen miles away. Ground-to-ground reception was possible from about three or four miles. Once the bird was airborne, however, as Canadian Wildlife Service biologist tracker Ernie Kuyt soon discovered, faint signals could be picked up from as far as fifty miles away.

The first young crane to quit its nest territory was R/W–Green (a small red band above a small white on its left leg with a large green band attached to the right leg; Kuyt writes out the color name for the large band and abbreviates the color of the smaller-size bands). Its parents flew from their Klewi River nest area in Wood Buffalo National Park on 17 September 1981 and traveled 175 miles southeast to a lake near Embarras, Alberta. Next day, Canadian crane expert Ernie Kuyt, flying out of Fort Smith, located the family still heading south, but thick clouds made visual contact impossible. The whooper family settled on a lake, so-called Smoky Lake after forest fires in the vicinity, near Fort Mc-Murray, after flying fewer than one hundred miles. On the third day, the airmen landed their float plane on Smoky Lake and watched the family feeding along the bank until a wildfire closed in, forcing them back to Fort McMurray.

Forest fires continued to hamper observations, but Canadian birdmen listened to the steady radio beep from R/W–Green, who foraged around the lake for four days. They noted, too, the passage of other migrants, including loons, ducks, and bald eagles, and spied river otters feeding around their moored aircraft. On 23 September, although plagued by fog, Kuyt and his pilot set off southward, following signals. Again, the crew did not make visual contact but judged that the birds were flying at about 7,000 feet altitude. They lost the cranes over Primrose Lake Air Weapons Range, straddling the Alberta-Saskatchewan border, after about 270 miles but knew that the whoopers were approaching a ground team eager to follow their route. Low cloud, fog, and rain dogged both sets of trackers. On 25 September, however, Kuyt's aircraft picked up the trail and followed the elusive cranes to Midnight Lake near Glaslyn, Saskatchewan, where for a time he switched to the ground team and discovered that receiving equipment was not working properly. It was here that the ground crew made initial contact and kept a close watch on the whooping cranes.

For two and a half weeks the family fed on wheat and barley stubbles and roosted in one of three wet areas near Midnight Lake. The birds established a simple routine. They fed on grain at first light, rested in the marsh around midday, returned to the fields, then flew back at dusk to a secure water site.

On 11 October, while flying between food and a roost, Klewi River chick R/W–Green struck a single-strand power line near Midnight Lake. Severely injured, the young male was rushed by experts to the University

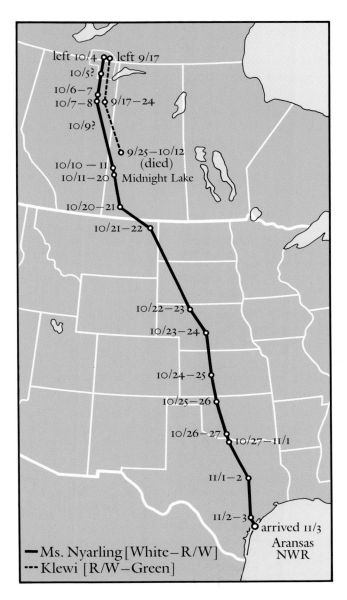

Fall 1981 Migration Route for Ms. Nyarling and Klewi (based on Aransas National Wildlife Refuge Annual Report, 1981, p. 33)

of Saskatchewan's Veterinary Clinic in Saskatoon, where it died a week later. Its parents reached the Aransas National Wildlife Refuge about ten days later.

An autopsy showed fractures in the spine and skull. The back injury had damaged nerves and caused leg paralysis. Interestingly, the heavier-than-expected seventeen-pound bird had ingested pieces of plastic wadding used in shotgun cartridges.

Kuyt recalled the distress felt by trackers and local residents, who had become crane enthusiasts. "The farmer on whose land the cranes fed for so long is almost heartbroken," he wrote sadly, admitting that "I find it difficult to read the autopsy reports and not see the sight of these stately birds striding through a Saskatchewan stubble field or at rest in a small pond, the juvenile in its customary position near the adult female."

Kuyt and colleagues speculated that a gust of wind may have pushed the youngster into the wire over which it had flown at least fifty times while foraging in the vicinity. It is possible that the chick lagged behind or flew a little above or below one of its parents on a short flight and simply didn't see the wire ninety feet above the ground. The family often passed within a few yards of this line on local flights, and on the day of the accident people had seen them fly *under* it as they went out to feed at 7:32 A.M. Chick R/W–Green may have injured itself a few hours later and lay paralyzed under the wire all night. It struggled to fly away as the team approached it next morning, watched by its parents who bugled anxiously two hundred yards away. Power lines were to figure tragically in further radio tracking of whooping cranes.[8]

Kuyt and the ground team switched to another crane family, whose chick, female (White–R/W) carried a radio whose signals another aircrew was monitoring. The three birds had set off from a nest territory along the Nyarling River, an intermittent creek in Wood Buffalo National Park, on 4 October. The third family, with the radio-tagged male chick, Green–R/W, nicknamed Alberta, after its natal territory in that province's northern edge, followed them on or about 16 October.

Difficulties with tracking equipment caused air observers to lose contact with the Nyarling family. On 6 October, however, searchers found them. The cranes had moved almost two hundred miles from their departure point. The following day, headwinds held them to merely twenty-five miles. But on 8 October, winds shifted and the whooper family headed toward Primrose Lake Military Range where Kuyt had earlier lost

contact with his Klewi crane family.

On a routine flight to check his Midnight Lake charges on the day before Klewi R/W–Green was crippled, Ernie Kuyt tuned his receiver to the Nyarling family's frequency, and in mid-afternoon he heard the first faint beeps emitted by the radio on White–R/W chick, so-called Ms. Nyarling. He checked the Midnight Lake family in their usual grain haunts, then sped in his aircraft after this new family and, according to signal strength, was closing rapidly when the beeping ceased. He realized that the crane trio must have landed. Next day, alerted by Kuyt, the trackers who had been pursuing but had lost this second radio-marked chick caught up with the whoopers about fifteen miles from Unity, Saskatchewan. In coordinating efforts to follow and watch Ms. Nyarling, Kuyt figured that this particular threesome faced the longest trip of any whooper family from the north end of Wood Buffalo N.P. to the Aransas National Wildlife Refuge in Texas. "It is unlikely," he said, "that any other family will have a longer migration route."[9]

Short flights to grain fields in Saskatchewan by the Nyarling birds reminded Kuyt of the tragic end to chick R/W–Green. Throughout the entire migration, human trackers feared for Ms. Nyarling's safety, especially when traveling birds dropped low looking for a suitable roost. In dimming light and overcast, wires seemed to loom everywhere. Conditions were most perilous as the cranes beat over intensively tilled croplands on the lower Plains, where power lines loop between irrigation sprinklers and pumps.

On 11 October, in the late afternoon, the Nyarling whoopers left the Unity-Reward area in Saskatchewan. This unusually late departure caused ground observers to wonder whether they had come too close and scared the birds. After a twelve-mile flight southwest the family landed in grainfields near Salvador, Saskatchewan, and stayed for nine days.

On 20 October, two inches of snow covered the ground; at 9:00 A.M. the Texas-bound cranes spiraled away, carrying good wishes from local people, who had been thoroughly briefed about crane behavior by tracking experts. Snow flurries and a low cloud ceiling hampered the aircraft. The cranes also appeared troubled by such icy conditions and landed on at least three occasions, then lifted above "cloud bottom" in mid-afternoon, reported Kuyt, only to descend close to his circling airplane toward a reservoir located about eighty miles north of the Canada-U.S. border. That night the whoopers used a mudflat behind a concrete dam of the

Russell Creek Irrigation Project. It was an unusual roost at the base of a coulee. They rested in about eight inches of water some fifteen feet offshore, sharing a narrow space with ducks and geese. The next morning the Nyarling family fed in wheat stubble near the coulee, then quite suddenly departed on a 150-mile flight.

Their highly unusual afternoon departure from Canada's Russell Creek Project almost fooled the aircrew, who scrambled after them and finally caught sight of three cranes at sunset. The birds were flying low, along the west fork of the Poplar River, obviously searching for a stopping place. They landed across the U.S. border in Montana about thirty-five miles west of Medicine Lake National Wildlife Refuge.[10]

Kuyt's aircraft was forced to return to Canada to pick up maps and gear left on what was supposed to have been a routine check and photo sortie. He and his pilot started anew the following day, found the cranes, turned back to clear customs, then caught up with the family, which was now airborne assisted by a northwest wind. The trio tracked across the southwest tip of North Dakota (near Bowman). At that point, the aircrew saw that rather than descending the three birds were spiraling repeatedly into a northwest wind and gaining extra altitude.

Alerted by Kuyt's plane the previous day, the ground crew had made it to the Montana roost site after driving all night. Customs agents passed them quickly through the "Gates of the Country" at 2:30 A.M., and the team dashed along a dirt road "filled with the sights," remembered one member, "of roadside mule deer, snowshoe hares, and a splendid display of the Aurora Borealis." Their vehicle drew up close to the roosting cranes at 6:00 A.M. and watched them awaken and fly off at 9:30 A.M. They then found out "that a crane can fly faster than a biologist can drive," said biologist Steve Labuda, doubtless thinking about innumerable turns to keep on the right heading, who failed to catch up with the birds for the next thirty-six hours.[11]

As he saw cranes climbing higher and higher in the early afternoon of 22 October, Kuyt and his pilot prepared to hunker down for probably a long journey, much longer than any they had tracked so far. They landed quickly at Bowman to refuel; while parked, the crew picked up signals from the cranes close to the airport. Biologist Kuyt made visual contact just before 3:00 P.M. as the white birds circled at 5,500 feet. For the next three hours, however, their quarry seemed to play cat and mouse, remaining invisible but well within radio range. The whoopers flew south at probably between 8,000 and 9,000 feet altitude, estimated Kuyt, above beaten and broken terrain. Like the whoopers, the airmen spotted the Badlands National Monument, creased by shadow-filled ravines and white, glittering cuestas. The aircraft droned on, crossing into Nebraska at 6:00 P.M., and finally its occupants glimpsed the threesome near the Niobrara River. The whooping cranes were descending, no longer gliding but flapping along in a line with radio-banded White–R/W in the rear. The whoopers beat southward for almost an hour after sunset and circled once over Merritt Reservoir, where Kuyt and the air team awaited them in the dusk. "We are unhappy that we have not seen them land safely," he reported, "but we can't stay in the area and we depart for Valentine, Nebraska." The birds had made a 9½-hour flight of approximately 464 miles from northeast Montana into north-central Nebraska.[12]

A sleep-deprived ground team sped toward Valentine but were to arrive too late to catch up with the cranes. Instead, Ernie Kuyt staked out the tired whoopers, who hunched in a pond chilled by night air. The Nyarling family stepped from shallow water at about 8:00 A.M., flew to an alfalfa field, and was disturbed by a vehicle into spiraling flight. As the birds slowly circled higher, Canadian-based trackers saw two additional whoopers straining to join up. The newcomers were probably subadults on the identical southbound route, but, failing to climb as efficiently, they fell behind, and the trio continued alone.

Kuyt studied flight maneuvers on this first journey. He noted, for instance, that after lifting off in the morning the whoopers flew round and round, spiraling to gain altitude and to test higher wind currents for both lift and direction. Once they reached a desired height, the big birds set their wings and glided forward and slightly downward until they found more lift and repeated the circling maneuvers. Once aloft, the cranes often flew in an echelon or single line with an adult leading and the chick either between parents or bringing up the rear. At low altitudes, usually toward the end of a day or when the air was cooler, Kuyt noted how the cranes propelled themselves forward with energy-sapping wingbeats.[13]

On 23 October, in Nebraska, Kuyt saw his cranes practice usual climb, spiral, and glide tactics, but headwinds pushed them north, not south, forcing them to sharpen their angle of descent in order to make headway. The family covered only 110 miles in six hours, reaching Oconto, Nebraska, where the ground team finally caught up with them. Next day the birds flew with tail winds another 200 miles in almost seven hours. Before they left Nebraska, however, the ground team noted that the long-shanked cranes "first left their roost pond walking upslope, flipping cow chips as they proceeded uphill." Turning over a dozen chips in the area where the birds had fed, biologists counted eight crickets, two spiders, and a grub. One of the birds, presumably the inexperienced chick, apparently had selected a fresh pile of manure and stirred it in an attempt to turn it over.

Weather in Kansas was dull and wet. Kuyt's aircraft kept surveillance. The whooping cranes, seemingly reluctant to fly, remained at low altitude. The men noted other migrants teaming up with the cranes. "I get the impression that we are on a busy highway with all traffic heading south," observed Kuyt, who saw flocks of sandhills beating toward Oklahoma. One sandhill family joined up with the whoopers and all headed south in tight formation, adult whoopers periodically giving way to sandhills and vice-versa at the head of the line. After about an hour the brown birds dropped away, said Kuyt, who noted that the whoopers made several stops that day. He speculated that flapping-type flight, which characterized much of their progress, tired them. They needed to land in order to rest and perhaps feed briefly.[14]

On 26 October, ground spotters watched their charges leave a roost on Oklahoma's Cimarron River, forty miles southwest of the Great Salt Plains National Wildlife Refuge, a traditional stopover for white cranes, and spend the morning turning over cow chips. Heading into a 10-m.p.h. wind, the family kept low and adopted spiraling, short glides, and some flapping to make 150 miles to southeast of Lawton, Oklahoma.

Unfavorable winds grounded the birds along the Red River between Oklahoma and Texas. Over the course of four days the whoopers made only short flights to glean millet, milo, and wheat. The team in the vehicle monitored them and saw how the big birds tried frequently but unsuccessfully to push south into a strong, persistent wind. Trackers grew worried about possible health risks from fungicide-dressed wheat on which the cranes were feeding. A cold front on 1 November enabled the trio to go on; they covered about 230 miles to a small stock pond near Rosebud, Texas. On this flight, Kuyt followed them over Fort Worth's eastern suburbs, and his pilot obtained clearance for the aircraft and the cranes from air traffic control near Dallas–Fort Worth airport. Commercial flights were diverted momentarily to permit crane passage.

The next day, the air team expected the now fatigued migrants to complete their long journey; but, although they had barely two hundred miles to go, they failed to reach Aransas. At 10:00 A.M., Kuyt heard from ground personnel that cranes were aloft. His aircraft shadowed them traveling south at 3,500 feet altitude, but by mid-afternoon the birds were exhausted. Approaching Green Lake, less than fifty miles from the refuge, Kuyt wrote: "We begin to note many other white birds . . . The whoopers begin to cross Green Lake but after a few hundred yards the three birds, obviously tired, return to the shoreline and follow it in a westward direction. The three cranes fly low over the water in a labouring fashion we have not often seen. At 4:55 the birds have had it; they unceremoniously plop down in a flooded field along the Guadalupe River close to Tivoli."[15]

On 3 November, a group of bird enthusiasts led by manager Frank Johnson, alerted by news of the Nyarling family's imminent arrival, watched from Mustang Lake's visitor tower, the highest vantage point in the area, as the territory's owners swung in to claim that lake for their winter home. Kuyt's aircraft was in position as the whooping crane family "flap-flying in a line astern, with the chick tucked in No. 2 position," crossed the refuge boundary around 8:00 A.M. Kuyt noted that "the cranes hesitate not at all, they know where they are and they land, fluff wing feathers a few times and begin to feed. It has all gone so matter-of-factly but I feel deeply touched now that it is all over."[16]

Watchers, positioned luckily to see the cranes land, "whooped" in victory as birds and aircraft flew past, completing a 31-day, 2,400-mile journey. Within thirty minutes the adult female twice presented her youngster with food. An Aransas family was "home" or, as the Canadians prefer to think, in their winter "resort."

In 1982, pleased with data from the first season's work, Canadian and U.S. experts made plans to follow the cranes south again. They banded four chicks with solar-powered radios and noted that transmitters on the two 1981 survivors (Nyarling and Alberta) were still functioning. They decided to follow two birds. An air and ground team was assigned to Ms. Nyarling, the chick tracked the year before, now a white-feathered year-old bird. Another set of monitors was designated to follow a new chick and its parents.[17]

On Wednesday, 15 September 1982, Ms. Nyarling left her subadult, or nonbreeding, area in Wood Buffalo National Park where she had summered in company with three other whooping cranes. A float plane tracked the four birds 447 miles into Alberta. The next day the four subadults added another 192 miles, and on 17 Sep-

tember they landed beside Devil's Lake, Watrous, Saskatchewan, an additional 174 miles southward. The foursome loitered in this region for twenty-four days, feeding on barley stubble for a few hours each day, then flying back to the lake to rest and preen. The ground team, which staked out the site, recorded that as the birds' stay became progressively longer whoopers fed less and loafed more, indicating that they were in good physical shape to continue migration.

On 11 October 1982, with favorable winds, the whooping cranes started to move but after only 39 miles alighted on the east shore of Last Mountain Lake, the oldest wildlife refuge in North America. Curious bi-

A radio transmitter being applied to a young whooper chick on Grays Lake, August 1979. In the early 1980s, a number of chicks in the Wood Buffalo–Aransas population received similar instruments that provided data about migration, food, and habitat. Photograph by Rod C. Drewien.

ologists watched the cranes fly up and down the Saskatchewan lake "as though [they] were searching for something." Finally they landed and the men remained close by until it was dark, satisfied that their charges had settled.

The ground vehicle and its equipment drew up half an hour before dawn but received no signal from Ms. Nyarling's radio. The tracker plane also drew a blank. Astonishingly, the four whoopers had left before dawn and vanished from human ken. One team member reported: "Visual searching from the ground and air failed to turn up any whooping cranes around Last Mountain Lake. Several thousand sandhill cranes which had been present on the lake the previous afternoon had also disappeared overnight. The whoopers had flown at night. Two days' search failed to recover the four cranes, and nothing more was heard of Ms. Nyarling until one week later."

On 18 October, a passing motorist saw something white beneath a four-strand roadside wire near Waco, Texas, more than 1,300 miles south of Last Mountain Lake. The bundle of white feathers on the edge of a harvested maize field turned out to be the radio-banded seventeen-month old Ms. Nyarling. She was dead. The young female had barely 300 miles to go to complete her first migration as an independent whooping crane. Instead she became a statistic—the second radio-carrying crane in consecutive years to end its life by hitting a power line.[18]

Trackers had developed affection for Ms. Nyarling. People had bustled after her as she followed her parents a year earlier and had cheered from the tower as she swung down to her parents' winter territory. There, observed by staff and visitors, she had learned to catch crabs, shrimp, and clams before migrating north again under parental guidance. Ms. Nyarling also reminded people to take nothing for granted when it comes to cranes. The four young whoopers had moved off under cover of darkness; somehow their restless wandering up and down the lake before roosting had perhaps indicated the desire to continue. This was not the only time that observers discovered that whooping cranes migrated at night.

After losing track of Ms. Nyarling at Last Mountain Lake, but before they learned of her tragic demise in faraway Texas, Labuda's team picked up a chick (White–Red) with its parents. This crane family, whose male adult Red/White/Red–Blue was the first whooper whose breeding age was known (four years), had come within sixty miles of Saskatoon, Saskatchewan, after

foraging in stubble farther north. On 15 October, under the watchful eyes of Canadian Wildlife Service biologist Kuyt and U.S. Fish and Wildlife Service pilot Bill Larned, the three birds spiraled upward and headed off, not south but north. By nightfall White–Red and its parents had traveled 142 miles and passed close to another crane family headed southwest.

On 16 October 1982, the White–Red crane family flew north another 68 miles, reaching the boreal forest's edge they had quit several days earlier. They swung about and after two days were back south near where they had begun their detour northward. The family lingered in the North Battleford region, roosting in a five-acre pond and foraging in nearby barley and wheat stubble. On 27 October, the whoopers began migration southward in earnest, covering 303 miles into lower Saskatchewan. Next day, they flew into the United States and landed near Beulah, North Dakota, forced down by bad weather. On 29 October, they traveled about 160 miles and landed near Eureka, South Dakota, where they lingered awhile. On 31 October, they teamed up with another whooper pair, and on 1 November headed almost 200 miles south into Nebraska's Sandhills, landing after dark 15 miles beyond Ainsworth.[19]

At first light, Labuda's crew failed to pick up the chick's radio signal. The birds had moved off; luckily, the trailing aircraft picked up a faint signal in the south and chased after the errant cranes. The day finally ended when the family alighted in a shallow bay of Fort Cobb Reservoir, in central Oklahoma, 504 miles south of the trio's previous roost.

The ground team pulled into the nearby community of Anadarko close to midnight, and at daylight they were positioned to watch adults catch small, shiny fish, probably shad, at a prodigious rate. Biologists counted sixteen finfish per minute being fed to the radio-tagged chick—about one every four seconds. Soon, the whoopers flew off, crossed into Texas before noon, and carried on until well after dark, coming to earth within thirty miles of Aransas National Wildlife Refuge.

At 10:12 A.M. on 4 November 1982, three whooping cranes touched down on their territory along Dunham Bay, having completed 2,727 miles in 26 days, three of which were spent flying 248 miles in the wrong direction! Monitoring cranes had turned up a wealth of new details and additional surprises. Trackers learned that cranes did move at night and did make very long nonstop flights. In this instance, the family had traveled the final 1,168 miles in a little more than three days.[20]

With data gathered about family and subadult behavior en route to Texas, experts turned attention toward the northbound migration route. They wished to determine the spring pathway, compare it with fall routes, examine and compare habitats, and identify hazards.

Two teams, similar to the ones operating southbound, arrived at Aransas National Wildlife Refuge on 25 March 1983. A film crew sponsored by the National Geographic Society joined them. After a long expectant wait, the family with chick Green–white/red, so-called Sass, headed out on 9 April. A second family with chick White–Red, or Lobstick, the one people had tracked earlier, left two days later. With six birds on migration and heading for the same objective, biologists characterized the daily flights as a race to see if Lobstick could catch up to and overtake Sass.

The Sass family made 155 miles the first day, landing beside a five-acre pond northeast of Austin. The next day the three cranes flew another 240 miles to Byers Lake, averaging close to 30 m.p.h. in nearly nine hours. By contrast, the same day, the Lobstick family, leaving with strong southerly winds, reached North Texas in one hop, flying 410 miles at an average speed of 47 m.p.h. and at times clocking 64 m.p.h. It landed about 40 miles west of where the leading family had been that morning, cutting the latter's lead to only one day.[21]

Neither crane group touched down in Oklahoma. The Sass family reached Hoxie, Kansas, on 11 April after flying almost 400 miles in eleven hours. The pursuing family made it to Hazelton, Kansas, a day later. Bad weather then hit cranes and humans. The teams lost contact with the crane families in rainy and overcast conditions. Picking up the signals was more a matter of luck and intuition, given abbreviated distances for receiving them from the birds on the ground. Without air coverage, the whoopers disappeared from the face of the earth.

Both crane families remained in Kansas. The Sass group was about 200 miles north of trailing Lobstick. On 14 April, the former fought 15-m.p.h. headwinds and beat 50 miles into Nebraska. Their average flight speed was below 10 m.p.h., and they landed in a pond half covered with ice. Next day, still flying into winds, they made 82 miles, then rested near Broken Bow and fed in corn stubble.

The Lobstick family left Hazelton on 16 April and made 85 miles to the Quivira National Wildlife Refuge, another sanctuary often visited by whoopers, where the adult male had paused in migration two years earlier. With little to eat, the birds pushed on the next day into stiff westerly winds, landing 93 miles north near Beloit,

Kansas. As the winds died at sunset, they left again, heading almost due west to Glen Elder, as if wishing to compensate for an easterly drift caused by earlier winds. The ground crew guessed that their brief thirty-minute flight carried parents to a recognizable track.

On 19 April, both families landed in North Dakota barely fourteen miles apart. The trailing group had overcome the time lag by spending more hours in the air. The two tracking teams rendezvoused in Williston to compare notes, assuming that spring migration was nearing its end.[22]

The Lobstick family was first into Canada. It had made up the Sass family's two-day headstart and crossed the border on 20 April about fifteen miles ahead. The Lobsticks' lead vanished abruptly, however, when the trio put down only fifteen miles into Saskatchewan. Watchers had seen that chick White–Red had developed a limp. Its condition worsened and may have affected the pace of migration. The Lobstick family remained close to Minton for ten days, under scrutiny from concerned trackers who came upon another radioed whooper subadult, Green–R/W, so called Alberta. Alberta had made fast progress, taking no more than nine days to fly from Aransas to southern Saskatchewan.

The same day that the Lobsticks flew into Canada, the Sass family made 320 miles. The latter covered another 384 miles on 21 April, sleeping on an ice floe in the Athabasca River near Fort McMurray, Alberta. The trio entered Wood Buffalo Park, having taken two weeks to traverse 2,391 miles, with ten days in flight and four days in rest.

Kuyt, U.S. Fish and Wildlife Service pilot Gene Steffer, and cameraman T. Mangelsen followed the family into the park on 22 April. In fact, the Sass adults and chick landed in a nonbreeding area that day and on the next were together on the actual nest site in which the chick had hatched almost a year earlier. Ernie Kuyt photographed the three birds near their 1982 nest island. When Ernie Kuyt carried out his first breeding pair count on 3 May 1983, he discovered Sass close to the place where her parents had led her, as if to show her where to remain, while they tended a new nest with one egg about three hundred yards from the old site in their territory eight miles away. This young female (Green–w/r) stayed in that nonbreeder area for most of the summer before moving about thirty miles by mid-September and teaming up with White–Red, whom researchers had also seen only a few miles from its birthplace in the park. Its parents built a nest but failed to rear a chick in 1983 and probably started out for Texas

Two crane families with two adult-plumaged whooping cranes stand in Saskatchewan grainfields en route to Texas in October 1987. Photograph by Brian W. Johns, CWS.

around mid-September, whereupon Sass and Lobstick fed in their territory before they, too, started out on 24 September 1983.[23]

Canadian researchers fastened miniature transmitters to six chicks in Wood Buffalo National Park in summer 1983. For the third successive year teams prepared to follow two birds on fall migration. By that time, however, only two of the six chicks were still alive. Wolves had reportedly fed on the others. Because of this high mortality, researchers decided to pick up a subadult instead of a ‘chick. Three other radio-tagged birds from prior years were alive. Two of them, Lobstick (White–Red) and Sass (Green–w/r), both named after small rivers draining their parents’ territories—had summered together in the nonbreeding area. Alberta, a two-year-old male, also survived. Lobstick, or White–Red, was the same bird trackers had followed to Dunham Bay on Aransas in 1982 and had tracked back north in spring 1983. The trackers readied to follow Lobstick south again. The fifteen-month-old bird was making its first unsupervised journey with its companion Sass, Green–w/r, also followed north, as we have seen; both carried transmitters.

Now the two independent young cranes left Wood Buffalo and reached Brownlee in southern Saskatchewan in four days, completing more than 700 miles. As expected, they paused in grain fields to rest and prepare for the journey ahead. For two weeks they fed on harvested wheat and roosted on stock ponds. As time passed they became restless, then at 8:45 A.M. on 11 October, with cold temperatures, clear skies, and good tailwinds, they finally departed. The companions flew no fewer than 475 miles at an average speed of 30 m.p.h. before setting down in a stock pond near Isabel, South Dakota.[24]

The tracking Cessna had followed this flight, circling slowly, above and to one side of Lobstick and Sass. Next morning the cranes flew across Nebraska and into Kansas. They had joined up with a sandhill crane flock and were still flying strongly when the airplane broke off contact at 7:00 P.M. Next day, on 13 October, the air team picked them up near Russell, Kansas. The young whoopers had continued to fly at least 75 miles after the aircraft had left them and were to complete another staggering 475-mile trek. They still seemed hell-bent for Texas, moving quickly into Oklahoma, but landed in a well-known stopover point, Salt Plains National Wildlife Refuge, where, on a hunch, the ground crew had decided to go. Due to headwinds Lobstick and Sass stayed at Salt Plains for nine days feeding on minnows in the northern end of the reservoir and foraging in wheat fields. A whooper family joined them.

On 22 October, the two cranes headed south once more. They left at 10:26 A.M. and 8 1/2 hours later landed next to a house on the edge of Garza–Little Elm Reservoir, east of Denton, Texas, a curious roost. They had flown almost 270 miles. From the Denton stopover the duo made it to Sealy, about 250 miles away, in eight hours. Staff from Attwater's Prairie Chicken National Wildlife Refuge drove over to see the illustrious birds, who passed the night just east of that refuge boundary. By 10:00 A.M. they were off again but missed Aransas by fifteen miles, landing in a freshwater inlet on Mission Bay, south of Blackjack Peninsula. Appearing content and in no hurry, the whoopers fed off the refuge before moving to winter quarters on 26 October. Three days later, a tracking team sailed down the Intracoastal Waterway to count cranes and discovered their birds; the subadults had separated, each returning close to its parents' territory. Lobstick and Sass made their first independent migration without mishap, in 32 days, covering about 2,537 miles and averaging 212 miles per day in 12 actual days of flying.[25]

While observers recorded the activities of subadults Sass and Lobstick, two other radio-tagged cranes, chick

Red–Yellow and chick Yellow–Y/R, made it to Texas in fall 1983. The migration of Red–Yellow was most remarkable.

Trackers intercepted this chick near Glaslyn, Saskatchewan, on 18 October and began to monitor its migration on 5 November, when a crane flock consisting of five birds flew into Last Mountain Lake, north of Regina. Two days later, Red–Yellow, its parents, and a subadult pair traveled 370 miles to Long Lake National Wildlife Refuge, North Dakota, shifted (picking up another whooper) to near Pierre, South Dakota, and on 9 November set out in a group of six on the longest apparent nonstop flight ever recorded—1,086 miles to the Texas Gulf coast. Strong tailwinds pushed airspeeds to 60 m.p.h., so that, after about 10 hours of spiraling and gliding, Red–Yellow and company hit the coast 60 or so miles north of Aransas. Heading southwest, this family was on Matagorda Island on 9 November 1983. Unfortunately, this flight could not be monitored during its entirety, so the large distance remains speculative.[26]

Canadian- and U.S.-based teams decided to follow crane migration north again in 1984, for the second successive spring. On 6 April, Ernie Kuyt's aircraft was in touch with no fewer than ten whoopers, including his favorites, Sass and Lobstick (heading north together), Alberta, and the two radio-carrying 1983 chicks. On the first day, pushed by extra strong winds, the whoopers sped into North Texas' Red River area, where a storm grounded them.

For a week progress north was painfully slow. Rain, overcast conditions, and stiff headwinds held most cranes to stop-and-go flights. Conditions worsened in Kansas, as they had in 1983, and the Red–Yellow flock (including Red–R/B and R/B–Red subadults) labored at speeds as low as 10 m.p.h., often at treetop level. Near Hays, Kansas, for example, Red–Yellow, who had flown across that state apparently nonstop the previous fall, struggled along and came down almost due east from its starting point; winds had pushed it off track.

As inclement weather abated, the whoopers quickened their pace and made some long-distance flights. Kuyt noted spiraling tactics, flight formations, and spacing of flock members; he was impressed by the cranes' ability to switch formations. On 18 April, Red–Yellow's four-bird flock flew 400 miles from North Dakota into Canada. Kuyt caught sight of them shortly after midday north of Big Muddy Lake, Saskatchewan, and watched the cranes land and briefly rest, then head northward. At about 6:00 P.M. he flew close to his charges, who had covered another 240 miles since their stop. They were speeding along at more than 50 m.p.h. on a northwest course when biologist Kuyt noted "that the single bird in the flock was falling out of formation a few times, then rejoined the other three birds. Three times the bird actually pecked at and grabbed a wing of one of the parents of yearling 19/83 [Red–Yellow]."[27]

Within a couple of minutes the four cranes, others had left the flock earlier, swung down and landed in grain stubble near Alticane, northwest Saskatchewan. They had flown for a good eight and a half hours; obviously, the non–family member, toward which chick Red–Yellow showed some hostility, had grown tired and communicated its distress to the lead bird.

On 19 April, Red–Yellow's group started out again but after several course changes landed and passed several days foraging in grain stubbles before departing in a northwest direction and leaving Red–Yellow behind on cultivated prairie lands. That afternoon, Kuyt found the chick airborne and solitary northeast of Turtleford, Saskatchewan. Red–Yellow drifted eastward and roosted. It worked back next day into the same area where it had stayed with its parents, leading observers to believe that it was checking out previous feeding sites. The youngster drifted slowly south-eastward, eventually choosing to visit a crane staging area near Krydor. Later, it made its way into Wood Buffalo National Park.[28]

United States Fish and Wildlife Service ornithologist Marshall Howe has recently summarized data from eight radioed whooping cranes monitored from fall 1981 through spring 1984. In the fall, whoopers commonly make a two-day flight from Wood Buffalo, younger birds generally preceding experienced breeders, into Saskatchewan's grainlands where they forage in harvested wheat and barley fields for days or even weeks in order to build up fat reserves for migration. They use a broad range of natural and humanly modified wetlands for feeding and roosting, walking or flying short distances to pick waste grain in routines that last for about twelve hours, starting at daybreak.[29]

Saskatchewan remains an important staging area for whooping cranes, who frequent glacial lakes and small potholes. Provincial biologists know of half a dozen lakes—Meadow, Witchekan, Buffer, Blaine, Last Mountain, Kutawagan—frequented by whoopers. Two or three of them are shared with large numbers of sandhills. Late September through early October is the time for whoopers to pass along a corridor linking Saskatoon with Regina, and six or more whoopers may turn up together at any one time with 25,000–50,000 brown

cranes, for example, on Midnight Lake or near Outlook, Kyle, and Cabri on the South Saskatchewan River.

In addition to Canada's prairie provinces, significant for both fall and spring, Oklahoma and Texas are important in fall months and Kansas and Nebraska in spring. There are indications that certain individuals make repeated use of larger marshes, such as Salt Plains National Wildlife Refuge, Oklahoma; Cheyenne Bottoms, Kansas; and Byers Lake, Texas. Lobstick family members have frequented Radisson Lake, Saskatchewan, in consecutive years, in both spring and fall. In 1983, subadult White–Red's spring trajectory deviated barely fifteen miles or so from its fall flight line between Cherokee, Oklahoma, and north of Saskatoon, Saskatchewan, a distance of 1,200 miles.

Observers speculate that while whoopers are opportunistic in using natural and constructed water bodies, which vary appreciably in size, more-dominant males may select pathways shown initially to them by parents, whereas less-dominant males and females may be more influenced by other cranes in selecting routes. This may account for some birds showing up in the same spots year after year.

One factor about migration is clear. Wetlands are essential. Natural lakes are most often visited in fall; in spring, whooping cranes often roost in croplands and pastures flooded by winter precipitation. Families tend to use marsh sites more frequently than do unaccompanied adults and immature birds, who glean a good two-thirds of their food in grainlands. Availability of animal protein in such wet spots may satisfy a chick's needs more completely. Wetlands are safe places with unrestricted visibility around roost sites, and such boggy places are usually more isolated and distant from houses and other buildings, which whoopers avoid due to human activities.[30]

Nebraska

Until 1974, no land along Nebraska's Platte River, a staging area in spring for upward of 500,000 sandhill cranes and a stopover for whoopers, had been set aside as a sanctuary. Allen made an appeal for a Platte River refuge in his *Whooping Crane* monograph, recognizing that primary habitat along the migration corridor was dwindling. His Audubon Society employer took practical steps in 1973 by using an estate bequest to purchase several hundred acres of riparian land for the passing cranes.

Two years later a challenge to the issuance of a permit for a dam in Wyoming on the Laramie River, a tributary of the North Platte, centered on water diversions, which litigants claimed had effectively reduced stream flow on the Platte River over the years by two-thirds or more. As development has siphoned off water, the width and number of sandbars in braided channels, preferred as roost sites for cranes, have decreased. Woody vegetation has encroached on many reaches of the river, restricting visibility for cranes and making wet meadows and open places harder to find. This hotly debated issue of habitat preservation for the endangered whooper and other river bird species gained momentum in the mid-1970s and remains a conservation issue.

An out-of-court settlement between the state of Nebraska and the National Wildlife Federation versus Basin Electric Power, who had pushed for the Grayrocks Dam on the Laramie River, resulted in the Platte River Trust. In addition to setting flow rates, the action established a $7.5 million fund for habitat preservation and refurbishment downstream. Currently, the nonprofit trust draws upon this fund in monitoring and restoring critical habitat for whoopers and other endangered species. Researchers have experimented with woodland clearances, roost site maintenance and creation, and wet meadow restoration along the Big Bend section (between Overton and Grand Island) on the Platte River. A thirty-four-day stay of a young female, so-called Oklahoma, in spring 1987 on this stretch, specifically in and around Audubon's Lillian Annette Rowe Sanctuary, and a family that lingered for several weeks that fall attracted public interest in the Platte River as critical habitat. Trust personnel are dedicated to conserving the wildlife spectacle of crane throngs sweeping over this water ribbon in the north plains. Their intent is to make habitat along the Platte River an essential component in the nation's heritage.[31]

The American Crane lives well in confinement. The first
pair of this species acquired by the Zoological Society of
Amsterdam was purchased in 1865 at the Antwerp sale,
being imported by Mr. Charles Reiche . . . although they
are never very plentiful in the animal market and of late
years have become very scarce.

—F. E. BLAAUW
A Monograph of the Cranes, p. 19

4. Propagation and Release
Trials with Captive-Reared Cranes

The following Cranes have been in the collection, but have never nested:

The American Crane (*Grus americana*)

The Canadian Crane (*Grus canadensis*)

The Wattled Crane (*Anthropoides carunculata*) a single bird

The Asiatic White Crane (*Anthropoides leucogeranus*)

The Demoiselle and Common Cranes have raised their young to maturity.

—DUCHESS OF BEDFORD

"Cranes at Woburn Park," *Avicultural Magazine* 6 (1907) : 26

Argument and disagreement persist in whooping crane conservation. One author has noted how the bird's many supporters fight about "what is the best road to its salvation." There was little dispute about the acquisition and development of a sanctuary at Aransas, the southern terminus for the big crane. A good deal of controversy, however, flared up and still persists about propagating this species. To move from the preservation of a wild animal in its natural home to breeding it in research centers or zoos is a radical step, an assertion of human intervention and control rather than withholding, to let nature take its own course.

Aviculture, that is, keeping birds for purposes of ornament and display, exemplifies a tradition of control. For centuries, kings, aristocrats, and gentlemen of leisure have confined, bred, and reared birds, developing a familiarity and appreciation for different orders and families. Being large, conspicuous, and handsome, cranes figured in private collections. They made impressive ornaments in the aviaries and grounds of stately homes, especially nineteenth-century estates.

Unfortunately, details about the care and keeping of cranes are sparse, although some British journals carried essays and notes about the care of cranes. People devoted more effort toward more tractable and fecund waterfowl and colorful pheasants. Such records of cranes that do exist tend to emphasize cross-breeding and rearing hybrids.

Zoological collections in England, Holland, Germany, and France also included cranes, and in some instances captive birds nested successfully. However, there is almost no information pertaining directly to whooping cranes. When avicultural magazines grew fashionable in the late 1800s, the "hooping," or "American," crane was already rare and disappearing quickly.[1]

Poultry science, another way of exerting human dominance, offers more scope. As we shall see, one ostensible reason for locating the crane propagation facility in Patuxent, Maryland, was because another establishment run by the U.S. Department of Agriculture in Beltsville specialized in breeding domestic birds. Experts used to rearing such fowl were able to offer suggestions about food, incubation schedules, treatment of diseases, and so on and provide equipment for starting up a program for breeding cranes and other endangered birds in captivity.

Captive propagation befalls organisms whose future cannot be ensured by conventional methods of legal protection and habitat management. It is really a last gesture, made when existence in the wild appears impossible. Through the federal Endangered Species Preservation Act of 1966 and the Endangered Species Act of 1973 as amended, the concept of captive breeding has gained strong support among wildlife specialists. These two laws charged the U.S. Fish and Wildlife Service with protecting and restoring those native animals and plants threatened with extinction. Established in 1965, the Endangered Wildlife Research Program, organized by the Fish and Wildlife Service and located at Patuxent Wildlife Research Center near Laurel, Maryland, has attempted to test those factors believed to limit a species' survival. It has also sought to establish captive populations of the most endangered birds and mammals in hopes of eventually reestablishing these species by releasing captive-bred individuals directly in the wild or transferring eggs or young to be reared by wild foster parents. Captive propagation, proponents argue, can produce stock for release; it can preserve genetic mate-

rial in times of high risk and allow the comprehensive investigation of key physiological or behavioral traits that may provide clues for the better management of wild populations. Also, captive breeding contributes to education by enabling the public to view and become knowledgeable about those species in greatest jeopardy.[2]

Patuxent Wildlife Research Center

In the 1950s, ideas about propagating whooping cranes surfaced among Canadian wildlife experts, notably Fred G. Bard and associates in Saskatchewan. Bard, who was director of the Museum of Natural History

Table 2. Captive Propagation and Release

1961	Propagation techniques begun on sandhill cranes at Monte Vista NWR, Colorado.
1965	Under auspices of U.S. Fish and Wildlife Service crane experiments transferred to "Endangered Wildlife Research Program" based at Patuxent Wildlife Research Center, Laurel, Maryland.
1967	First whooping crane eggs (6) transferred from Wood Buffalo National Park, Canada, to Patuxent for artificial incubation and hand rearing of chicks.
1969	Artificial insemination techniques developed at Patuxent.
1971	Fourteen five-month-old Florida sandhills released near Lake Okeechobee, Florida; all died within three months.
1973	Biologists pair off whooping cranes at Patuxent.
1974	Double-unit pens built at Patuxent for Mississippi sandhill cranes; extended later to include whoopers.
1974	New rearing methods (dowels) employed at Patuxent for feeding young cranes.
1974	Release of a pen-raised male Florida sandhill on Paynes Prairie, Florida.
1975	First whooping crane egg laid at Patuxent (one female produced three eggs). The chick, Dawn, lived for fifteen days.
1975	Three Florida sandhills liberated, including the 1974 recaptured male, on Paynes Prairie.
1976	Three hybrid sandhill × whooper crosses reared at Patuxent, including so-called Ghostbird, the sole survivor.
1976	Methods developed at Patuxent for the cryogenic preservation of crane semen.
1976	One pen-reared female Florida sandhill liberated on Paynes Prairie.
1976	One parent-raised greater sandhill crane released at Grays Lake NWR, Idaho.
1977	Two Florida sandhills released at Paynes Prairie.
1978	Whooping crane eggs incubated and hatched; chicks reared at Patuxent by selected sandhill cranes. Young birds at Patuxent remain full-winged.
1980	Eleven greater sandhill cranes set free at Grays Lake.
1981	Nine parent-raised Mississippi sandhills released in Jackson County, Mississippi.
1981	Trial release of Patuxent-raised female whooping crane, so-called Too Nice, at Grays Lake; recaptured after five months.
1982	Second release of the same whooping crane female at Grays Lake; recaptured five months later after death of potential wild mate (75-1) and failure to establish firm bonds with other male birds.
1984	Seven of thirty-nine whooping cranes, mostly breeding-age females, die at Patuxent from eastern equine encephalitis; 1975–1984, total of ninety-three whooper eggs laid at Patuxent: thirty-five were sent to Grays Lake; eighteen chicks have been raised and retained in Maryland's captive flock.
1984	Twenty-one parent-reared greater sandhills released at Grays Lake.
1985	Experimental release of five puppet-reared greater sandhill cranes from Necedah NWR, near Baraboo, Wisconsin.
1985	An additional thirty-three Patuxent-raised Mississippi sandhills released in Jackson County, Mississippi, since 1982; nineteen survive in the wild as of 1987.

Table 3. Captive Whooping Cranes at the Patuxent Wildlife Research Center

	Adult	Young	Total		Adult	Young	Total
1966	1	0	1	1978	19	3	22
1967	1	5	6	1979	19	3	22
1968	5	7	12	1980	20	0	20
1969	12	5	17	1981	19	1	20
1970	14	0	14	1982	18	7	25
1971	14	3	17	1983	24	10	34
1972	17	0	17	1984	28	5	33
1973	17	0	17	1985	31	7	38
1974	17	4	21	1986	38	2	40
1975	20	0	20	1987	35	6	41
1976	18	1	19	1988	38	8	46
1977	19	2	21				

SOURCE: *Grus Americana* 27, suppl. no. 1 (1988): 2.
An adult bird is at the San Antonio, Texas, Zoo, and one is at the International Crane Foundation, Baraboo, Wisconsin, for a total of 48 whooping cranes in captivity.

in Regina, on the flight path for cranes, developed an early interest in the whooper from working with Fred Bradshaw, the last person recorded to visit a whooper nest near Unity, Saskatchewan, in 1922. Bard and colleagues publicized the plight of the species and with help from the National Audubon Society, notably John Baker and Robert P. Allen, in the 1940s they urged Canadians in the prairie provinces to protect the few remaining white birds. Preservationists interested farmers in observing rather than shooting the tiny population of whoopers that turned up sporadically in that province's grain stubbles during spring and fall passage.

In the following decade Bard and aviculturist friends in Canada and the United States talked openly about more direct ways of saving whooping cranes. The Whooping Crane Conservation Association (WCCA), founded in 1961 from a consortium of aviculturists, biologists, business people, and zoo and museum staff, including Bard—all whooper enthusiasts—was and still is an important body for airing views about ways of conserving the species. Opinions expressed at meetings, held annually since 1963, have covered a wide range of topics. Bard, a WCCA charter member, proposed the idea of using sandhill cranes as foster parents for setting up a second migratory population. Another WCCA "crane brain," Ernest L. Paynter, director of wildlife in the Saskatchewan Department of Natural Resources, chaired a session on whooping cranes at a Federal-Provincial Wildlife Conference, Vancouver, B.C., in 1956, in which a plan was presented for captive propagation. He, too, added his clout for more intensive management.

One suggestion was to remove one egg from the normal clutch of two and carry it away for hatching and rearing. The actual implementation of this suggestion about breeding and rearing whoopers fell to federal wildlife biologist Ray C. Erickson. With cooperation from Canadians and encouragement from WCCA members and others interested in propagation, Erickson and colleagues hypothesized that taking one egg from each clutch would not compromise the productivity of the wild population.

Data from Aransas winter counts suggested that usually one not two chicks per family arrived in Texas, although in most cases female cranes laid two eggs. In short, one chick almost invariably succumbed. The removal of one egg from a nest, Erickson proposed, would not significantly depress the numbers of wild cranes, particularly in times of low water on the nesting grounds when the chances of two chicks surviving in a nest were slim to none. In hatching and rearing these so-called surplus birds, a new population could be established. Whooping cranes raised in captivity in turn would breed, and their progeny could be released to bolster numbers in the wild flock.

The available evidence also suggested that the core of experienced breeding pairs in Canada grew slowly due to inexplicable losses prior to the age of breeding. Nobody knew where these immatures summered. Erickson's logic, therefore, could be extended from chicks to subadults. One could perhaps mitigate the effects of this low rate of maturation by capturing younger birds and holding them in captivity, then release them back into the wild flock as they grew older (see Table 3).[3]

Initial experiments with the capture and retention of juvenile sandhill cranes at a federal center in Monte Vista, Colorado, in the early 1960s did not go well. United States Fish and Wildlife Service experts concluded that hatching eggs rather than the capture of wild birds would be a more manageable proposition—reducing the costs and dangers of shipping cranes long distances and also lessening risks of introducing diseases and parasites into a captive flock.

In February 1965, a bill sponsored by U.S. Senator Karl E. Mundt of South Dakota authorized the creation of an Endangered Wildlife Research Program to continue experimental propagation at the Patuxent Wildlife Research Center established in 1936. The endangered wildlife program had ready access to expertise in poultry science and animal pathology and to important collections of live animals and specimens in the nearby Washington, D.C., area. Greater sandhill crane (*Grus canadensis tabida*) nests at Malheur NWR in southeast Oregon and at Grays Lake NWR in Idaho supplied eggs for incubation and the rearing of chicks. Additional eggs from the Florida (*G. c. pratensis*) and the endangered Mississippi (*G. c. pulla*) subspecies of the sandhill crane provided extra stock and, in the latter case, have helped build back the population of Mississippi sandhills.

Beginning in 1960, crane research involved all aspects of hatching and rearing, including artificial incubation of eggs at different temperatures and humidity, supplying food to chicks, and treating them for diseases, so that workers could anticipate problems that actual breeding of the whooping cranes at Patuxent would pose. These early years made researchers hopeful that techniques applied to sandhill cranes both in the wild and in captivity could be repeated on their larger, endangered cousin. With these favorable results, Erickson and associates successfully urged the Whooping Crane Advisory Group (WCAG) to support the proposal of taking one egg from several whooping crane nests in Wood Buffalo National Park. Researchers at Patuxent were ready to begin captive propagation.[4]

Optimism stemmed from two factors. First, crane biologists found that after they removed one egg most wild sandhills continued to incubate the remaining egg and often fledged the chick. It was, therefore, possible

A regimen of swimming enables captive-born whooper chicks at Patuxent Research Center to exercise and grow normally. Photograph by author.

to remove an egg without seriously impairing reproduction. Second, procedures for the removal, transport, and incubation of eggs and the subsequent rearing of crane chicks also appeared feasible; tests with various subspecies of sandhill cranes under different conditions had helped to establish and refine methods for the care and handling of young birds.

In May 1967, CWS biologist Ernie Kuyt, accompanied by Ray Erickson and others, flew into north-central Canada and removed six of the olive-buff eggs with dark spots from the total of seventeen in nine whooping crane nests. Five of the elongated eggs, about double a larger-sized chicken egg, hatched at Patuxent, and four chicks were reared to six months of age. In 1968, half of the total egg production of whoopers in Canada went to the U.S. facility in Maryland. Nine of the ten eggs taken hatched, and seven chicks were reared—one more than in the wild for that year.

Three more years (1969, 1971, 1974) brought the total of whooping crane eggs removed to fifty; thirty-seven chicks hatched in captivity and twenty-three lived for at least six months. During the same five-year period (1967–1974) the average young produced by the wild whoopers each year increased to 6.0 compared to an average 4.1–5.1 for three ten-year periods back to 1939. Erickson was delighted. These statistics showed that egg removal from Wood Buffalo NP did not jeopardize the production of young in the wild. No adults had deserted their nests because of egg removal. Indeed, the population growth rate of wild whoopers had increased during the five-year period when eggs were taken from an average of less than one bird (0.84) for the previous thirty-one years to three birds per year.[5]

In 1975, toward the end of the first decade of experiments at Patuxent, twenty-one whoopers lived in pens on that 4,200-acre well-watered and partially wooded tract. Nineteen birds had hatched out from eggs flown in from north-central Canada; two others had come through different channels: "Canus," named after the epigram Canada-U.S., had been picked up with an injured wing as a fledged chick in Wood Buffalo NP on 11 September, 1964. "Tex," the offspring of Crip and his second captive mate, Rosie, was hatched in the San Antonio Zoo. The initial challenge of incubating and hatching eggs had been met, although losses from disease, accident, and diet-related malformations of the legs of young cranes plagued initial years.

The next step was to encourage captive birds to breed. A self-sustaining population of whoopers at Patuxent would blunt criticism about tampering with nature and draining vital genes away from the wild flock; in fact, once the cranes nested under controlled conditions, researchers could turn to the most constructive and fulfilling task of all—acclimating the birds to the wild. Finding ways to return whooping cranes to their natural habitat was, after all, the basic objective for captive breeding.[6]

The first whooping crane hatched from parents in the propagation facility emerged from an incubator just before 7:30 A.M. on 29 May 1975. Nicknamed Dawn, she, like Rusty, was an important boost for Patuxent staff and attracted media attention from all over the world. Dawn was the first chick produced by the flock at Patuxent. She was the progeny of parents whose pen had been artificially illuminated to copy the longer summer days in native breeding grounds. Handlers had artificially inseminated the female with the male's semen after she had produced a first egg on 18 April. The tiny crane chick was fed a specially designed diet and placed indoors with turkey poults for company and to keep it from imprinting on humans.[7]

Unfortunately, the new crane lived for only fifteen days. Dawn suffered from a congenital deformity that twisted the right foot outward, inhibiting movement. Despite the bird's legs being taped to improve posture, Dawn refused to eat and died.[8]

Gee Whiz, male offspring of Tex, remains at Baraboo on display for visitors. Photograph by Comstock

Erickson recognized that the procedures established for raising sandhill cranes were only generally applicable to whoopers. The endangered cranes were proving much harder to raise. In 1975, when Dawn was born, six year classes lived at Patuxent. Canus was a 1964 chick. Three birds represented the 1967 age group, including Tex, shipped in from the San Antonio Zoo and placed with Canus. Additionally, six cranes were alive from 1968, including the female laying the first eggs, four from 1969, three from 1971, and four from 1974. Six pairs had been isolated in breeding enclosures; one of them had produced Dawn and an additional two eggs that didn't hatch.[9]

The Maryland facility received no more Wood Buffalo eggs until 1982 when two were flown in to add representation from selected nesting pairs. Both hatched and one chick fledged. Two reasons contributed to the decision to withhold eggs from Patuxent. First, a new experiment was launched to establish a second wild flock by placing eggs from Canada under foster-parent sandhill cranes in Idaho, thereby conserving time, energy, and money in raising and releasing captive whooping cranes. Second, Patuxent was on its way to becoming self-sustaining. A second five-year-old female began to lay in 1976; she and the earlier fertile female produced five eggs that year. All five were held initially in incubators; two of them were shipped to Grays Lake, Idaho (but did not hatch), and the remainder were kept in Maryland. Personnel managed to hand-rear one surviving chick.

Between 1975 and 1985, 197 eggs were laid at Patuxent, including a record 34 by five females in 1983. One hundred and twenty-five, or 63 percent, were retained by the captive rearing program itself, resulting in 86 fertile eggs, 66 chicks, and 28 fledged birds. An additional 73 eggs were transferred to Grays Lake and produced 17 young for the Rocky Mountain, or western, flock.[10]

Successful breeding at Patuxent has shifted toward refining techniques for incubating whooping crane eggs and rearing chicks. Once biologists had learned to keep their charges alive and built up the flock, they gave more and more attention toward breeding and to increasing the fertility among those captives old enough to reproduce successfully; but it was a step-by-step process.

Egg Transfer and Chick Rearing

Since it was designed in 1966, a dark-colored fiberboard suitcase lined with plastic foam insert sections that act as molds for crane eggs, and three hot water bottles to maintain an appropriate temperature for incubating the eggs, has carried both sandhill and whooper eggs from nesting grounds to the Maryland research center. This hand-carried container measures 20 × 14 × 10 inches, suitable as carry-on baggage that can be slipped under the seat in a commercial aircraft. A courier, initially Erickson himself and, since 1975, Elwood Bizeau from the University of Idaho and Ernie Kuyt of the Canadian Wildlife Service, takes charge of the bird eggs after Kuyt transfers them from a helicopter that is used to land near nests in Wood Buffalo Park. For whoopers this switch from nest to incubator is made in Canada in the last days of May. Bizeau and Kuyt carry them to the United States. In 1988, they transported twelve eggs in two suitcase incubators bound for Grays Lake aboard a chartered Piper Cheyenne. Two additional incubators with nine live and six nonviable eggs were given to two

Patuxent-based researchers at Edmonton airport.

During the flight from Canada to the United States, couriers monitor the status of the eggs. They check on the temperature around them by reading a thermometer fitted into the incubator and may move the incubator lids, which are used as a bellows to release surplus heat. It is vital not to overheat the embryo; embryos can take subnormal temperatures but will die if they are overheated. Ambient temperatures should remain between 94° and 98° F (34.5°–36.7° C). The hot water bottles supply heat, and wet sponges also packed inside each suitcase release humidity. It is important to place the eggs so that the large end with the air cell is positioned toward the handle on the top of the case. Ten eggs per case can be transported horizontally or vertically, but the smaller, pointed end should not be held upward. Movements to switch a case from an upright position to a horizontal position, or back again, should be slow and deliberate, for jostling can damage delicate embryos.

Two or three hours into the flight the temperature within the suitcase will begin to drop and more hot water is needed to recharge the three bottles. Therefore, on the long flights from Edmonton, Alberta, to the Baltimore-Washington airport or to Grays Lake via Great Falls, Montana, and Jackson, Wyoming, the courier must be ready with spares and have access to water of about 120°F (56.6°C).[11]

Prior to being placed in a large wooden Petersime Model 4 incubator in Patuxent's incubation unit, the newly arrived crane eggs are disinfected. The incubator at Patuxent is set at 37.7°C and 55 percent relative humidity. The machine turns the eggs mechanically at two-hour intervals. Each egg is checked twice daily until staffers hear peeping from within. When the egg is pipped or very near pipping, that is, when a small hole made by the chick's bill appears, the egg is placed in a smaller hatcher unit that is held at a slightly lower temperature but higher humidity until the chick struggles free of its shell. This hatching process takes from one to two days. After the crane chick pierces the shell, it begins the long ordeal of chipping a circle around the shell until finally it kicks itself free of the egg and, exhausted, usually sleeps.

In the early years all whooping cranes at Patuxent were hand reared. Over the years, by trial and error, experts familiar with young cranes drew up guidelines for rearing these birds, including treatments for life-threatening situations. Today, a caretaker transports the newly hatched crane from the hatcher, in which it has dried for several hours, to the chick building, weighs it, gives it injections to ward off infection, and sets it down in an 8 × 8 foot pen. This carpeted enclosure is equipped with water jugs, heat lamps, and bowls of specially prepared food and is the crane's first home. A stuffed crane model in a brooding position and another model of a crane head, which is suspended by a cord over the food, are important visual clues for the chick to identify with, and, most important of all, all chicks are placed in pens next to a live crane for at least a week in order for them to imprint on a living and moving crane. Plexiglass separates each youngster from the adult and prevents possible injury.

Cranes are especially pugnacious in the early weeks of life, and they will chase and peck each other. Biologists have learned to place young chickens or turkey poults in pens in which there are groups of crane chicks. These domesticated birds provide exercise for the cranes as the former move and dodge away from attacks. The result, according to one observer, has been "much exercise but little injury." Also, poultry scratch and make a fuss over food and attract crane chicks to search for tidbits.[12]

After four days the chick is allowed to come and go at will into an outdoor exercise enclosure, except in rain or cold or at night. The live adult is kept next to it. A few meal worms cast into the area often stimulate the bird to search for food—the aim is to keep it active. Swimming now is featured in an exercise schedule that keepers set up after the crane is a week or ten days old. A little guidance may be required to keep the fluffy gangling crane afloat and upright as it paddles vigorously in the water.

Unexpected problems in the early years associated with too little exercise and an excessively rich diet caused abnormalities to feet and legs. Unusually fast growth in early life, defined currently as a more than 10 percent increase in body weight per day for two or three days consecutively, created deformities in the young birds and often resulted in death.

Problems with diet stemmed from imbalances in the volume and type of food that cranes learned to consume. Acting as surrogate parents handlers must teach crane chicks to eat and to drink, and in the early years of the captive program youngsters tended to ingest either too much or too little and suffered from growth-related problems.

Ultimately, experts with a background in poultry science devised the right balance of proper nutrition, and crane behaviorist Cameron Kepler, who joined the Patuxent program in 1973, worked hard to establish appropriate procedures for feeding the right nutrients to small, fast-growing chicks. Initially, Kepler concentrated in getting chicks beyond that tender age when mortality was highest. For example, in 1974, nine of the thirteen eggs collected in Canada hatched, but five whooper chicks died within a month and the remainder grew ill. Food was available but the birds were reluctant to feed.

Kepler tested ways of inducing chicks to eat a carefully balanced diet. He made up wooden dowels resembling parent crane beaks, colored them, and watched chicks, initially sandhills, aim pecks at them. From this experiment, Kepler devised a red-colored dowel, which was suspended over bowls of mash and which swung into the food under the force of frequent pecks. The tiny cranes obtained food as the dowel swung into the bowls and lifted out mash. Within a few days each one had learned to feed on its own.[13]

Today, cranes are given a commercially prepared "starter" food mixed with grit, then, around day 35, switched gradually over to special pellets. Usually it takes three to four days for the youngster to be taught how to obtain food and water, but there are always slow learners. At the beginning, at least six times a day or as often as once an hour, a caretaker hides behind a screen with an armhole in it and, disguising the hand in an orthopedic stocking, holds a puppet crane head and pushes it through the screen. The caretaker dips the puppet-crane bill into water then into a food bowl. Encouraged by "parenting" sounds from the hidden human, who manipulates the fake crane head in a realistic manner, the chick pecks at the puppet's bill as if it were its true parent and pulls off food. If the chick is shy, a piece of red tape stuck on the bill can usually lure it to begin pecking. When the crane is a few days old, a pulley arrangement enables the operator to manipulate the head while standing outside the pen.

Handlers are instructed to avoid usual contact with young birds and avoid giving parent-type calls when cranes can see them. Current efforts to imprint cranes use taxidermically prepared brooder models and heads of sandhill cranes that have been dyed white to resemble whoopers. Having a live bird for the chicks to see encourages young cranes to socialize with their own kind and to avoid imprinting on human keepers. Turkey poults, which scratch about the enclosure, may also attract crane chicks to investigate food sources. The beak dipped into a water source also supplies necessary fluids, or for slow learners a red-tipped syringe may be held out from behind a screen and the chick persuaded to peck at droplets forced from the end. The objective is to familiarize the crane with food and water set out in its pen and get it to feed on its own.

After whooping cranes are at least seventy days old, a time of rapid growth, workers move groups of them into larger outdoor pens with shelters where they pass the fall. About December, the flock manager, Scott Hereford, switches them to enclosures where they remain for sixteen or seventeen months until as subadults they begin to show associations that are hoped will lead to pairing. Behaviorists watch birds to see how they link up with potential partners. Vocalizations and evidence of standing together in close physical proximity suggest possible pairs. If sexually compatible, these birds are moved to 45 × 65 foot breeding pens where isolation and combinations of physical barriers, including net screens, shelters, and shade, give them the security and sense of being in a territory in which mating and nest building can ultimately take place.[14]

Staff members James W. Carpenter, a veterinarian charged with day-to-day handling of cranes, and Scott R. Derrickson, who now works in the breeding facility for the National Zoo, which handles rare and endangered animals at Front Royal in Virginia, reviewed mortality characteristics for the first fifteen years of crane operations in the United States. Between 1966 and 1981, forty-one whoopers died at Patuxent, 32 percent from infectious diseases as downy young. An additional 20 percent, or eight birds, succumbed to parasite infestations, and the same number died from abnormalities associated with growth. A further 7 percent succumbed because of pugnacity or fighting within the flock, and the remaining 21 percent died from a variety of causes, including predation by a fox, surgical shock, and ingestion of foreign objects.

Bacterial infections, such as *Salmonella, Streptococcus,* and *Bacillus,* have been the major causes of deaths in thirteen, mostly very young, cranes. Researchers are well aware that hatchlings are extremely susceptible to infection, and they take precautions to sterilize equipment and fumigate pens. Staff cover their shoes or boots with plastic overboots as they enter the chick-rearing house in order to minimize the risk of carrying in parasites from other pens or locations.

Anatomical abnormalities resulting in curled toes, misaligned legs, and deformities in the hips have caused eight deaths, mostly of birds four to seventy days old. Stress, debilitation, and loss of appetite were the immediate causes of death. As discussed earlier, modifications in procedures governing hatching, rearing, and feeding have countered these growth-related problems. In the

wild, such problems rarely if ever occur because crane chicks paddle, walk, and run vigorously to keep up with their tall, long-striding parents.

One rare and inexplicable death during this fifteen-year period involved an egg-producing pair. The male killed his mate with whom he had shared a pen for seven years. Initially, Patuxent personnel attributed the female's wounds, in the head, eyes, and neck, to trauma engendered by a storm. They speculated that she had taken fright and somehow injured herself, after which her alarmed mate had turned on her. The male, subsequently nicknamed Killer, was united with a second female. Observations confirmed that the two cranes were compatible and after several weeks the new pair was enclosed in a pen. Killer later murdered his second mate. He still lives at Patuxent but will never share his pen with another crane. Killer is sexually imprinted on humans and does not behave normally toward other cranes.[15]

Most deaths (68 percent) occurred among "downy young," that is, cranes only a few days old. Adults comprised 24 percent of the deaths, or ten of forty-one birds, while subadults totaled just 7 percent. In sum, once crane chicks have passed through the critical phase of early growth, their chances for survival in captivity increase. Adults die from a variety of causes, including accidents whereby they injure themselves in their pens or, as in the case of Killer's mates, from rare attacks. In 1981, twenty whoopers lived at Patuxent, eleven of them hatched out from fifty crane eggs collected at Wood Buffalo National Park. The remaining nine cranes were produced by the captive birds (after 1975) within the propagation facility. By 1988, the population had risen to forty-one birds.[16]

Rearing began at Patuxent with little background data, except from zoos in New Orleans and San Antonio in which the famous couple Crip and Josephine had been housed. Historically, aviculturists, bird fan-

ABOVE: The captive breeding facility at Patuxent. Paired cranes are placed in pens provided with screens and lights that are turned on in early spring to facilitate breeding. Photograph by author.

LEFT: Rearing techniques for whoopers at Patuxent include heaters, food dispensers, and model cranes. The live sandhill crane in the foreground helps the distant chick to imprint on cranes, not its human guardians. Photograph by author.

ciers, and zoological institutions have kept cranes in animal collections. But there has been little sustained effort to breed them and none with the objective of producing young that can be released ultimately into the wild.

Understandably, mistakes were made and lessons learned during Patuxent's pioneer efforts. Critics argue that too many birds died from pen-related injuries or rearing infections when better facilities and equipment, an X-ray machine for example, or extra space and air conditioning would have reduced losses. Funding was low in the first years, but since 1980 the facility has made major strides in improving pens, equipment, and the technology geared toward survival and productivity.

Reproduction and Fertility

Once Erickson and associates established a reliable means for hatching Wood Buffalo eggs and rearing chicks, they turned attention to older cranes within the captive group. They needed to know how to help pair off and assist adult cranes to breed. Ethologist Kepler's major breakthrough involved the sexing and pairing of captive whooping cranes. He noted, for instance, that four dominant birds in the flock produced a "unison call" different from that uttered by other members. Knowing that among the similar looking whooping cranes males tend to be physically larger, more aggressive, and socially dominant, Kepler concluded that the four birds were males. His surmise came from studies by another Cornell-trained ornithologist, George Archibald, who investigated the importance of vocalizations among cranes in the genus *Grus*.

The whooper's trumpeting call, which sometimes carries in excess of a mile, is made extra piercing and resonant by the bird's long trachea, or windpipe. The special unison call is a loud duet between male and female that is used to show assertiveness and often to claim territory. In making this call, the male stands stiffly, drops his wings to reveal black primaries, and with head and bill raised utters two notes as his partner, also standing erect with her head and bill upright, makes three shorter higher-pitched notes. Often the calls appear to run together so that at a distance vocalizations seem to come from one bird when in fact they come from a pair—cranes familiar and compatible with one another. These trumpeting calls begin when a crane is between eighteen and twenty-four months old and are a way in captivity of determining gender without recourse to blood analysis or physical examination.

Kepler divided the whooper flock, all of whom were at least four years old, into four pairs and isolated them.

He selected two more pairs in 1975 and another two consisting of two-year-olds in 1976, thereby setting the stage for reproduction in captivity.

Six years after the propagation experiment began at Patuxent, heterosexual pairs among the thirteen birds had been identified. But the practice of holding birds together in a large pen, in the same way for sandhills, was not sufficient to stimulate reproduction. Kepler concluded that in such a grouping whoopers, unlike sandhills, tended to form "dominance hierarchies" not pairs, so he proceeded to redesign the enclosures in order to optimize pair formation and bonding. Pairs or likely pairs were removed from general enclosures to smaller breeding pens when about two years old.[17]

Kepler also noted that "it is not enough to place males and females together, even though they appear compatible." Variation existed among individuals. Some females appeared to be more dominant than the males with whom they associated. Other birds showed sexual incompatibility. It therefore took careful and unobtrusive monitoring by Kepler and others to arrange birds so as to maximize their reproductive potential.

Kepler never did witness successful copulation between courting pairs and concluded with other experts that the process of rendering a crane flightless makes it difficult for males to mount and balance for successful mating. Some cranes at Patuxent are tenotomized, that is, one wing is surgically altered to prevent the bird from opening it fully. This practice minimizes chances of a crane escaping over the barriers between the open pens. Unable to get the whooper to mate because of imprinting and tenotomy, biologists fell back upon the practice of artificial insemination.

To date, all fertile whooping crane eggs produced in the Patuxent Wildlife Research Center have been attributed to a routine of insemination whereby sperm from a specific male crane is placed inside a female. This practice begins before the breeding season and takes place two or three times a week until an increase in day temperatures in mid to late May terminates the crane's reproductive drive. Recently, however, fertile Mississippi sandhill crane eggs have been obtained, and eight pairs of whooping cranes are being left full-winged in hopes of producing fertile eggs.

In captivity, by removing an egg from the nest as soon as it is laid, a crane may be induced to lay four or five times more eggs than in nature. A greater sandhill holds a record at Patuxent for eighteen eggs in one season. Among whooping cranes, productivity has never been that high; however, in 1978, the third season of egg laying, three cranes laid twenty-three eggs, nineteen of which were fertile. A year earlier a Patuxent whooper produced nine eggs in five clutches. Potentially high recruitment to the overall population from inducing long-lived birds like whooping cranes to reproduce in Patuxent has been a major point used to justify the propagation experiment. People speak of a captive pair being sixteenfold more productive than if it is left in the wild—birds will live longer and will be induced to lay more eggs in propagation units.

Between 1977 and 1984, The Patuxent whooper flock laid 176 eggs, and, except in 1980 and 1981 (when they produced 6 and 11, respectively), they laid more than 20 eggs annually with a high of 34 in 1983 produced by five females. Seventy-one, or 40 percent of the total, were used to assist the cross-foster experiment in Idaho. Patuxent eggs resulted in seventeen young wild whooping cranes. The balance of the fertile eggs (75) remained in Maryland and resulted in twenty-seven new cranes.

Several factors influence reproduction, including hormones, temperatures, and day length. The installation of lights over pens stimulates breeding by replicating the longer days in the northern nesting grounds. Manipulation of this photoperiod commences in mid-February when lights are turned on before dawn and switched on earlier and earlier until crane pairs receive close to 24 hours of illumination, equivalent to the length of a June day in Wood Buffalo National Park. Researchers are confident that this extra illumination helps bring cranes into breeding condition. They note that females under lights begin to lay eggs earlier and produce more than others not stimulated by this manipulation.[18]

Biologists remove eggs as cranes lay them in order to stimulate replacements. Experiments with both sandhill and whooping cranes show that taking eggs on a daily basis maximizes the number a female will lay. Toward the end of the nesting season staff may leave an egg for the bird to incubate; however, to minimize the risk of losing a precious whooper egg, only sandhill crane eggs are set out. The whooping crane eggs are placed under carefully selected sandhill crane pairs.[19]

Parent-Raising

Captive propagation experts favor the practice of allowing cranes themselves to incubate eggs and rear chicks in captivity. That means that some cranes may tend young of their own or of another species. For example, at Patuxent, sandhill cranes are given whooper eggs or hatchlings to raise, and whooping cranes have raised young sandhill cranes. This method of captive-rearing

stems from a consensus that any candidates for release into the wild must be young cranes who have associated and, it is hoped, bonded with others of their kind, imitating as far as confinement allows characteristics helpful for survival. Parent-raising gives both adults and young the experience of the natural reproductive cycle and assists with proper socialization and imprinting, which some experts regard as a problem when species are mixed in pens or held close together. For adults, fulfilling the drive to reproduce—nest and rear chicks—reinforces pair bonds while giving experience in incubating, hatching, and feeding. For chicks, constant supervision by crane parents helps them bond correctly, keeps them wary of humans, and, if they remain unpinioned and able to fly, may also contribute to what biologists term "natural fertility," that is, the ability to copulate successfully without recourse to being artificially inseminated. Parent-raising also gives chicks more and better opportunities for learning to forage more expertly.

By inspecting potential breeding pens in winter before nesting occurs, workers close up any holes, pick up debris that cranes may swallow, and eradicate briars, thistles, and other weeds. They check on feeders, water dispensers, shelters for shade, and so on, to make sure there are no rough edges against which birds may hurt themselves.

When the nesting season begins, pairs who are ranked highly because of a good parenting history receive a whooper egg. The egg of an endangered crane is switched with their own egg or a dummy egg the pair has been incubating. Whooping crane eggs are supplied only to those "excellent" sandhill crane pairs who have demonstrated strong attachment to their young in previous seasons and who have a record of at least two years of good parenting. Cranes will not be ranked lower for losing an egg or a chick if severe weather floods the nest or chills the chick. So far (1988), Patuxent researchers have used only sandhill cranes for tending whooper eggs and chicks.

A flock of "brooder" sandhills provides parents for both the endangered whooping crane and the Mississippi subspecies of the sandhill crane, *G. c. pulla*. Whenever possible highly rated pairs are selected, but if a top-ranked duo is not available one of the "good" pairs may be used. The sole hybrid remaining at Patuxent, a male called Ghostbird, born from a greater sandhill mother and a whooper father (Canus), has turned out to be a model parent. He is the outcome of an experiment to ascertain whether whoopers and sandhills could be bred

Tex, produced by Crip and Josephine in the San Antonio Zoo, is shown at Baraboo, Wisconsin. The photo was taken by her "mate," ICF Director George Archibald, Summer 1981.

together. During the nesting season this handsome, tall, gray-and-white crane attacks handlers and other birds viciously while tending chicks with great solicitude. In 1986 he was a highly ranked bird and raised an endangered Mississippi sandhill chick. This high score earned him the distinction of rearing a whooper chick in 1987.

Workers establish a routine of minimum disturbance and maximum quiet around crane enclosures during spring, especially ones used by whooper pairs. Once a day, a three-member team enters the enclosures of those birds raising chicks. One member handles the chick, gives it shots for its first four days and weighs it, checks its breathing, eyes, legs, and may collect a fecal sample for lab analysis. This person also replenishes food and water and removes any egg shells. The other two people act as guards, fending off aggressive adults. They risk serious injury from piercing beaks and kicking legs as crane parents seek to drive them away from their nest.

Whenever possible, the chick is examined away from its parents and is set down away from the exit in case it may be trampled as adults charge after the handlers. Once the youngster is large enough to use cylindrical feeders set out for the adults (at about 50 days), rations are no longer supplied daily. Whatever its size or age, staff check the young crane visually each day for any signs of illness or injury. Sitting or lying on the ground for long periods is one indication that a chick is having difficulty.

As the young birds approach sixty-five days of age, they are examined to see whether "brailing," a method of flight restraint, is needed. Brails, plastic loops placed over the wrist, immobilize a wing and prevent the crane from flying. Construction of flight pens, enclosures covered with mesh, obviates the need for brails or pinioning to prevent flying, except when birds are being transported and held in confinement prior to release.

Artificial Insemination

Inducing birds to lay fertile eggs is obviously a prerequisite for propagation. A number of problems, however, may keep sexually mature individuals from reproducing in zoos, aviaries, and other places. For example, male cranes may be unable to copulate correctly due to pinioning or other techniques used to inhibit flight. Adults may be behaviorally incompatible, or certain birds may be imprinted upon humans and fail to establish effective pair bonds.

All these factors have come into play at Patuxent. Operations on the wings of the first-generation cranes in order to make them flightless made it extremely difficult for sexually active males to mount, balance, and copulate successfully. Behavioral problems posed by Killer have already been discussed. He will never be released with a female again. Tex, a female whooping crane hatched in the San Antonio Zoo, transferred to Patuxent, and then loaned to the International Crane Foundation in Baraboo, Wisconsin, was imprinted so strongly on humans that, as we shall see, ICF director George Archibald decided to play the role of male crane. He worked closely with the female after her real crane consort, the dominant Canus, failed to get her to bond.[20]

Artificial insemination (AI) is one solution to these various problems among captive cranes and is the crux of the whole program at Patuxent. Since 1969, an enormous effort has been made to establish procedures that reduce stress to cranes and the risks of injury to handlers, while maximizing chances for the eggs that whoopers lay to be fertile.

Three methods are used to inseminate birds—cooperation, massage, and electrostimulation. Raptor specialists and falconers often employ the first type, which requires that a bird is imprinted upon a human handler and essentially treats the human as its mate. The male bird "cooperates" by voluntarily ejaculating semen on clothing or into a receptacle from which the handler transfers it to a female bird. The large size and long legs of the cranes make it impractical for them to mount human keepers.

Semen is normally collected and transferred among whoopers by the "massage" procedure, which can be applied to both imprinted and noncooperative birds. An operator and an assistant massage the individual's back, thighs, and vent area in order to cause ejaculation in males and increased receptivity in females. Although the operation takes only a few seconds, there may be a good deal of stress associated with capturing and handling, and, compared with the former cooperative procedure, massage is riskier for both cranes and keepers.

The third method of electrostimulation, by which an electric current is applied to the genital region, causing spasms and the ejaculation of semen, is not used much on nondomestic birds except waterfowl and is not employed in artificial insemination for cranes.[21]

Insemination procedures at Patuxent begin with regular handling before the actual onset of the breeding cycle in order to lessen distress to the crane from being grabbed and manipulated. After the start of the spring breeding season, a three-member team works through the breeding pens three times a week to extract seminal fluids and deposit them in females. An operator and an assistant edge the bird into a corner and capture it. One man then cradles the head beneath his legs with the bill toward the corner of the pen. Facing toward the back of the crane, he bends forward, stroking the thighs and legs in a circular inward motion. A second person positioned behind the bird massages its back, tail, and vent, pushes the tail up, exposes the cloaca, and squeezes forth semen into a glass collection funnel. The third person records details of the operation. The entire process takes usually thirty seconds. The female is treated in a similar fashion but a syringe is used to deposit the semen from the male, a portion of which is retained for laboratory analysis of semen quality. Female cranes receive AI massage and insemination three times per week during nesting season and after they lay an egg.[22]

Staff members acknowledge that fertility rates among whooping crane eggs fluctuate from year to year, ranging from a respectable 83 percent to merely 33 percent. The timing, quality, and quantity of seminal fluids and placement of them in the female's reproductive tract factor into this variable success. Also, operator familiarity with massage techniques affects egg viability. Usually, the same team works together from one year to the next to familiarize the cranes with the human handlers and to establish knowledge about each bird so that the insemination routine is smooth and effective. In the early 1980s, experts admitted that "fertilization currently remains the biggest bottleneck in propagating large numbers of whooping cranes in captivity."[23]

Current efforts to retain full-winged birds, that is, whooping cranes raised by "parent" sandhills and capable of flight, are one step toward natural reproduction, which will lessen the labor-intensive, time-consuming AI. Naturally, the power of flight is essential for the final step of releasing cranes back into the wild. Hence, covered pens and brailing the wings to prevent flight have become more common in recent years as they provide extra flexibility in efforts to improve natural fertility and for experiments in crane releases.

Another goal of Patuxent's animal physiologist George F. Gee, who pioneered AI in cranes, is to preserve crane semen in order to enhance or restore genetic diversity. For a dozen years or more Gee has experimented with the best ways to obtain semen, freeze it, and subsequently thaw it for actual use. In a study published in 1985, he achieved 50 percent fertility in eggs laid by sandhill cranes artificially inseminated with semen subjected to freeze and thaw techniques. Gee concludes that cryogenic methods of storing crane semen in straws at very low temperatures make it possible to use such vital genetic materials over the long term.[24]

Current research based in Los Alamos National Laboratory, New Mexico, shares Gee's aim of maintaining as much genetic variability as possible. Geneticist Jonathan Longmire is working on "genetic fingerprints" for Patuxent whoopers. DNA research with blood samples enhanced by laboratory and photo techniques established bands of genetic material whose patterns vary from bird to bird. Closely related individuals show similar band patterns. Naturally, experts hope to pair off birds with dissimilar "fingerprints" in the belief that their offspring have the best hopes of surviving.[25]

Releases of Captive Cranes

From the early 1970s through the mid 1980s, a number of captive-reared cranes (all except one were sandhills) found their freedom in the wild. Most of the birds failed to adjust and perished. However, biologists learned a great deal about methods of releasing cranes, including at what age and in what numbers they should be set free and when and where it was best to do so. Cranes must learn a great deal if they are to survive without human care. Other birds, especially wild cranes, not biologists, are the best "teachers." But humans can give liberated cranes a real chance to live long enough in order to learn the ways of other cranes and to adopt important behaviors that may lead to pairing and nesting in the wild. But the challenge has been enormously complex.

Captive-raised cranes must be taught to identify and consume wild foods; they must learn what is dangerous and how to avoid predators; and, important for the long term, they often must learn to migrate and achieve an understanding of the social life in their wild counterparts. So far, only sandhills have been put through this school of hard knocks, and few individuals of this species have survived the dangers and accidents that comprise its curriculum, except for Mississippi sandhills, who comprise now between one-third and one-half of the resident population in the wild. Only one captive-reared whooping crane has been released, but it was recaptured due to the premature death of a potential mate (see the Grays Lake section).

More than one hundred sandhill cranes hatched in Patuxent, belonging to three races, have flown free. The story began in 1971 when thirteen captive-reared youngsters of the Florida race were taken "home" and released near Lake Okeechobee. Author David Zimmerman characterized this abrupt release and the subsequent loss of all the birds as an ill-conceived scheme, poorly executed and doomed from the start. The cranes were hand-reared and very tame. They seemed to be unable to forage adequately, followed human investigators about, and begged for food until within a few weeks they disappeared one after another.

Three subsequent releases of greater sandhill cranes in Grays Lake NWR, Idaho (1976, 1980, 1984), turned up much more useful and conclusive data for optimizing release strategies, particularly for migratory situations. Survival rates remained low and not as catastrophic.

Grays Lake, Idaho

The Grays Lake experiments began in August 1976, when a single parent-reared greater sandhill crane was set free in the national wildlife refuge. This subadult, hatched in 1975 and kept semiwild by placing it in a five-acre pen with wild-trapped parents, was flown to Salt Lake City, Utah. Biologists released it in Idaho the next day. The crane adjusted smoothly to life in the huge marsh, foraging in nearby fields on grain and insects. At night it flew to roost with wild sandhills.

Biologist Rod Drewien, who had assiduously monitored sandhills in this area of southeastern Idaho for about twenty years, judged that the youngster "never completely integrated with other sandhills." It tended to follow rather than mix with conspecifics and fed on the edges of crane flocks. Drewien color marked the bird with a green tag on the left leg and a red tag on the right and so was able to spot it among the hundreds of other sandhill cranes that use Grays Lake for both nesting and migration staging.

He observed the Patuxent-raised bird for the last time on 17 October 1976, together with sixteen sandhills in a grain field. Large flocks of gray-brown cranes had already streamed south toward Colorado and on to wintering grounds in New Mexico. Only this small group dallied in Idaho, and by the morning of 18 October only six cranes remained. The Patuxent bird had left, presumably flying with the ten missing birds. Except for a possible glimpse of a crane resembling this individual in a large flock some eight hundred miles south in New Mexico's Bosque del Apache NWR in late December of that year, Drewien never spotted his greater sandhill crane again.[26]

On the afternoon of 18 June 1980, a new batch of eleven Patuxent-reared greater sandhill cranes (*G. c. tabida*) arrived at Grays Lake. Researchers immediately took the weary birds to a release site in the northwest sector of the 22,000-acre preserve and set them free. The site was a flat meadow with an expanse of bulrush and

A banded whooping crane chick in Wood Buffalo NP Wilderness, July 1977. Photograph by Rod C. Drewien.

cattail on the east, which provided cover. Open sagebrush country lay to the west; close by was a barley field kept baited with grain to which Patuxent keepers had habituated the cranes. The birds' new home is the summer quarters of upward of three hundred wild sandhill cranes.

Craneman Rod Drewien checked each bird's activities by attaching a colored and numbered band to one leg and a small radio transmitter to the other. He observed the new cranes from a blind close to the release site and used a scanning receiver to monitor radio signals.

Over the summer four of the eleven birds (one had succumbed in transit) died. Three of them were one-year-olds. One of these, plus a three-year-old, probably starved to death. Drewien saw that two of them tended to be loners and subsisted almost exclusively on natural foods obtained near the release site. Other cranes supplemented their diets by flying to nearby grain fields, where they associated with their wild counterparts and assumed the latter's activity patterns.

One of the released birds died of severe head wounds that it received after intruding into the territory of a wild crane. On another occasion Drewien saw a native crane chase a new bird and strike it repeatedly, but the newcomer managed to escape. Wild sandhills won almost all such hostile encounters with the inexperienced Patuxent group.

The Patuxent survivors foraged in the marsh and the barley fields. They tended to associate more with each other than with wild cranes. Older birds in particular seemed to prefer the company of those with which they had been raised. Drewien noted how they were submissive to wild cranes. Patuxent sandhills also spent more time searching for food, allocated less time to alert behavior, and sought to avoid trouble with the more dominant wild counterparts.

One bird, however, female no. T27, adopted wholly different behavior from the very first and became the only Patuxent bird to "go native." On the morning of 20 June, Drewien watched with a mixture of curiosity and increasing anxiety as she "wandered along westward into the sagebrush-grass uplands." The inexperienced crane passed that day in the exposed area west of the lake and roosted for the night. Next day, the biologist caught up with T27 again, "walking aimlessly in the hills." Finally, the young crane stopped her trek west into the arid uplands and flew toward the marsh. Her "walkabout" continued, however, as she skirted the water and ambled southward, choosing to roost in a small wood on an intermittent creek. Still walking south, the hapless T27 roosted the next night in a ditch more than four miles from the release site. Such a perambulation courted disaster by inviting interest from marauding coyotes or hungry golden eagles, but she remained unscathed. On 23 June, the captive-raised female came upon a group of wild subadult sandhill cranes and joined the flock. From that day onward T27 grew into a wild crane. She attached herself to the sandhills, particularly to one bird, presumably a male.

Such individualistic (and dangerous) behavior paid off. Within a week after her release young T27 associated exclusively with wild individuals of her species. She lived with them on and around the marsh and was the last of the Patuxent survivors to leave Grays Lake. Moving to a staging, or assembly, area on the southeast side of the refuge, close to the headquarters, she joined a big flock in soaring flight at noon on 6 October but landed after circling overhead for twenty minutes. Other cranes pushed south that day, but T27 remained.

At 11:34 A.M. on 9 October, Drewien saw T27 link up with another flock of spiraling sandhills. Half an hour later he lost sight of her as twenty-eight brown-colored living gliders set sail. They headed southeast, tiny specks high above him. Drewien located T27 nineteen days later on the edge of another important federal sanctuary, Monte Vista NWR at the southern end of Colorado's San Luis Valley. The Patuxent crane was with another bird, possibly the one she had teamed up with in that first week. Both cranes remained at Monte Vista until mid-November, then headed along the Rio Grande into New Mexico, possibly setting down in Bosque del Apache NWR, a common roosting spot for cranes, including her parents, who had been captured on that refuge.

In late January 1981, Drewien picked up the signal from T27's solar-powered radio in New Mexico and found her again as she flew back into Monte Vista on 13 March. On this occasion the radio signal carried only a few hundred yards as the antenna was broken. The signal was good news. T27 had survived her first migration and was backtracking again with companions. She passed at least nine months in the wild, making two long flights over unfamiliar territory. Drewien had the good fortune of finding her alive the second winter on the same site north of Bosque del Apache NWR—with a male crane. Her radio no longer worked. It is hoped that she is still alive, leading in her turn young cranes down the mountain flyway.[27]

Possibly, other Patuxent sandhills survived as did T27. Six of her cohorts survived the first summer and were seen leaving the refuge together on the afternoon of 5 October 1980. Despite patient searching on sandhill wintering grounds, however, Drewien has never been able to locate any of them again.[28]

In the most recent release of Patuxent-raised greater sandhill cranes at Grays Lake in 1984, biologists changed strategies, basing them on lessons from the 1980 release and from work with sandhill cranes in Mississippi. First, they selected young birds. Nineteen of the twenty-one parent-reared cranes were only a year old; the other two were two years old. Experience suggested that younger birds fared better, as bonds they had built in captivity appeared less firm than those between older birds. They were more likely, therefore, to integrate into wild flocks. Second, the experiment was a "gentle" or "soft" release. Rather than merely tagging the new cranes and liberating them upon arrival as had been done four years earlier, the refuge staff constructed a conditioning pen, a 25 × 50 foot pentagon-shaped enclosure with a netting roof. The purpose was to familiarize the pen-raised greater sandhills with their new environment. This enclosure, set up in the northwest corner of Grays Lake, the site of the first release, was home to the birds for about a week. The twenty-one cranes arrived in three batches. Each individual received plastic leg bands, a neck collar, and a radio before it entered the enclosure.

Drewien and others watched what happened. Initially, the Patuxent-born cranes wandered about and pecked at the radio tags they carried. After a couple of days in confinement, the new arrivals preened, fed, and loafed, settling down to normal activity patterns. From the fifth day until release, the cranes grew more restless. They pecked at the wire barriers, carefully watched wild counterparts who drew near or flew over, and demonstrated what Drewien interpreted as boredom.

As soon as personnel opened the enclosure the sandhills ran or flew off toward the marsh. By the third week most of them had established a summer area in and around the haunts of wild cranes. All but one of the Patuxent group, crane no. 5, remained within two miles of their conditioning pen. Nine of the twenty-one birds lived long enough to migrate.

But there was bad news. Within six or seven weeks, thirteen Patuxent cranes had died or disappeared. Predation and aggression on the part of wild sandhills claiming territories on Grays Lake factored into losses. Crane no. 19, for example, a female released with seven others on 25 June, was immediately attacked and severely beaten by an angry wild male that was already paired. Finally she escaped and stumbled away but probably died shortly afterward. Four birds in this second batch were unable to fly. One of them disappeared after a day or two; another lasted more than a month. Two other flightless individuals likewise stood no chance.

Wild cranes beat up other fully winged birds who trespassed into their territories; almost all encounters over food or space between captive-raised cranes and wild cranes resulted in defeats for Patuxent birds. Drewien noted how the 1984 birds behaved like the earlier cranes. They avoided conflicts, adopted submissive postures in the presence of wild sandhills, moved about more, and took up positions on the periphery of wild flocks. This trait cost no. 10, a Patuxent female, her life. On 30 June, five days after her release, an observer found no. 10 standing on an open hillside about one

and a fourth miles from the enclosure. She was associating with a group of twenty to thirty wild cranes but stood a little way from the flock. As a golden eagle swung in, the wild birds bunched together, a tactic designed to frustrate aerial attack. No. 10 never moved. She was a perfect target, isolated and unsuspecting. The eagle's talons hit her at the base of the neck, killing her almost instantly. By the time biologists walked to the hill the predator had started to feed on the carcass. Eagles were believed to have taken other soft-released birds that year, a cause of mortality not documented in 1980.[29]

Drewien was disappointed to discover that, although some birds mixed with wild sandhills, they tended to remain with their own captive-raised cohort. He discerned no close associations with native cranes. As wild birds came together in or near grain fields in late August, signaling the end of summer and preparation for migration, Patuxent cranes joined them. Biologists tracked crane no. 4, the first released bird to migrate shortly after noon on 6 October. Crane no. 4's flock teamed up with a larger one and, climbing higher and higher, flew across southwestern Wyoming. Birds streamed over the lofty Uinta Mountains at an altitude of more than 11,000 feet before sunset, then planed into the Green River drainage system in Utah where they landed, some 220 miles southeast of Grays Lake.

Other Patuxent sandhills joined wild flocks for migration. Two released birds also departed together unaccompanied. But after an intensive search, Drewien could locate only two (cranes no. 4 and no. 23) in Colorado's San Luis Valley. Another bird turned up in late October about sixty-one miles southwest of the normal migration route. It was crane no. 16, who had left Grays Lake in the company of wild birds on 7 October.

Later, Drewien observed cranes no. 4 and no. 23 in usual wintering habitat south of Albuquerque, New Mexico. The following April, no. 23 reappeared in the San Luis Valley, and no. 5, who had not been located all winter, turned up near Farson, Wyoming. Thus, a minimum of two of the nine Patuxent migrants survived their first winter in the wild, and two others were possibly still alive. One survivor was sighted at Grays Lake in September 1987.

Drewien and associates were disappointed that survival seemed so poor, concluding that the birds' refusal or incapacity to become integrated into wild flocks was costly. Wild-hatched sandhills appeared to shun the newcomers, who tended to group together. The "soft" as opposed to "hard" release seemed to provide a small advantage, but in both experiments most birds died within six weeks. The biologists recommended that future releases should be made with individual birds spaced some distance apart in order to force integration with wild migratory birds. An alternative would be to capture wild cranes and place a guide bird in a pen with a captive-reared bird. In this way, a "buddy system" might develop and enable the inexperienced crane to emulate the ways of wild brethren.[30]

Florida's Soft Releases

Soft releases in nonmigratory situations have been the most successful method of returning cranes to the wild. Biologists, such as Stephen A. Nesbitt with the Florida Game and Fresh Water Fish Commission, argue that the provision of food and water in situations where pen-raised birds integrate gradually with wintering or resident wild cranes without the burden of migratory flights is the best hope for survival and, ultimately, for reproduction.

Nesbitt has experimented with both hand- and parent-reared sandhills in Florida since 1974. Although the number of birds tested in the mid through late 1970s was small, evidence suggests that cranes can learn the necessary skills to live for months at a time in the wild and that parent-raised birds that do not demonstrate tameness or dependency on humans adjust quite well, to the point of pairing off and nesting.

Nesbitt's first bird, a male hand-reared sandhill crane (not from Patuxent), no. 53, was liberated in January 1974 on Paynes Prairie south of Gainesville, Florida. It remained around the release site but proved too tame, to the point of trailing after hikers, and was recaptured. No. 53 survived for about four months in the following year when it was released with two additional captive-reared cranes. However, it was picked up again and returned to captivity because it was too tame.

Nesbitt and co-workers achieved better results with no. 16, a parent-raised female sandhill, released in August 1976. This bird roamed gradually and linked up with wild birds, assuming their characteristics of wildness.[31]

The real momentum for experimental releases was linked with the whooping crane recovery team's decision in 1980 to further consider the option of establishing a third flock in the United States. Four years later the recovery team selected three eastern areas for study, including four nonmigratory sites—Georgia (1), Florida (3)—and a migratory site in Michigan and Ontario, Canada. The state of Florida possesses about 20 million acres of wetland habitat, much of it in public owner-

ship, plus a population of some 4,000–6,000 resident Florida sandhill cranes from which to select foster parents. Equally important, there is strong support from the state's wildlife authority for a new whooper flock.

In late 1980, Nesbitt began transplanting migratory greater sandhill crane eggs in order to confirm Rod Drewien's research in Idaho, which suggested that migration in cranes is learned not innate. In order to pave the way for a possible whooper flock, Nesbitt needed to be sure that any whoopers raised from placing eggs in nonmigratory Florida sandhill nests would remain within Florida, preferably close to their natal areas. In order to test this hypothesis, he selected eggs from a migratory subspecies of sandhill and placed them in nests of a nonmigratory subspecies.

From spring 1981 through 1984, Nesbitt placed nineteen eggs of migratory greater sandhill cranes, the same subspecies that Drewien used for experiments in Grays Lake, into twelve nests of the sedentary Florida subspecies. Six eggs came from wild greater sandhills in Wisconsin; thirteen were supplied by captive greaters at Patuxent. Hatching and fledging success was low. Only two young cranes survived from two of the twelve nests, but, as anticipated, the youngsters did not migrate even after consorting with members of their own subspecies who pass the winter in Florida.

A recent shipment and release of parent-reared greater sandhills from Patuxent to northern Florida also suggests that in cranes migration is learned, not instinctive, and confirms that it can be suppressed. Nesbitt released fifteen Patuxent greater sandhills in April 1986 and noted that they remained close to the release site. They did in fact respond to the arrival of migratory counterparts in winter by flying about seventy miles southward, but, when their wild associates headed north again, the released birds did not fly out of Florida with them but moved back to about thirty miles from the release area but farther west. In January 1987, a new batch of Patuxent-reared greater sandhills behaved like Florida sandhills. Twelve of the twenty-seven total Patuxent-reared cranes died after a few weeks of freedom, mostly from striking fences or power lines or being taken by bobcats. Inexperience, Nesbitt believes, results in early losses; the newcomers have no other cranes to guide them. But the important point was made: the Patuxent birds remained nonmigratory, even after coming into contact with migrants of the same subspecies, an event that whoopers would not experience in the Sunshine State.

Nesbitt and others are confident that several sites in

Canus, patriarch of the captive flock at Patuxent and sire of numerous whooping crane offspring in that federal facility. Photograph by author.

Florida will make excellent homes for whooping cranes. One possible strategy for building a new flock consists of placing the majority of birds, if not all, in a soft release. This would circumvent heavy mortality that can occur in the first weeks of life in a cross-foster situation and resolve the possibility that such individuals may have an identity crisis (unless, of course, they are misimprinted in the rearing process in captivity).

Problems of hatching and rearing chicks not encountered in the Idaho experiment include the timing of egg transfers to Florida and the availability of wild sandhill foster parents. The Florida subspecies of the sandhill crane breeds earlier than other subspecies and much earlier than whooping cranes in Canada. "Floridas" begin to lay eggs in early January, with a peak in mid-February through mid-March, when whoopers are still on winter grounds in Texas. Most of the tests of egg transfers from wild greater sandhill cranes to Florida were made after mid-April when the nesting season for Florida sandhills is well advanced. Any transfer of eggs from Wood Buffalo, Canada, would be in late May and would create difficulties in finding satisfactory, well-experienced parent Floridas (who usually are among the first pairs to lay).

An alternative would be "recycling," that is, removing clutches from Florida sandhills to stimulate renesting enough times, probably at least twice, in order to gear the foster parents into synchrony with whoopers but without having the sandhills leave the area or abandon breeding efforts. The major assumption, of course, is that whooping crane chicks raised by Florida sandhills will know they are whooping not sandhill cranes and will identify one another as potential mates as well as accept released parent-raised conspecifics as partners.[32]

Mississippi Experiments

Efforts spearheaded by dedicated biologist Jacob M. Valentine, Jr., to safeguard the endangered Mississippi race of the sandhill crane have concentrated on soft releases of young cranes into the 18,000-acre Mississippi NWR (established in 1975) in Jackson County, within the bird's ancestral range. Beginning in January 1981, with nine (eight young of the year and one two-year-old) parent-raised birds from Patuxent, which has housed this subspecies since 1966, injections into this sandhill population have helped stabilize numbers in its historic southeastern Mississippi range. An infusion of eggs and young birds from the federal propagation program combined with habitat protection and management, notably thinning woodlands and creating wetlands,

have successfully slowed a decline in the wild population.

In the initial 1981 experiment, biologists helped the new cranes to adjust gradually to a nonmigratory situation by holding them in large enclosures for about a month before they removed flight restraints. All nine birds placed in a 200-acre predator-proof pen in moist prairie interspersed with woodlands survived the first five months of freedom after they were allowed to fly. Supplemental food in the pen enabled them to become familiar with their surroundings and fly freely between the "home" enclosure and the native habitat.[33]

Through December 1986, almost half of forty-one released sandhills survived one to six years; long enough to pair off and breed with either released or wild conspecifics. In 1987, for example, five of nine nesting pairs had at least one captive-reared member. With about forty Mississippi sandhills in the Patuxent flock capable of producing a dozen or so young per year, biologists are confident that numbers of this most endangered of native cranes can be bolstered upward from the fifty to sixty or so in the wild. *Grus c. p.* inhabited Gulf prairies and wetlands from Louisiana to at least Alabama. Now, however, cranes no longer breed in Louisiana or Alabama; efforts to preserve this endangered subspecies are concentrated in Mississippi. Once consolidation of the population has occurred, other releases may proceed in other Gulf states.

In addition to honing techniques for the soft, or gentle, release of sandhill cranes, which may be applied to whoopers, experts have tested other methods. One of them includes placement of eggs under Florida sandhills held in an enclosure. These "brooder" adults raise Mississippi sandhill crane chicks from eggs laid at Patuxent and subsequently permit their offspring to fly out of enclosures on their own accord. Another method is switching fertile for infertile eggs in wild Mississippi nests. This technique has not been as successful as hoped due to low survival rates among chicks. Predation from coyotes, dogs, and crows and accidents with vehicles factor into Mississippi sandhill crane losses, which occur mostly in the first year, but the precise reasons why so few wild chicks survive at all are matters for speculation.[34]

In general, experts agree that young cranes are most likely to adjust best in the wild. Encouraging results may be obtained if managers place them in communal pens in Patuxent, then switch to secure enclosures in Mississippi until they acclimate to new surroundings. Upon release, open pine woods and savannah country is best for the cranes; food is set out on an unlimited basis until cranes cease to visit their former enclosure.

It is also preferable to release birds in winter when cranes are in groups or flocks and have lessened territorial behavior associated with breeding. It is difficult to calculate how much time is required for inexperienced cranes to associate with and be accepted by wild flocks. Individuals adjust in different ways.

Experts conclude that releases in Florida and Mississippi give most reason for optimism. In such nonmigratory situations cranes are able to learn social skills important for associating with wild birds and recognize new foods, habitat, and dangers without being forced into journeys covering several hundred miles before the onset of winter. Migration inevitably takes a toll on inexperienced birds whose wild counterparts either have made similar travels before or receive assistance from parents who guide them to staging and wintering areas.

Puppets in Wisconsin

One way of providing role models, albeit a very attenuated way, is for human guardians to act as cranes without their charges imprinting on them. A recent experiment in Wisconsin has drawn upon the sandhill crane's ability to learn from the moment it pips the eggshell through fledging and early independence.

In 1985, Rob Horwich puppet-reared five greater sandhill cranes on the grounds of the International Crane Foundation (ICF) at Baraboo. Working with ICF director and crane ethologist George Archibald, Horwich devised an incubation, hatching, and rearing schedule to maximize the chick's sense of being raised by a parent bird while in fact being tutored by humans. The idea of the crane puppet, a false crane head covering the keeper's arm and hand, is to assist the chick from its earliest hours in identifying itself as a crane. Mirrors, taped brood calls, and live cranes in pens, now used in Patuxent, were used to teach the hatchlings to begin to feed and to respond only to cranes not humans.

As his birds grew, Horwich donned a costume hiding his head and face, a cloth fold to brood the chick in, and a puppet head affixed to his arm and headed his "family" on walks. Huge and ungainly looking, this "parent crane" introduced his charges to insect and plant foods. After the sandhills became bigger, he transported them about fifty miles to Necedah NWR, a staging area for migratory sandhill cranes, and set up a camp, complete with an enclosure, shelters, feeding trays, and his tent, in which he lived as "mother crane." Again, the costumed biologist guided his birds around their new home and, as they developed flying skills, urged them

into the air by running along towing his brood of flapping brown young. Soon the birds left the enclosure and practiced short circular flights above the refuge.

All went according to plan, except that, as time passed, the ever-larger chicks regressed, loafing outside his tent. Fledged cranes were waiting for "Mama" crane to appear, he recalled, and demanded food. At this juncture Horwich took radical action in order to wean his brood. He closed up the camp and abandoned the young, forcing them to forage on their own. After hanging about the site the sandhills began to drift away and fend for themselves. Within a couple of weeks three of the reared birds turned up southwest of Necedah, heading toward the Mississippi River, away from normal flight paths.

Horwich worried about intervening to "save" his charges. Finally, deciding to do so, he drove his VW camper three hours in their direction and eventually located a radio-banded male named Noah, who was associating with a flock of domestic turkeys on a farm and reportedly had dashed inside a barn when frightened. Donning his costume, Horwich called the crane over, loaded him into his vehicle, and drove back to Necedah. Once out of the camper, Noah spied a passing flock of wild sandhills and scrambled after them. Relieved, Horwich quickly departed.

Within a few days, Noah had linked up with the three surviving released chicks, who had begun to forage with wild sandhills. Two birds, one of which was Noah, headed south toward Jasper-Pulaski NWR, an important stopping area for migratory sandhill cranes. There the two released birds separated and disappeared, as had two other birds with which Horwich had lost contact along the Mississippi River.

Four of five puppet-raised sandhills turned up again in spring 1986. Two renegades returned from the direction of the Mississippi River, having wintered in some unknown locality. Noah was identified near Green Bay; his companion at Jasper-Pulaski NWR also came back to the Necedah area. Only Medusa, a bird who seemed to integrate with wild birds from the start, has never been seen again. Horwich hopes that Medusa is alive, perhaps heading into Canada in some wild flock.[35]

Noah was sighted in Florida in mid-January 1987. Transmitters on the other ICF cranes had begun to run down, but Horwich was pleased to note that at least one of his puppet-raised sandhills was alive. Unfortunately, a second similar test with puppet techniques in 1986 was aborted at the very last moment after a new batch of captive-reared sandhills tested positive for *Salmonella*. Fearing that this bacterial infection could be spread among wild birds, Horwich and colleagues were forced to delay the release and, after subsequent treatment and testing, decided not to liberate them. The small sample and failure to repeat the experiment has clouded hopes that this release method may become more acceptable to propagationists. Current ICF procedures for raising cranes intended for release involve isolation, crane models, and puppet feeding.[36]

Baraboo, Wisconsin

George Archibald loves cranes but not as embellishments around some stately home. His affection goes well beyond that blue-blood penchant for elegant bric-a-brac. Cranes have strong characters that command respect. It is their grace, color, bearing, individuality, and longevity that attract and sustain the interest of this Canadian-born birdman.

George Archibald has devoted himself to the welfare of the earth's cranes ever since he encountered them in Alberta on a game farm where he worked one summer. Doctoral work at Cornell University on crane taxonomy revealed by vocalizations and behavior put him into contact with another crane expert, Ron Sauey; together the young ornithologists founded a center for crane research and conservation in Wisconsin.

For the last fifteen years Archibald has been a peripatetic ambassador for all cranes. He has alerted officials in Japan about red-crowned cranes nesting on Hokkaido. He has promoted sanctuaries for several species in China, discussed propagation techniques for Siberian cranes with experts in Russia, and notified authorities in Korea about the importance of the DMZ for wintering white-naped cranes.

As director of the International Crane Foundation located at Baraboo, north of Madison, Archibald admits good humoredly that although the present 160-acre site has become home for all fifteen species of cranes—thirteen have bred—its whooping cranes have been more or less "basket cases."[37]

Since its establishment in 1973, ICF has accommodated five whoopers; now there is only one. Three of them were potential mates for the behaviorly impaired female called Tex, and the fifth, her single offspring, so-called Gee Whiz, continues to attract appreciative comments from people who visit Baraboo's "crane pod" where he is on display.

Tex captured America's heart when she danced in public with Archibald, who, knowing that his crane "mate" was sexually imprinted upon humans, decided to try to bring her into a breeding state so that she

Table 4. Baraboo Whooping Cranes

1976	April	Nine-year-old Tex is shipped to ICF from the Patuxent Wildlife Research Center, Laurel, Maryland.
1976	Fall	Tony (alias Georgette, George II, named after George Douglass of the New Orleans Zoo) arrives from Audubon Park, New Orleans, Louisiana.
1977	9 April	Tex, who is "paired" with ICF director George Archibald, lays her first egg. It is infertile.
1977	Fall	Angus (alias George), the second potential mate for Tex, is shipped from Audubon Park.
1978	27 April	Tex lays a second, fertile egg, but the chick fathered by Angus dies just before hatching.
1979		Tex lays a soft-shelled egg.
1979	24 May	Angus is injured after hot air balloons overfly ICF.
1979	16 August	Angus breaks a leg.
1979	7 October	Angus dies.
1980		Tex does not lay.
1980	13 August	Tony found dead of abdominal hemorrhage.
1980	October	Patuxent–Red 16, so-called Tux, arrives from Patuxent.
1981	20 April	Tux dies after becoming lodged in his pen. Tex does not lay.
1982	April–May	Archibald devotes dawn to dusk hours working with Tex.
1982	3 May	Tex lays a fertile egg.
1982	1 June	Gee Whiz hatches.
1982	22 June	Tex killed in her enclosure by raccoons.
1987		Gee Whiz shares an ICF enclosure with a female red-crowned crane.

would lay an egg. Tex's preference for humans, especially dark-haired men, over cranes goes back to when she struggled out of an egg in San Antonio Zoo in 1967. She was the daughter of Rosie, a wild-caught female injured on migration near Lampasas, Texas, and was fathered by Crip, the most famous of all male whoopers. Crip had been paired with Rosie after his mate Josephine died in 1965. Moved from New Orleans to San Antonio in 1966, Rosie excited San Antonio Zoo director Fred Stark by hatching out two eggs the following spring. One of the chicks died, but Stark lavished care on the other, to be named Tex. He fed it with mealworms, calcium, and other goodies and kept an almost constant watch over the tiny crane. After a couple of weeks and not long before he died of a heart attack, zoo director Stark relinquished his charge to Ray Erickson, who carried the young whooper back to Patuxent.

Tex turned out to be a disappointment as a member of the breeding flock. The crane had been in the federal facility for eight seasons before Archibald offered to work with her at ICF. He also contacted Audubon Park in New Orleans, where two potential mates for Tex lived (Tony and Angus). His idea was to pair off with Tex himself, then use one of the males, a crane called Tony (1957 offspring of Crip and Josephine), as a semen donor for artificial insemination.

One-half of the plan worked. Tex responded well to her new premises in Wisconsin. She bonded with Archibald, who set up an office in her enclosure and spent hour after hour in her presence. Tony arrived from New Orleans about a week after Tex and took up a pen near her. Archibald noted that the two cranes even danced together. But Tony proved a very aggressive bird and also a poor semen donor. Only 7 of 138 attempts to collect semen from him in a five-year period resulted in excellent samples. On 13 August 1980, the male whooper Tony was discovered dead in his pen.

Tex blossomed. In 1977, her second year at ICF, she courted Archibald, who replicated her leaps and gestures until she laid an egg. In April of that year, George began to notice how restless his crane was growing, so he opened the gate of her pen and followed the white bird up a hill to a nearby hayfield. Tex claimed that hillside as her territory, built a flimsy nest, and, with Archibald by her side, laid her first egg. Then she walked down the hill and back into her pen again. Archibald was pleased. Although the egg was infertile, he had persuaded Tex to lay her first egg after ten years in captivity.

In April 1978, Tex laid her second egg. Interestingly,

nine days prior, Ektu, her stepmother and her father's third captive mate, also laid an egg in San Antonio Zoo. That year, remarks Georgette Maroldo, Crip's biographer, that patrician among whoopers "could have had the distinction of being both father and grandfather." Ektu, from a Canadian egg hatched on Patuxent, experienced difficulties in pairing with Crip; her 1978 egg was fertile, but its embryo died of an infection.

Tex's egg was also fertile after Crip's two sons, Tony and Angus, had acted as semen donors. Angus, who also hailed from Audubon Park, New Orleans, like his sibling, carried the previous genes of his mother, Josephine, and had arrived in Baraboo in advance of the 1978 breeding season. Archibald describes Angus as a flawless bird—well proportioned, behaviorally well adjusted, and even tempered. From early March through mid-May, Angus furnished the semen that Archibald injected into Tex, which resulted in her second egg being fertile.

The following year, Ektu laid no fewer than eight eggs (five were fertile), and it was while incubating number five on 27 March 1979 that Crip, Tex's sire, "got up from the egg, walked to the stream at the far end of the enclosure for a sip of water, and suddenly fell over dead." Within two months, a tragic accident struck down his 22-year-old son Angus.

On 24 May, literally out of a blue sky, a "flock" of hot air balloons passed over ICF premises. The odd, menacing objects terrified the cranes. Angus smashed into the fence of his enclosure and broke off a part of his upper mandible. His beak never healed. Workers began to force-feed the big crane, but in mid-August, while being fed, Angus pushed against his restraints and broke a leg. Despite intensive care, the admirable whooper never recovered. He rallied briefly, then slowly weakened as his leg failed to set properly. Angus stopped unison calling with Tex in early October and died on the seventh of that month. He had been at ICF less than a year.[38]

The staff were heartbroken by this tragic, needless accident. They had lost a crane in his prime. There was Tony glaring coldly from his pen, but he was a broken down bird, unlikely to sire progeny. Archibald continued to work with Tony, but it was hopeless and, shortly after the second male's unexpected death in August 1980, George called Patuxent for assistance. On 29 October 1980, Patuxent–Red 16, shortened by ICF staff to Tux, arrived in Baraboo to be Tex's third mate.

Archibald calls Tux a sad case who lived barely six months before succumbing from apparent trauma after he became lodged in Christmas trees used to wall off the sides of bird pens. Tux was a stunted bird, a poor semen donor, and as unlikely to contribute to Tex's reproduction as Tony had been.

In 1982, with only Tex remaining, Archibald decided to give the female whooper his undivided attention. She had failed to lay eggs at all for two years. From April through most of May, he quite literally moved in with her, passing each daylight hour in her presence. Archibald was there when Tex awoke to bugle at the dawn and stride off toward her favorite spot on the hill. The ICF director danced with her, helped patrol the environs, chasing off would-be human trespassers. Archibald moved a small shed out in the field, beside the spot Tex had chosen for her nest. The human rested, foraged, and talked to her. Then he noted that her abdomen was starting to swell gradually, and he arranged for fresh crane semen to be flown out from Patuxent to Madison and trucked to Baraboo two or three times per week. Archibald began to inseminate Tex using donor sperm from an unmated male, Killer, and grew increasingly sure that she would lay an egg.

On 1 May, George noted that Tex seemed lethargic and ate little, so he stayed on hand as the egg formed inside her. Two days later at 3:00 P.M., after the crane had sat on the nest for one and a half hours, an egg appeared. Archibald recalled: "I removed it immediately, replaced it with a sandhill egg filled with plaster of paris, and put Tex's egg under an incubating pair of captive Florida sandhill cranes." He hoped that his "mate" would lay another, but after a couple of weeks Tex started to wander out of the nesting territory; one egg was all that she was able to produce.

Archibald shifted attention to the unusually narrow, crinkle-ended egg. He candled it after two weeks by shining a bright light against the shell and saw an embryo darkening the inside. It was losing weight, however, at a dangerously high rate, so Archibald placed it in a mechanical incubator and turned up the humidity. Fluids continued to waste away, until finally, in desperation, ICF staff followed the suggestion of University of Wisconsin poultry science expert Bernard Wentworth and submerged the egg in freezing water, causing it thereby to swell again after it pulled moisture inside the porous shell.

Gee Whiz crawled out on 1 June 1982. A number of well-wishers were on hand, including Faith McNulty, who had flown in from New England to witness the birth of this important crane. Gee Whiz, named out of sheer relief and after George Gee, specialist and crane physiologist at Patuxent who also came to Baraboo to

see the newly hatched crane, flourished only after life-saving liquids were forced into him. Staff members took over the duties of feeding and rearing.

On the night of 22 June 1982, three weeks after her chick hatched, Tex died. That evening Archibald was scheduled to appear on "The Tonight Show" with Johnny Carson, and news of her death spread. Raccoons had ripped a hole through the nylon flight netting in her cage and attacked the terrified female. "All that remained next morning was her beak," remembers Archibald, and one of the culprits, a large raccoon that workers had killed. Another two cranes died in successive nights despite round-the-clock vigilance and an electric fence looped around the pens. 'Coon hounds were called in and tracked down the marauders. It was the first instance in the ten-year history of ICF that raccoons had caused problems; incredibly, Tex was the first victim.[39]

Gee Whiz is the single whooper among 112 cranes on the ICF site along Shady Lane north of the city of Baraboo. He is one of the display birds housed in an oval-shaped set of cages, each screened from the next, in which a dozen species are penned. Visitors walk past these crane pens, observing endangered Siberian, hooded, and red-crowned cranes and learning the names of individual birds and the distinguishing marks of each species. Most people pause beside the "whooping crane" enclosure and are puzzled by the marked differences in size and appearance between its two residents. In fact, a female red-crowned crane named Zha Long has been placed with whooper Gee Whiz in order to reassure him that "he is a crane," explains Archibald, who does not think he is imprinted on humans. Both birds were born in Baraboo and are paired although there is no conclusive evidence that the whooping crane has mated with his female companion of a closely related but different species. Superficially, they look alike. They are white in color, but the male whooper is much taller and is more assertive than the red-crowned female. He struts aggressively toward humans as they approach his pen, picking at the wire and uttering low guttural threats on the boundary of the enclosure—his territory.[40]

Too Nice

To date, only one whooping crane, a female hatched in Patuxent in 1978 from parents in Wood Buffalo NP, has been released into the wild. In the first years at Grays Lake, Idaho, when prospects for the egg transplant and foster-parent-rearing looked most promising, biologists recognized a potential problem. After five years it was clear that a sex ratio heavily favoring male whoopers had developed, which threatened future breeding. In 1980, three males established summer territories on Grays Lake. All of them originated from the first hatching in 1975; all three were unpaired as few females had survived, and those that did failed to return to the marsh. Consultation among officials in Patuxent and Idaho brought about an agreement to ship a parent-reared female crane to Idaho in order to introduce her to a territory-holding male.

On the evening of 25 April 1981, Too Nice, named by Patuxent behaviorist Scott Derrickson because of her coy behavior if not outright indifference before a potential mate, arrived in Grays Lake NWR. Difficulty with airlines and an unscheduled deplaning in Chicago made it too late to place the three-year-old female in the enclosure specially constructed for her in the north end of a male whooper's territory. Biologists held her overnight. The holding pen measured 24 feet by 40 feet and stood 8 feet high. Vegetation within the enclosure included cattails and bulrushes native to the wetland plus a small patch of upland meadow. A feeder stocked with barley to which the female had been preconditioned at Patuxent was also set in the enclosure. Nylon netting covered the roof.

Conditions seemed ideal. Although the female was too young to actually mate, people hoped that she would associate and pair with the wild male, who would lead her to winter quarters. Only one problem was unanticipated. Too Nice had molted her flight feathers a few days before she arrived at Grays Lake, probably in response to artificial lights used to stimulate egg laying among the Aleutian race of Canada geese in a nearby pen at Patuxent. The roof netting was unnecessary, because she could not fly, but helped guard against avian predators.

At 7:45 A.M. on 26 April 1981, Too Nice entered the special pen. She bathed, inspected her enclosure, and within a few minutes received a visit from the male, 75-1 (named for his year of hatching and nest number in Wood Buffalo), who had watched the entire construction procedure and even visited with a life-size silhouette of a crane placed there after completion. Having been deluded into thinking it was a crane, the male had ignored the decoy as he fed on barley scattered around the new pen. This time the white crane was real, and the two whoopers looked at each other intently.

During the first day, 75-1, or Miracles, as Rod Drewien called him, flew back and forth to the enclosure no fewer than sixteen times. Clearly, he was interested in this new crane who paced about the enclosure nervously. Similar activities in ensuing days brought the two birds closer together. Once Too Nice danced briefly as Miracles remained nearby. He sped off to the other end of his territory and began to chase sandhills, thereby enlarging his chosen area. It was not clear whether this was a response to Too Nice. Was he trying to impress her or get out of her way, or was acute aggression toward sandhills an indication that he was imprinted on the gray-brown species? Biologists could only speculate. Meanwhile, the female whooper was unsettled and tried repeatedly to get out of the enclosure.

On 4 May, biologists opened the pen after workers banded her and placed a radio on her leg. Immediately, Too Nice, still unable to fly, walked south along the entire length of the male's territory. He joined her; they walked, fed, and socialized and then he moved away to chase sandhills. The female headed into deep vegetation and grew secretive. She remained hidden in a section of Miracle's territory for almost a month when, to the relief of biologists, she began to fly once more.

While the male crane showed casual interest in his potential mate, he directed a great deal of aggression toward sandhill neighbors and on one occasion was observed to knock a bird out of the air and beat it severely, possibly fatally. This behavior puzzled observers, who could only speculate that Miracles was directing aggression away from Too Nice to more easily recognizable sandhills. Perhaps he was confused, aroused by the presence of the female yet somehow unable to express the appropriate behavior that would result in pair formation.

Once Too Nice regained her powers of flight, she moved east of the male's territory into grain fields, consorting there with sandhills and occasionally with Miracles. Experts watched for clues of bonding. On July 26, the wild male landed near Too Nice and gave a unison call, to which she responded, indicating mutual regard. Unfortunately, this was the only vocalization that suggested bonding between the pair. For most of the summer, Miracles continued to attack sandhill cranes while the female roamed about his territory and nearby areas. She also associated with two other whoopers who had moved in to feast on barley in staging area fields.

Since no pair bond had formed, craneman Rod Drewien, who had assiduously followed all these activities, set out to capture the female in early October 1981, assisted by Keith Day. He watched as a young male, 79-10, passed the entire day with Too Nice. When evening came, 79-10 flew to his roost alone leaving the

Patuxent female to join a group of sandhills. Unwilling to risk losing this bird as migration from the valley was in full swing, Drewien moved into the marsh that night. Shining a bright light into the female's eyes, he was able to dazzle her long enough to grab her. She was airlifted back to Patuxent the following day. Her expected mate, Miracles, left Grays Lake eleven days later with two other whooping cranes.[41]

Although biologists were disappointed by the pair's apparent unwillingness or inability to establish firm bonds, they were pleased that Too Nice survived for more than five months on the Idaho marsh. She came to look like a wild-born whooper and for all intents and purposes behaved like one. Experts concluded that she would have left Grays Lake with other cranes, but they didn't want to risk losing her in winter or have her wander off to distant summering grounds the following year, as cross-fostered females had done.

They were less sanguine about the interactions between Miracles and Too Nice. Initial interest cooled quickly as the male made off after sandhills and as the flightless female grew secretive. Interactions later on seemed more casual, and, although Miracles never grew hostile, he demonstrated no attentive regard that characterizes a good pair.

Undeterred, officials decided to try again in 1982. Shipped by air to Salt Lake City, Utah, then transported by vehicle the remaining hundred or so miles, Too Nice arrived for the second time at Grays Lake on the evening of 2 April 1982. Next morning she was placed in the same enclosure in the territory of the same male, who had returned from New Mexico for his sixth season, the oldest survivor of the cross-foster experiment.

High water that spring inundated her pen, but the female whooper was able to eat from the barley feeder and loaf on a platform added to the enclosure to keep her out of the shallow water. Miracles quickly took up duties as observer. Calling elicited no response from her, so he flew over the enclosure repeatedly, then landed on the nearest dry land some seventy-five yards away and studied the new arrival. Biologists released Too Nice from a pen on 3 May, and she quickly trekked south as she had done a year earlier. Ignoring the presence of the male, who flew to join her, she plodded steadfastly out of his territory into a dense stand of willows. Too Nice remained several hundred yards south of 75-1's selected area for the next ten days. The male again began attacking sandhills. Although the two cranes were well aware of each other's presence, they remained separated.

A new, welcome sign appeared 6 May, when Miracles began to pile together bulrushes and cattails. Drewien saw him on 13 May in his haunts. Two days later Miracles was discovered hanging in a barbed-wire fence, dead from an apparent collision.

Too Nice remained in the patch of willows. She moved to more open haunts in early September when biologists noted that she had injured a wing. Although the young male, 79-10, from the previous summer accompanied her for short spells in grain fields, observers concluded that no real bonds were established and captured her on 6 October for shipment back to Patuxent.[42]

It was a bitter disappointment to lose Miracles, the senior member and most dominant male whooper of the Grays Lake program. He was in prime breeding condition and was the only crane ever observed to initiate nest construction. His liaison with the introduced female puzzled biologists. In the second season, he appeared to have elicited little or no response from the four-year-old female; and, although obviously interested in her and passing much time maintaining a territory, 75-1 stayed away from Too Nice. His tragic and unexpected death terminated further efforts to release captive-bred female whoopers into the wild.

*Upon the place of their return they confer a peculiar dis-
tinction. Amid the endless mediocrity of the commonplace,
a crane marsh holds a paleontological patent of nobility,
won in the march of aeons, and revocable only by shotgun.
The sadness discernible in some marshes arises, perhaps,
from their once having harbored cranes. Now they stand
humbled, adrift in history.*

—ALDO LEOPOLD
A Sand County Almanac, p. 103

5. Second Flock in Idaho

JULY 26, 1859

The rode kept the valley till noon, sometimes would go over the hills, but it is prairie & should think it the same valey. We nooned by a large pond [Gray's Lake] which is at the head of the valey. I should think the pond was somewhere between 2 & 5 miles across. It is hard to tell. I would not like to say, eny how. Flags & rushes grow at the edges of the pond & at places extend some distance. It is full of ducks & I saw 3 swans. Shot at them several times but was to far off. In the afternoon the rode kept arround the pond for 4 or 5 miles, then followed up a ravine & went over the hill into a nice little valley watterd by Antelope Creek. (CHARLES CUMMINGS)[1]

As I travel north along Idaho 34 (the state's outline is embossed on route markers), it is clear that there is to be a shift in the weather. Weather governs the life of cranes in southeastern Idaho. Cold and snow, evidence of winter's tightening grasp, push flocks southeast over mountainous Wyoming and Utah toward wider spaces in Colorado's San Luis Valley and the warmer reaches of the Rio Grande in New Mexico. In minutes, a summer storm can chill a chick just out of the nest by blasting through a marsh's secure curtain of bulrush and cattail, splattering its down with ice-cold rain or snow, even in July, and causing it to die. Sandhill cranes raise their young in an open, high wetland called Grays Lake, named after a half-Iroquois man employed by the Hudson Bay Company, John Gray. Originally named Grays Marsh or Grays Hole, this site in southeastern Idaho is the center for an effort to establish a second population of whooping cranes.

The day after the autumn equinox is early for a major storm to hit Soda Springs, the town nearest to the "large pond" described by Charles Cummings. But coffee talk in Ender Café, a spot for plant workers and local ranchers, is about a Pacific cold front that has dumped snow on the Cascades and is headed across the Columbia River plateau toward this community. Tomorrow, folks say, the snow line will be down to 5,500 feet, below the altitude of this former stopping place on the Oregon Trail, whose natural alkaline waters old boys imagined tasted of beer. Certainly, on the roadside going north out of town the sky is as dark as the spoil tip. Grays Lake, almost thirty miles away, is six hundred feet above Soda Springs, and in that high country winter is just around the corner.

Flares from phosphate plants shine eerily against dark snow-flecked hills, but after a mile or two the country opens up and glows. It is a shaggy land of earth-tone brown, blue, and candle-flame yellow, which aspens take from harvested grain fields nearby and paste to huge chunks of exposed basalt from which they sprout.

As the odometer ticks away, high-country trees come near to the road. Every mile or so a kestrel flicks from a telephone pole leading the eye toward hummocks of unplowed land. Curved like huge blisters and perfectly rounded, these volcanic intrusions in an ancient uplifted seabed resemble tumuli, relics of some great civilization.

The cloud-filled road appears blocked by a whalebone of hills that breech from the stained waters of Blackfoot River Reservoir, another meeting ground for cranes. I drive toward the barrier, pass along five miles of unfenced switchback, and slow down every now and then to avoid knots of white-faced cattle who share this range with mule deer, the biggest native animal. Like the road, a buck zig-zags in front of me, then bounds away into grass and sagebrush, once home for pronghorn antelope and bison, ancestral prey of Shoshone Indians, who lay claim to this hunting ground.

All around, the country is hard and rugged. I catch the first glimpse of a broad hollow that grows into Grays Lake. The vehicle swings around the final curve on the lake's south shore, and Caribou Mountain fills the eastern horizon. Today, this second-highest peak in southeastern Idaho wears a shroud of cloud and snow that billows in white waves. Flakes coat the roadside, whirl out over hidden waters, and cascade on a broad, flat wetland. Grays Lake seems more prairie than water. From a distance, vast stands of brown and green plants could be mistaken for grass stretching out to bony hills in the north.

A knot of gadwalls upend in a lead, several coots peck compulsively at the water's surface, and an eared grebe bobs for a moment then dives. Above, a Foster's tern momentarily beats against the piercing wind until an air draft flings it away. This marsh dweller must head out soon, leaving a bigger northern harrier, tacking higher up, to eke out a living in this prairie-sea of tightly spaced marsh plants.

Remote and lonely, this 22,000-acre marsh is an important nesting ground for sandhill cranes. Next April, as winter loosens its hold, brown cranes will return, build nests, raise young, forage with them in surrounding barley fields, and then guide them several hundred miles south during the hardest months. Crane experts mark out nest sites, observing how pairs establish and patrol territories and how successfully they reproduce. One of them, Roderick C. Drewien, has watched sandhill cranes on Grays Lake for twenty years. He knows these birds and can tell you which pairs are reliable parents, how successfully they feed and tend their chicks, when they will leave, and where they will go.

Drewien has three homes: one on Grays Lake from which he checks on nesting activities, a second at Colorado's Monte Vista NWR on which many of his birds pause for several days or weeks as they pass on migration, and a third on Bosque del Apache NWR, near Soccorro south of Albuquerque, New Mexico, about 850 miles south of Grays Lake. He uses this latter refuge to study sandhills in winter quarters until the birds begin to retrace their path to nesting grounds. On occasion, Drewien travels south from Bosque into Mexico to search for tagged cranes in Chihuahua. Some birds choose to move that far south for food and to get away from disturbances in the Rio Grande Valley.

In size, Grays Lake cranes are almost as big as whoopers, and a male sandhill may stand as tall as a female whooping crane. These stately birds belong to the Rocky Mountain population of a subspecies called the greater sandhill crane (*Grus canadensis tabida*). This tall, migratory subspecies nests in the United States from southern Oregon and northeastern California eastward through the Great Basin and range country into glacial

lakes and moraines in Wisconsin and northern Minnesota. The mountain population nests in remote valleys and alpine meadows above 5,000 feet in five states (Idaho, Wyoming, Montana, Utah, and Colorado); Idaho holds the largest concentration. After declining precipitously to a few hundred in the early portion of the century because of marsh reclamation, human disturbance, and overhunting, numbers of this special race of sandhill crane have recovered to twenty thousand or so. Largely as a result of Drewien's research, greater sandhills were selected for an imaginative program to establish a second flock of wild whooping cranes. They have become foster parents for whoopers.

Working out of the Idaho Cooperative Wildlife Research Unit in Moscow, Drewien completed a doctoral dissertation in 1973, titled "Ecology of Rocky Mountain Greater Sandhill Cranes." For several seasons he had studied the nesting success of greater sandhills, including some 250 pairs at Grays Lake, Idaho. Grays Lake cranes did unusually well, fledging 78–92 percent of young. Drewien and co-workers captured and banded several hundred birds and tracked them on migration. The route that Grays Lake cranes took carried them over thinly settled areas where little or no hunting occurred.[2]

With an ample supply of foster parent sandhills and details about the reliability of specific pairs, Drewien analyzed the physical parameters of the proposed transplant site in Idaho. He discovered that conditions were similar to nesting territories used by whooping cranes in Canada, although the effects of a higher elevation, 6,385 feet in Grays Lake compared to less than 1,000 in Wood Buffalo, were undetermined.

Grays Lake National Wildlife Refuge was established in June 1965 for waterfowl protection. The vast marsh consists mostly of hardstem bulrush (*Scirpus acutus*) and cattail (*Typha latifolia*) and nurtures about five thousand ducks belonging to five key species and about half that number of Canada geese. Drewien's research proved that the broad, shallow, thickly vegetated 18,000-acre lake bed, over which the U.S. Fish and Wildlife Service has direct control, provides habitat for what is probably the largest concentration of nesting sandhill cranes in North America. Authorities selected this highly productive, unpolluted crane marsh for whooping cranes because they could monitor human access and activities on the nine-by-four-mile valley wetland. In addition, Grays Lake lies on the western edge of the whoopers' known range, although there is some debate about the accuracy of the historic record. The fact that state authorities in Idaho, Colorado, and New Mexico supported a foster program for whoopers also contributed to building a well-rounded plan for bringing back one of America's most endangered birds.[3]

Grays Lake sandhills migrate to other federal refuges along a relatively short flyway compared with that of their Canada-U.S. counterparts. Drewien has spotted a significant number of banded cranes at Ouray NWR on the Green River in Utah, essentially a long day's flight from the Idaho site. About another day's journey southeast brings the migrants to Monte Vista NWR in Colorado's wide barley-filled San Luis Valley. Drewien speculated that adult sandhills would guide their whooper chicks to this refuge and its environs, feed on stubble as they did around Grays Lake, and rest in 14,000 acres of refuge wetlands. After a few weeks, crane families would spiral up and glide toward their winter destination in a sward of green marking New Mexico's middle Rio Grande Valley. Sandhills home in on Bosque del Apache NWR—the final link in a protective chain of federal lands in which cranes encounter suitable feeding and roosting spaces.

Sandhill cranes begin to nest at Grays Lake in late April and early May, about the same time that whooping cranes settle on mostly two-egg clutches in Wood Buffalo National Park some thirteen hundred miles farther north. The experiment called for transplanting whooping crane eggs into sandhill crane nests, a task that required well-planned logistics. Nest cycles of specific pairs would be monitored and well-incubated eggs from Canada would be flown into Idaho and placed in sandhill nests at a similar stage in the incubation schedule. In sum, nest synchrony keyed on the Idaho wetland, a known migration corridor, and federally protected winter quarters with other state management areas close by appeared acceptable to Canadian, U.S., and state authorities. With Drewien's background data, field experience, and familiarity with crane habitats to rely upon, authorities gave the go ahead for the foster program (see Table 5).

1975 Foster Experiment

In 1975, "cross-fostering" at Grays Lake got underway to an inauspicious start. On 13 May, when nest building and egg laying should have been in full swing, Rod Drewien found pairs of sandhills merely loafing on breeding areas. Much of the lake was iced in, and abundant snow on the surrounding hills made the scene look like mid-winter, not early spring. The sandhills had flown in, but such unseasonable conditions set back the breeding cycle by about three weeks. He found the first nests on 17 May, and ten days later all sixteen color-marked pairs, dependable and experienced breeders selected to raise the first whoopers at Grays Lake, had established their territories. Riding an airboat into the rapidly thawing marsh, Drewien began to remove an egg from every crane nest so that he could later switch the remaining one with a whooper egg. When a pair deserted their nest after he had finished only half his task, Drewien decided to leave the remaining nests alone and wait for CWS craneman Ernie Kuyt to fly in from Wood Buffalo with the precious cargo of whooping crane eggs.

Three days later, Drewien was on hand to greet the chartered plane, which touched down in Idaho Falls. Then Drewien and Canada's pick-up man for Wood Buffalo, Ernie Kuyt, assisted by Elwood Bizeau, University of Idaho and U.S. Fish and Wildlife Service, transferred the rare whooping crane eggs to a helicopter for the final forty-mile leg to headquarters on Grays Lake's eastern shore. The biologists landed at 1:10 P.M. and immediately prepared to carry the fourteen crane eggs to sandhill nests staked out in the marsh. By 7:00 P.M., all of the whooper eggs were in the appropriate sandhill nests. The single egg in seven nests was exchanged for a whooper egg; in the remaining seven nests with two eggs, one was stolen and replaced with a whooping crane egg dutifully marked. Drewien would remove the second sandhill egg after the parents had returned and settled into their incubation routine. He didn't want to risk further desertions this early in the nesting cycle.

Happily, the weather smiled on this first egg transplant. Clear, sunny conditions and temperatures in the seventies eased the transfer. Next day Kuyt and Drewien flew over the nests; all of the eggs except one were safe under sitting birds. Their aircraft startled a pair who stood nearby. Thereafter, Drewien kept a diligent but unobtrusive watch over the nests with whooper eggs. On 3 June, the first egg hatched; and a week later nine newborn whooping cranes were on Grays Lake. Three eggs were infertile, and two more disappeared from their nests, probably lost to predators.

Throughout June, Drewien devoted most of his waking hours to the welfare of the nine chicks. He noted that young whoopers responded to their parents, who fed them and saw to their needs. They hid at the sounding of adult alarm calls and followed obediently upon hearing typical "purrr" sounds. Families stayed together, the parents accepting their foster chicks.

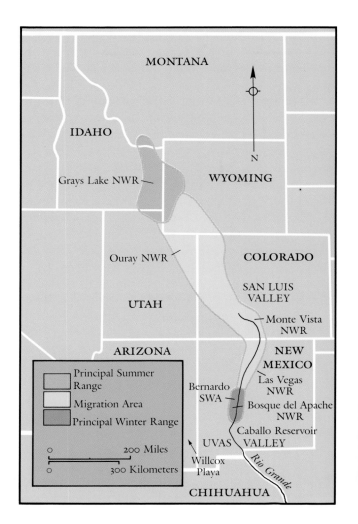

Summer and Winter Ranges and Migration Route of Whooping Cranes Introduced into the Rocky Mountain Region, 1975–1985 (based on U.S. Fish and Wildlife Service, *Whooping Crane Recovery Plan*, 1986)

ABOVE: A 52-day-old whooper chick raised by sandhill parents, Grays Lake NWR. Photograph by Rod C. Drewien.

RIGHT: The tall, snow white whoopers stand out among their more numerous sandhill cousins. This bird, a member of the second flock, mingles with sixteen sandhill cranes on Bosque del Apache NWR, December 1984. Photograph by Rod C. Drewien.

Drewien watched one male shelter his youngster during a rain shower, and observed another attack a steer that approached his whooper colt. Experience has shown, however, that, rather than run into vegetation and squat in response to alarm calls, most whooper chicks tend to move into shallow water and run or swim off, making it easier for watchers to spot them.

June was cold and wet. Snow on the twenty-fifth probably caused chick 75-9 to die. Drewien caught a final glimpse of it with adults before the storm but could not find it thereafter. By early July, Drewien knew the whereabouts of six growing whooping cranes and turned up two more (75-6 near dense cattails and 75-4 in a small marsh) by 11 July.[4]

July turned out to be perplexing. Although parent-chick responses were satisfactory, the presence of cattle in wet meadows caused some youngsters to panic. Chick 75-1, who Drewien nicknamed Miracles because he managed to extricate himself from so many difficult situa-tions, followed his parents into lightly grazed sections of their territory with no apparent problems. But when cattle were allowed into areas held by other families, such as 75-3 and 75-5, neither whooper chick was seen again. Drewien talked with staff about eliminating cattle from such critical areas. Later an agreement was reached to keep livestock out until the chicks had fledged.

Drewien also discovered another problem—fences. On 31 July, he observed Miracles struggling to get through a six-strand wire fence. While foraging with his parents, who usually jumped up and flew over such ob-stacles, the youngster, still unable to fly, pushed into the sharp-edged strands, became snagged, and panicked.

The problem was a serious one. Miles of barbed-wire fences criss-crossed sandhill territories. Young sandhills, being smaller and less ungainly than their whooper rela-tives, had seldom been observed in such difficulties with wires. To ensure the safety of the whooping cranes, fences on little-grazed portions of the refuge would have to be removed, and others would have to be changed from six to three strands. Both suggestions caused considerable debate.[5]

Miracles and His Cohort

For Drewien and others who monitored the foster-reared cranes, month after month, the experience was filled with gut-wrenching ups and downs. Fences and power lines became a constant concern, as did hunters and predators. Every storm was followed by a vigil to see if a whooper chick survived; each new season brought its own anxieties. The crane handlers would pass weeks or months without sighting a particular bird. Some returned to familiar locations, others turned up in distant and completely unexpected places. In case after case, however, whooping cranes disappeared. Drewien would receive calls from helpful people who had discovered carcasses, and, in some instances, he could determine the cause of death. But many birds simply vanished, and each loss brought sadness.

The life and experiences of Miracles typify the range of problems encountered by other foster-reared cranes in the Grays Lake experiment and by their human overseers. Miracles outlived all other 1975 birds and seemed on many occasions the most likely candidate to finally initiate the mating ritual. Over the seven years of his life, he was one of the most consistently observed cranes in the experimental flock, whether at Grays Lake, on migration, or in winter haunts in New Mexico's Rio Grande Valley. People knew where to find him, and, in the end, his remains were the only ones recovered out of the 1975 cohort.

This remarkable whooping crane hatched out on 5 June 1975. Other crane families were relatively sedentary, preferring to remain within four hundred yards or so of the nest site, but, as soon as cattle turned up or fencing crews disturbed them, his parents led the rapidly growing chick half a mile or more away from its natal territory until such threats passed. This tough youngster ran alongside wary adults, who were prepared to quit their preferred area and did so on a number of occasions in July, even staying away for a day or two until they were fully satisfied that it was safe to return.

On one such occasion, Drewien noted two stray dogs nosing toward the birds. Alertly, the brown parents guided their offspring to familiar haunts in the marsh. Generally, they roamed about a good deal in both marsh and meadows and visited grain fields around the edge of the marsh, introducing Miracles to his first taste of barley. It was on one of these forays that Drewien and his boss, at Grays Lake on a visit, spotted the young whooper tangled in a wire fence that bisected its territory. Daily foraging forced Miracles to negotiate this cruel hazard; and, on at least six occasions, while his parents stood by watching anxiously, he experienced difficulties in getting through the strands. Miracles' chances improved considerably as he learned to fly, and by mid-September he was covering up to seven hundred yards a day in flight.

On 1 August, Drewien ran Miracles down and subdued the 57-day-old youngster, who like other whoopers put up a good fight when cornered. Fully experienced in catching young cranes, Drewien held out his hand for the bird to peck, then grabbed its legs quickly with his free hand and secured its beak. Both feet and bill can inflict deep wounds on handlers, and birds can cut themselves while flailing their legs. After capture, Drewien placed a 3 1/4-inch-wide yellow plastic band marked A01 on Miracles' upper leg above the tibio-tarsal joint, in the same manner later used for the wild flock in Canada.[6]

Chick 75-6 had its own trouble with wire fences. This young whooper lived a more sedentary life than Miracles, but in late August it walked with adults to a nearby grain field whose owner, angered by pilfering, chased them away. Chick 75-6 ran straight into a chicken-wire fence and became snagged. As the rancher moved in, the terrified whooper managed to get free and promptly ran away with its parents. The family kept clear for a few days, then returned. Staff baited a safe

Table 5. Whooping Cranes Fostered by Sandhill Parents, 1975–1984

1975 Cohort: 14 eggs—9 hatchlings, 5 fledglings

75-9	Last sighted 24 June 1975; may have perished in storm (rain and snow) of 25 June; not found with parents 26–30 June (P.R. No. 1, p. 7).
75-3	Last sighted on 7 July 1975, after cattle were allowed to graze in its territory (P.R. No. 2, p. 2).
75-5	Last sighted on 12 July 1975 after cattle let in to graze on its territory (P.R. No. 2, p. 2).
75-8	Last sighted on 3 September 1975 when it was 88 days old (P.R. No. 3, p. 5).
75-6	Last positive identification on 8 October 1975 in Grays Lake NWR; reports of a fifth whooper in Colorado and New Mexico indicate that 75-6 or 75-8 survived migration (P.R. No. 4, pp. 4–5).

Table 5. *(continued)*

75-12 "Ulcers" last positively identified on 10 May 1976 in San Luis Valley, Colorado (P.R. No. 6, p. 4); believed to have summered in 1976 near Green River Valley in northeastern Utah and southwestern Wyoming; possibly the second whooper sighted on Ouray Refuge in Utah in August 1976 (P.R. No. 7, p. 2). A fourth subadult also reported near Bernardo, New Mexico, on 6 October 1976 (P.R. No. 8, pp. 4–5).

75-4 "Pancho" vanished on winter grounds in New Mexico during November 1980 (P.R. No. 17, p. 34).

75-7 "Corny" last sighted on 2 March 1981, 4 miles north of the Rio Grande, Alamosa County, San Luis Valley, Colorado (P.R. No. 17, p. 43).

75-1 "Miracles" found dead 15 May 1982, in a barbed-wire fence at Grays Lake. Had last been seen 13 May (77-17 also died in a barbed-wire fence that summer—24 August) (P.R. No. 18, p. 39).

1976 Cohort: 17 eggs—11 hatchlings, 4 fledglings

76-6 10 October 1976—barbed-wire fence collision, Monte Vista NWR (P.R. No. 8, p. 5, Table 1).

76-16 Remains found 29 May 1977—collision with a power line near Lonetree, Wyoming.

76-15 18 March 1983—apparent power-line collision, San Luis Valley.

1977 Cohort: 30 eggs—20 hatchlings, 4 fledglings

77-10 Remains found 22 October 1977—barbed-wire fence collision northwest of Alamosa (P.R. No. 12, pp. 5–7).

77-7 } Last seen fall of 1977 (P.R. No. 12).
77-12 }

77-17 24 August 1982—entangled in barbed-wire fence, northeast of Bear Lake NWR, Idaho (P.R. No. 18, pp. 6–8).

1978 Cohort: 18 eggs—14 hatchlings, 3 fledglings

78-9 Last seen 15 April 1979 near Eckart, Colorado (P.R. No. 15, p. 34).

1979 Cohort: 24 eggs—16 hatchlings, 8 fledglings

79-12 13 October 1979—killed by golden eagle, near Rangely, Colorado (P.R. No. 15, pp. 29–30).

79-11 Last seen 13 March 1981, Monte Vista.

79-9 Remains found 16 August 1981, northwest of Pinedale, Wyoming; cause unknown (P.R. No. 17, p. 45).

Patuxent no. 2 15 July 1982—avian tuberculosis, San Luis Valley.

79-10 13 March 1986—avian tuberculosis, Belen State Refuge, New Mexico (P.R. No. 86-2, p. 5).

79-4 14 April 1986—apparent power-line collision near Oxford Slough, Idaho (P.R. No. 86-2, p. 6).

1980 Cohort: 15 eggs—11 hatchlings, 5 fledglings

80-17 Remains found 9 April 1981 near Monte Vista NWR—apparent power-line collision (P.R. No. 17, p. 3).

80-5 Last seen 2 May 1981 near Cody, Wyoming (P.R. No. 17, p. 45).

80-2 Last seen 20 January 1983 at Bosque NWR—apparently hit power line in San Luis Valley, recovered enough to continue migration but succumbed to winter weather in New Mexico due to weakened condition, severe limp (P.R. No. 18, p. 35).

1981 Cohort: 12 eggs—5 hatchlings, 0 fledglings

1982 Cohort: 27 eggs—19 hatchlings, 7 fledglings

82-8 Last seen 12 October 1982 in San Luis Valley, presumed dead (P.R. No. 18, p. 35).

82-15 Remains found 11 April 1983 in Alamosa County, Colorado; cause unknown (P.R. No. 18, pp. 35–36).

82-13 23 January 1984—lead poisoning; captured at Bosque, died at Albuquerque Zoo.

Patuxent no. 5 14 May 1986—avian tuberculosis, contracted in Monte Vista, died at Albuquerque Zoo where it was taken for treatment.

1983 Cohort: 28 eggs—26 hatchlings, 19 fledglings

Patuxent no. 8 Last seen 11 October 1983, presumed dead.

83-9 Spring 1984—apparent power-line collision, San Luis Valley.

83-17 Spring 1984—apparent fence or power-line collision, San Luis Valley.

Patuxent no. 13 Spring 1984—apparent power-line collision, San Luis Valley.

83-15 21 January 1985—captured and taken to Albuquerque Zoo for treatment of bacterial infection associated with outbreak of avian cholera; cured but later died after hitting pen fence and breaking a leg.

83-14 Shipped to Patuxent after hitting fence or power line in spring 1984 and breaking wing, which was later amputated; died October 1987.

1984 Cohort: 32 eggs—25 hatchlings, 13 fledglings

84-10 Late September 1984—degenerative heart condition.

References P.R. refer to progress reports by Roderick C. Drewien. Whooping crane label numbers refer to year hatched and nest number at Wood Buffalo, Canada, but not to band number.

place on refuge lands with grain and relieved antagonism between cranes and man.[7]

Mingling with sandhill flocks that clustered in fields around the refuge, Miracles, attended by his parents, fed daily on barley supplied by refuge staff. That September three other whooper-sandhill families gobbled up grain near the headquarters. An additional family remained on the lake's northern end away from throngs of incoming brown cranes. Drewien noted its secretive habits in the deeper recesses of the marsh. He believed that its chick, 75-7, was underweight, and he proposed that grain be placed inside the family's territory. A sixth family, with whooper 75-8, also lived in an isolated undisturbed section. Drewien saw the trio on 3 September, after which they may have left Grays Lake. In any event, it was the last confirmed sighting of 75-8.

Migration was unusually late in fall 1975. Drewien speculated that the prolonged spring cold, which had delayed nesting, contributed to birds' loitering on their breeding grounds and eating refuge grains. The continuing presence of young whooping cranes forced postponement of the autumn waterfowl hunt. Poor weather also delayed departure. Cranes do not like to fly in bad conditions, and in 1975 the birds hung around the lake as a succession of cold fronts swept through southeastern Idaho from late September through mid-October.

The first whooper (75-7) left on 8 October in the company of twenty or so sandhills and a little more than a day later was observed five hundred miles southeast close to Colorado's Monte Vista NWR. Drewien was pleased. The youngster had picked up cues from parents and was following them to their traditional wintering grounds. Miracles was the second youngster to go. He quit his Grays Lake home on 14 October and, with his parents, headed off into low cloud, rain, and snow. Two other whoopers followed with their foster parents on 15 and 16 October.[8]

All three young whooping cranes made it to important stopover areas in Colorado's San Luis Valley. Miracles was foraging unconcernedly in barley alongside his parents on 20 October and remained in the general area of Monte Vista NWR for almost three weeks.

Drewien also moved south and was relieved to find four '75 whoopers (nos. 1, 4, 7, and 12) and possibly a fifth occupying southern Colorado's barley lands. Foster chicks stayed from sixteen days to just over a month before moving on. Tracking young whoopers in San Luis Valley posed unexpected difficulties for Drewien, because the increasingly popular practice of plowing up

stubble caused the cranes to vary their flights to procure food. As farmers plowed first one field and then another, the sandhills would move, continuing their quest for waste barley.

On 7 or 8 November, Miracles and his parents spiraled "downhill" from Colorado toward the sharp band of green lining the Rio Grande's floodplain below Albuquerque. Bosque del Apache NWR, a final stopover for many sandhills, lay only 250 miles south of Monte Vista NWR, but Miracles landed about 40 miles short of this objective. On 11 November he was sighted in a marsh complex in the Bernardo State Waterfowl Management Area. Bernardo, New Mexico, became Miracle's home for the remainder of 1975.

Two additional whooping cranes did go on to Bosque, and a third turned up on Edeal Dairy land near Los Lunas about twenty-five miles north of Bernardo. Drewien received many reports of other possible whoopers and attempted to find their foster parent sandhills, but with fourteen thousand brown cranes in the middle Rio Grande Valley this task proved impossible.[9]

During the course of winter 1975–76, Drewien observed that, although the foster parents were very protective of their whooper young, other sandhills began to harass the chicks, chasing and pecking them. No damage resulted, but foster parent families tended to shy away from the center of flocks, preferring to be on the periphery or on their own. Chick 75-1, however, was a large bird and not only held his own but also went on the offensive against the hostile sandhills.

Miracles also learned to cope adeptly with threats posed by duck hunters on his wintering grounds. Whereas at Bosque del Apache, hunting was carefully controlled and organized, conditions at Bernardo made life more hazardous for cranes. Some hunters shot illegally into flocks of sandhills, including the one with which Miracles foraged. One man who was apprehended claimed that sandhill cranes were "large gray ducks." In addition to illegal hunters, 75-1 had to fly over a legal firing line every day to his parents' feeding area, which was off limits to hunting. Drewien suggested that the young whooper learned to handle these threats from his foster parents and that a captive-reared crane released into the wild would not likely fare as well.[10]

While other foster parent families stayed in the same area throughout the winter, 75-1's family left its initial winter home on 17 January 1976 after the corn supply ran out. The trio foraged at Veguita, about seven miles northeast of Bernardo, for three days, then flew five

miles farther north to Belen State Refuge, where they joined up with an estimated 2,500 sandhills, who had also left Bernardo.

Drewien observed normal chick-parental behavior in all four surviving foster families throughout the winter and noted that almost all feeding took place in agricultural fields, primarily corn and alfalfa. Miracles and 75-4, nicknamed Pancho by the Edeal family, the two largest whooper chicks, easily defended themselves against aggression from sandhill cranes and foraged among them without being driven off. The smallest chick, female 75-12, whom refuge managers Richard Rigby and Gary Zahn called Ulcers due to innumerable anxious moments she gave them during the goose hunting season, remained submissive; her family always occupied an area away from the main body of a sandhill flock.

Miracles left Belen Refuge with his foster parents in early afternoon on 18 February and was sighted twice that day on his way north. He was first located in Colorado's San Luis Valley on 28 February on private lands northwest of Alamosa. Over the course of a month this young male began to assert increasing independence. He foraged among sandhills up to a hundred yards away

As winter closes in on Grays Lake, crane watchers leave the refuge headquarters on the southeast shore, a good location from which to observe whoopers, and follow the migrants south into Colorado and New Mexico. Photograph by author.

from his foster parents. This behavior was in keeping with normal sandhill juvenile behavior, although observers expected that whoopers, like sandhills, would remain with their parents throughout migration back to Grays Lake and only then go off on their own.[11]

In fact, only one (75-7) of the known survivors was believed to have completed the migration with foster parents. Pancho soared with his above the San Luis Valley on 4 April, only to land again as his parents and the rest of the sandhill flocks headed northwest. Miracles was with his family in the same valley on 8 April, but a few days later the sandhill pair turned up in Grays Lake without their 1975 offspring, who remained near Alamosa through 10 May, as did the small and submissive 75-12, Ulcers. This early separation is not unusual among sandhill cranes; neither is loitering along the migration route. In early May 1976, only twenty-five sandhill stragglers remained in the San Luis Valley after the main cohort had pushed well to the north.

Late spring and early summer 1976 proved hectic for Drewien and associates, who prepared to receive and set out new whooper eggs while checking on the survivors from 1975. None of the four whooping cranes returned to Grays Lake, but reports of them came in from a large area of the Rocky Mountains frequented by greater sandhill cranes. Three whoopers were finally identified in the summer: Pancho turned up in a meadow near Melville, Montana, where two ranchers kept an eye on him, let him forage in their barley fields, and kept away potential disturbances; 75-7, so-called Corny because of his preference for corn on Bosque, summered on Ouray NWR, Utah, and on nearby private lands where Ouray Refuge manager H. Troester monitored its activities; Miracles came closest to Grays Lake, spending the entire summer about twenty miles south, where a farmer first reported him on 11 June feeding with a flock of sandhills in his grain fields.[12]

The fate of 75-12 was less clear. Drewien had a soft spot for Ulcers and she worried him. On wintering grounds in Bosque to which her parents had guided her, the shy, slender 75-12 was often bullied by nearby sandhills, and being a smaller less developed bird she backed away from squabbles and never asserted herself. Most submissive of the four survivors, she relied on her parents, and Drewien grew increasingly concerned about her fate once the adults made off to Grays Lake. He predicted that Ulcers would have a difficult time fending for herself and speculated that the bird would become a loner. He was correct. From Colorado, a crane looking like Ulcers headed north as far as Ouray

NWR on Utah's Green River, a day's journey southeast of her birthplace and within the migration route and summer range of greater sandhill cranes. Although never positively identified, it seems that she flew in on 2 June, confined her activities to 40–80 acres of marsh, and remained there throughout the summer. She made no effort to team up with immature sandhills, as Miracles did north of her, but seemed content to forage quietly in hidden wetlands.

Ulcers simply retreated from the world of cranes, although Corny may have joined her for a short time. Such solitary behavior was never practiced by sandhill juveniles of her age. Except for unconfirmed reports along the Utah-Wyoming border in August and September, 75-12 turned into a ghost. Nobody could confirm her existence or prove that she was dead. Feisty and full of themselves, her brother cranes migrated back to New Mexico. There, in early October 1976, near where Miracles lived, crane watchers spotted two sandhills and a single white crane who called, "then flew north and disappeared." It may have been Ulcers on that afternoon near Bernardo; if it was, 75-12 made, as expected, her unobtrusive exit.[13]

Miracles remained with flocks of sandhills from mid-June until early October; roosting in a wet meadow, he foraged in nearby agricultural fields. The only non-sandhill-like behavior that Drewien observed during the summer in 75-1's case was his tendency to move away from sandhill cranes while they loafed during midday hours in order to forage on his own in wet places.

On 3 October 1976, Miracles started his second migration south with a flock of several hundred sandhill cranes and, three days later, turned up in the San Luis Valley. Pancho, who had summered in Montana, arrived in that Colorado stopover about the same time. Plumaged white, the two young males inhabited similar areas, including the same field in which they would feed side by side for the next five weeks.

The two whoopers teamed up and migrated from Colorado in a sandhill flock, passing over Albuquerque on 15 November (having been last seen the day before in the San Luis Valley). Somewhere in the mid Rio Grande Valley they parted ways; Pancho turned up on the Bosque del Apache Refuge on 16 November, while Miracles was sighted next day on Bernardo State Waterfowl Management Area where he had initially wintered with his foster parents. Roosting at night along the Rio Grande, 75-1 had once again to run the gauntlet of waterfowl hunters on his way to feeding grounds on state lands, but observers never found him in especial danger.

After staying at Bernardo through December 1976, the aggressive Miracles decided to move. First, he flew south several miles to agricultural fields around Lemitar, where nearly 3,400 sandhills had gathered after abandoning Bosque NWR during the snow goose hunt. He left Lemitar briefly for Bosque during the second and third of January 1977 but returned on the fourth and remained until the end of the month. On 31 January, Miracles flew back to Bernardo, stayed for two weeks, and then proceeded north to Belen State Refuge where he spent the remainder of his stay in New Mexico. Also in Belen at that time were two juvenile whoopers from the previous summer's egg transfer (and for a brief time a third juvenile), and Pancho, or 75-4, who had also been wandering between Bosque, Lemitar, Bernardo, Los Lunas, and Belen.[14]

Drewien noted similar behavior patterns between subadult whoopers and sandhill cranes; however, whooping cranes showed little affiliation on wintering areas with individual sandhills or specific flocks. The young whoopers sometimes joined up with a sandhill flock, then left again to feed on their own or join another group that happened nearby. The two large male whooping cranes often foraged with sandhills because their size and aggressiveness gave them the upper hand against their cousins. On a daily basis, these birds were seen to threaten, chase, and peck any sandhills who came too close or were occupying feeding areas that the whoopers wanted to keep for themselves. Observers counted 138 encounters between Miracles and sandhills between October 1976 and March 1977, of which the whooping crane won all but two or three. Corny, or 75-7, smaller than both Miracles and Pancho, kept to more solitary ways (it had also summered alone or perhaps for a time with Ulcers in Utah) as it was frequently harassed by sandhills. Nonetheless, when 75-7 did attempt to defend itself, it often won the encounter.[15]

On 4 March 1977, whooping crane subadults Miracles and Pancho left Belen State Refuge in New Mexico. Miracles appeared in the San Luis Valley the following day (Pancho was sighted five days later) and took up temporary residence in the southern portion of Monte Vista NWR. Drewien was particularly interested in watching for any indications that the three subadults still under observation (Miracles, Pancho, and Corny) were forming pair bonds with sandhills with whom they had been raised. At this early age, however, he found no evidence of sandhill–whooping crane bonding. On the other hand, evidence was mounting that whoopers recognized each other. Pancho struck up a relationship with a juvenile whooper, 76-15, which was still accompanying its foster parents at Monte Vista. The subadult migrated to Grays Lake with the juvenile and its sandhill parents and on two occasions was observed displaying, dancing, and vocalizing near the juvenile, but he got little response.[16]

Miracles, who had on occasion foraged and even flown in the same flock as Pancho the previous fall, was seen feeding with Corny near Monte Vista Refuge on 8 April 1977; later, both cranes took off, soaring above the valley to begin their way north. The association was brief, however; Corny returned to summer grounds near Ouray NWR in Utah, while Miracles turned up on Grays Lake NWR on 2 May 1977.

All three 1975 birds molted their flight feathers during May and June. It was clearly an anxious time as their behavior changed markedly. Miracles and Pancho, both at Grays Lake, kept each one to himself in marshes or nearby meadows, never far from cover. Only rarely did they feed on crops as sandhills did, preferring instead to remain in more aquatic habitat. The two-year-old whoopers gradually became more conspicuous and fed in meadows and roosted with sandhills. Only toward summer's end, however, did the young males begin to forage more on agricultural fields with brown cranes. This solitary behavior contrasted markedly with their activities as yearlings when they frequently associated with sandhills. Drewien also noted that both two-year-old whoopers and the year-old (76-15) at Grays Lake rarely associated with each other, although Pancho did strike up a relationship with another whooping crane chick (77-17) family.[17]

Pancho began using an area near the territory of 77-17's foster parents in late July; by mid-August, the older whooper had taken to approaching the family, only to be driven off by the adult male. After retreating, Pancho would once again approach. Gradually, he worked closer and closer and even joined the family briefly before being chased off. By mid-September, 77-17's parents had finally accepted Pancho's presence and chased the whooper only occasionally. During this latter period, Drewien observed the subadult displaying, dancing, and vocalizing to the chick, which did not respond. When the foster family migrated in early October, 75-4 remained behind at Grays Lake.

On 23 December 1977, Pancho found 77-17 and his foster parents again near Polvadera, New Mexico, and began to forage and roost with them. He remained with that family, occasionally displaying and vocalizing to the juvenile and chasing off other sandhills

A sandhill crane nest with two eggs, Grays Lake NWR, May 1971. Rod Drewien's research into nesting success provided the essential data for the transfer and fostering of whooping crane eggs and young that began in Grays Lake in 1975. Photograph by Rod C. Drewien.

that attempted to harass 77-17 until 13 February 1978, when Pancho and the family left the area for separate destinations.[18]

Miracles left Grays Lake on 10 October 1977 and was at Ouray NWR, some 210 miles south in Utah by next morning. He continued south that same week to the vicinity of Monte Vista and by mid-November was back at Bernardo, where he had spent much of the previous two winters. His sojourn in New Mexico proved routine as he moved primarily between Bernardo and nearby Polvadera, feeding on agricultural crops and moving among sandhills at will, not forming any specific association. In early January he moved south to Bosque where he remained until migrating north toward the end of February.

By mid-April 1978, for the first time, all three survivors from the 1975 whooper cohort had returned to Grays Lake NWR. Miracles occupied the same general area he had selected the previous summer, that is, a southeastern portion of the lake, within a mile of where he had hatched. As in 1977, Miracles spent most of his summer alone and fed primarily in the marsh and nearby meadows. He became particularly fond of a bulrush-covered pond and begin driving off sandhills, including two breeding pairs whose territories came under the whooper's control. One of the pairs had incubated whooping crane eggs.

75-1's activities represented the first territorial behavior that experts recognized among cross-fostered cranes. Although Pancho also made a few attempts to defend a territory, his aggression was not nearly so vehement or consistent. Corny, while restricting its activities to a specific location, made no moves to defend it. Drewien estimated Miracles' new territory to be between sixty and eighty acres.[19]

Miracles remained in his territory until he migrated in mid-October 1978. After spending nearly a month in Colorado's San Luis Valley stopover, he returned to his Bernardo winter haunt in New Mexico on 21 November. Like four of six other subadults in the Rio Grande Valley that winter, 75-1 moved about more frequently than in previous years, flying primarily between Bernardo and Bosque and eventually up to Belen State Refuge. Sandhills and snow geese were also more mobile; and Drewien attributed increased movement to inclement weather, exhaustion of food supplies at Bernardo, construction activities over a large area of Bosque, and failure to cut down enough corn and milo on that refuge to supply hungry birds during poor weather.

As they had the previous winter, Miracles and Corny

occasionally foraged together, sometimes joined by 76-7, while all three were at Bosque; but these associations lasted only a few hours. Observers were obviously hoping for signs of growing pair bonds and had surmised from their behavior that both 75-1 and 76-7 were males. Although Miracles and Corny did not live up to biologists' hopes, Pancho was proving more interesting. On 8 January 1979, this bird once again encountered 77-17, in whom he had been so interested in summer and winter 1977. The two birds spent just over a month in the same area, spending much time feeding and loafing together and occasionally going to roost with one another. Although it was still the older bird, Pancho, who showed most attraction, the younger bird also appeared to seek out the elder's company on occasion. On 10 February, however, Pancho left the area for Belen State Refuge.

Winter associations between whooping cranes came to naught on would-be breeding grounds in summer 1979. Once again, all three 1975 cranes—they proved to be males—came back to Grays Lake, as did 76-15, who had also been there. Once again, contacts between whoopers were few as each took up its respective area and kept apart even from sandhills. Miracles shifted his territory slightly southward but still proved to be most aggressive, chasing and pecking trespassing sandhills. Although such activities lessened somewhat after May, he remained master of his chosen domain until migration. Sandhills were not his only victims; in early July, he successfully hunted down an adult coot (*Fulica americana*), striding around with it in his beak and pecking at it occasionally before commencing to feast on it.

Pancho also returned to his territory and defended it against sandhills. Both Miracles and Pancho were at that time judged to be males, while 75-7 was thought, incorrectly, to be a female since it was a somewhat smaller bird, was more passive than the others, and did not exhibit territorial behavior. During the following winter in New Mexico, however, biologists concluded that all three 1975 birds were males, based on their unison calls.

Unison calls were given on several occasions when whoopers found and temporarily associated with other whoopers. Despite these brief affiliations, observers saw no evidence of pair bonds forming. In summer 1980, Corny also established a territory at Grays Lake and began defending it. Thus, all three 1975 birds had finally defined breeding territories; Miracles in 1978, Pancho in 1979, and Corny in 1980. Their preference to remain in respective areas throughout the summer season at Grays Lake meant a relatively solitary life but was to be expected since they were males. On a very few occasions two would be seen together in grain fields; more frequently they would be associating with sandhills; but mostly each whooper kept to himself.[20]

The preponderance of male whooping cranes at Grays Lake made it clear that pair formation and breeding would be difficult. Biologists at Patuxent and at the Idaho Cooperative Wildlife Research Unit, therefore, devised a plan to introduce a captive-raised female to Grays Lake and place her between the summer territories of Miracles and Pancho in 1981. In November 1980, however, whooping crane Pancho vanished from winter grounds at Bosque NWR in New Mexico. Drewien believes the whooper he saw on the refuge on 29 November was Pancho; if so, it was the last time the bird was seen. Because this crane was so consistent in movements in and around the refuge and was sighted so often, Drewien was forced to conclude that the 5 1/2-year-old male whooper was dead, possibly shot, although this could not be confirmed. Corny, meanwhile, spent a routine winter moving between Los Lunas, Bernardo, Bosque, and Belen. He migrated northward from the vicinity of Los Lunas with the first major sandhill migration on 13 February 1981. Observers found him in the San Luis Valley of Colorado in early March but never again located him, either in Colorado or in Idaho. He, too, was presumed dead, a possible victim of a power line. The loss of two of the original 1975 birds was compounded on 9 April by the discovery of the remains of a 1980 juvenile beneath a power line just north of Monte Vista NWR. It and five sandhills, whose carcasses were found nearby, had presumably died after crashing into wires.

Miracles became the sole known survivor of the 1975 cohort and was one of four whooping cranes to return to Grays Lake in spring 1981 (12 others were known or believed to have survived spring migration). When Miracles arrived back at Grays Lake on 10 April 1981, he immediately became the object of intensive study. As had been done on his wintering grounds in November, biologists carried out a precise time-budget analysis of his activities in daylight hours. Their study was part of a larger project to learn more about whooper activity in general and about this experimental flock in particular. Because Miracles was the oldest surviving bird and showed the most potential for breeding, he garnered a great deal of human interest. In addition, an understanding of his specific situation was important as experts had

chosen him as the most likely mate for captive-bred female Too Nice, brought from Patuxent into Grays Lake that spring.[21]

The experimental release of the three-year-old captive-reared female was described in the preceding chapter. Miracles was interested in the Patuxent female and at no point showed any aggression toward her. The two frequently watched each other from a distance and occasionally foraged together. At one point in late July, 75-1 landed near his potential mate, began to preen, and then gave the unison call. The female responded in kind and both began to preen again. Within a short time, however, Miracles took off again, and, although the two birds were frequently together for short periods after that, they were not observed unison calling again that summer or during staging for fall migration.

What impressed observers about 75-1's behavior during this period was his preoccupation with guarding and defending his territory and his extreme and frequent aggression against sandhill cranes. On one occasion in May, he harassed a sandhill pair on his territory for almost an hour, charging and flying in pursuit of them. He finally beat the male sandhill to the ground and continued pecking at him with his bill. The sandhill managed to fly off, only to be knocked out of the air. As he hobbled away, the whooper continued to beat him. The sandhill was not seen again and Drewien believed it may have died from this encounter, although he never found any remains.

The female whooper was captured and returned to Patuxent in early October, and Miracles migrated south later that month. Once again he spent a routine winter, partly at Bernardo but primarily at Bosque NWR where observers continued to analyze the timing and duration of his activities. His frequent associations with 76-15 at Bosque, where they were often joined by a third whooper, continued to raise hopes that Miracles would prove a success at breeding. 76-15's sex remained undetermined at that time, although its behavior led observers to believe it was female; it always summered in the same area at Grays Lake but had not set up a defended territory. Despite these associations, no evidence of pair bonding appeared; if 76-15 was a female, she was the only one on Bosque that winter. The six other whoopers present on the refuge were all males (picked up with a broken wing in March 1983, 76-15 turned out to be male).

Miracles arrived back at Grays Lake on 10 April 1982 and once more became the unwitting set-up for biologist matchmakers. They brought the Patuxent female

The body of an adult male whooping crane, so-called Miracles, who collided with this four-strand barbed-wire fence, on Grays Lake NWR, in May 1982. Photograph by Rod C. Drewien.

back to the marsh and reacquainted her with the seven-year-old male. Miracles again became aggressive, defending his territory and showing a distinct interest in the female. He watched her and called frequently. During the first week of May, observers twice saw him gathering nest material, although the female was paying him little attention. No nest was ever completed for, just over a week later, Drewien and colleagues found Miracles tangled up in his oldest nemesis, a four-strand barbed-wired fence. He had apparently died of trauma engendered by hemorrhage and shock. Analyses of his carcass indicated that he had been in good health and showed only an insignificant level of one pesticide (DDE) in his system. The wire fence divided his territory, and observers had never seen him have any difficulty crossing it on previous occasions. Because of mortalities associated with barbed-wire fences, all new fences on the refuge are now built with three strands and old ones have been modified accordingly. Miracles' prepared body is on display at the Grays Lake Refuge headquarters.[22]

To compound the misfortune, a second whooper, 77-17, the one in whom Pancho had taken a protective interest some years earlier, died after hitting a fence south of Grays Lake. A rancher reported the dead crane hung up in a four-strand fence in late August near Bear Lake NWR.

The initial 1975 cohort whose grasp on life lasted almost seven years, taught Drewien and associates a great deal about the cross-foster experiment. Earlier expectations that parent-chick bonds would be strong and that fledglings would receive guidance in order to learn where to migrate and how to subsist in a winter range were all confirmed. The young whoopers behaved as normal young, and their parents protected them. They feasted successfully on grain, flew in sandhill flocks spiraling upward as high as 12,000 to 13,000 feet to sail over Utah's Uinta Mountains on journeys to and from their natal marsh, and learned to forage on their own once spring heralded a new nesting time for their parents.

Questions remained, however, about survival rates and a skewed ratio of males to females among surviving birds. Females, like 75-12, appeared to "float," not establish territories, and, as years passed, failed to return to natal areas. On the other hand, many male birds, after one or two seasons, came back to Grays Lake and defended territories. They were more confident in encounters with sandhill cranes and some, like Miracles, turned into veritable crusaders, battling their cousins, even killing them, within and around the borders of their territories. Smaller whoopers, like 75-12 and 75-7, in its earlier years, proved timid. Both passed their first summers as subadults away from sandhills and selected aquatic habitats as their haunts. Birds recognized one another, even teamed up, but failed to sustain an association that might have led to pairing.[23]

The 1975 transplant also served to identify problems that affected survivorship. Some, like fences and disturbance from cattle, were more or less unexpected. In subsequent years such factors contributing to whooper mortality became clear and substantiated, and new ones, particularly predation on Grays Lake itself, resulted in forthright efforts to eradicate coyotes and foxes.

Predators

Between spring 1975 and spring 1986 a total of 264 eggs from Wood Buffalo and Patuxent were directed to the foster program at Grays Lake. Seventy-six (28 percent) failed to hatch, of which 40 percent were infertile, 30 percent contained dead embryos, and 30 percent were

taken by predators. Predators also took a toll on chicks. Of the 107 chicks that died before they could fly, predators accounted for a minimum of 28 percent.

The topic of egg and chick predation and a need for predator control has grown more and more important as the foster experiment has progressed. Two basic reasons cause this concern: First, the overall number of terrestrial predators has increased as a result, experts believe, of such federal policies as banning widespread and consistent use of 1080 sodium monofluoracetate baits in 1972. Second, in seasons of low water or drought (1976, 1977, 1978, 1981, 1986, and 1987, especially), whooper eggs and chicks together with those of resident sandhill cranes are more vulnerable to mammals gaining access to the marsh. Conditions of low water have been a recurrent concern in the eighties so that the number of eggs to be brought from Canada has been decided close to the time of shipment in respect to actual and projected water levels during the critical months of June and July.[24]

Part of the uncertainty stems from the disposition of water in the lake bed itself. Water in Grays Lake is owned and controlled by the Bureau of Indian Affairs, which uses the natural lake bed for storing spring runoff, then withdraws it for irrigation. Lake levels are thus subject to the control of an agency over which the U.S. Fish and Wildlife Service has no direct authority, but with which agreements have been made. The intent is to draw off sufficient water for agricultural needs yet retain enough to supply food and restrict predator access during the critical time of incubation and chick raising.[25]

In the first year of foster parenting at Grays Lake, 1975, observers attributed the disappearance of two whooper eggs to predators. In subsequent years, through 1984, another dozen eggs vanished, mostly taken by coyotes, who also killed at least twenty-three and possibly as many as fifty-eight flightless young. Grays Lake had a problem that biologists had hoped would not exist. Prior to the banning of compound 1080 in 1972, coyotes and foxes were uncommon on the marsh and at least 75 percent of sandhill pairs with eggs raised one young. During the second transplant season in 1976, however, water levels reached drastically low levels and the issue became all too clear. While making egg runs, Drewien spotted a coyote in the marsh munching sandhill crane eggs. Animal damage control (ADC) was instituted immediately.[26]

In 1977, full and immediate response was hard to generate without cooperation from various agencies and landowners. By the time control operations got under-way, a coyote pair had pilfered twenty-six crane nests, including three with whooper eggs, and had wrecked all Canadian goose nests along a two-and-one-half mile stretch of shoreline. Ravens also stole at least one whooper egg from another three nests.

By the third summer for transplants another drought had set in, causing even stronger impacts from maraud-ing canids. During spring overflights, ADC personnel picked off twelve coyotes, but, as Drewien worked on setting a record batch of thirty whooper eggs under fos-ter parents, he spotted a coyote in the bulrush zone usu-ally too deep for the animals to traverse easily. That summer at least one egg (from Patuxent) and sixteen flightless young disappeared; most it seems made meals for coyotes and red foxes who ranged freely across the dried-up lake bed. Conditions were so bad that refuge staff started up pumps to supply drinking water for wild cranes.

The discovery of a coyote den containing pups within a mile or so of territories from which eight whooper chicks vanished confirmed worst suspicions: Grays Lake staffers had an epidemic on their hands. They requested and received permission to intensify control measures, using traps and M-44 "coyote-getters" that pump cya-nide into the mouth of an animal tugging a scented device. They stepped up ADC throughout summer months but drought gave predators the upper hand; coyotes zig-zagged across the open marsh and used cover adeptly. Only five whooping crane chicks lived to migrate in early October 1977. Five cranes from thirty eggs was a disaster.[27]

In spring 1978, water levels increased markedly as did efforts to combat coyotes. Before the haul of special eggs arrived, ADC staff killed sixty-five coyotes, and ranchers hit an additional thirteen. But cold weather and drier conditions in June and July conspired to limit chick survival. ADC staff found an active coyote den on the marsh's western edge whose elusive diners de-stroyed sandhill nests, some of which usually received whooper eggs. Fourteen young cranes hatched from eighteen eggs that arrived, but only three whooping cranes lived to fly out of the Idaho refuge.

Drewien discovered evidence of one pair's vain effort to protect their chick. He found body feathers from an adult sandhill intermingled with tracks and scat of ei-ther a coyote or a large fox in one foster territory. The adults survived, but the young whooper vanished, and ADC people went back to work, removing seven coyotes and seven foxes from the refuge during the summer.[28]

Grays Lake looked more than ever like a proper lake in 1979. In January, moisture levels exceeded the ten-year average. Drewien received twenty-four eggs (19 from Canada and 5 from Patuxent) in late May and early June for placement in foster sandhill nests. Sixteen whooper chicks hatched and half of them fledged, in-cluding the first young from Patuxent eggs. Drewien was pleased with this survival rate. At 33 percent this was less than half of what he had recorded for Grays Lake sandhills six or seven years earlier, but it was double that of the previous year.

Aerial hunting had removed thirty-one coyotes dur-ing late winter and early spring and contributed to hatching success. In late June, coyotes were judged to have grabbed three chicks, and Drewien thought that at least some of these canids had arrived with sheep that were trailed in for summer grazing. Agents trapped two coyotes. In late August, the remains of another well-grown whooper revealed the work of a coyote or a fox. Probably the same mammal killed 79-13 as it came in from its roost to a meadow feeding site on 2 September. Staff placed coyote-getters around its carcass; the preda-tor returned but never triggered any control devices.

Experts were frustrated but hopeful that with adjust-ments and correctly operating M-44's they could hold back coyotes and foxes, when a new predator appeared. On 13 October 1979, a nine-member party of deer hunt-ers spotted whooping crane youngster 79-12 with its parents over Angelo Ridge, five miles west and eight miles south of Rangely, Colorado. A golden eagle, North America's largest predatory bird, capable of knocking down ducks, geese, and great blue herons, circled above the migrating trio. Suddenly, it folded its wings, dived, and struck the juvenile whooper with its talons. The youngster planed an estimated thousand feet down to earth, hit a juniper tree as it landed, and survived for about ten minutes after the hunters found it. Subsequent examination showed that eagle claws had fatally ruptured the crane's liver. In all other respects, the whooper was in excellent physical shape and had completed 250 miles of its southward flight before fall-ing prey. Golden eagles are known to harass and kill mi-grating demoiselle cranes, much smaller birds, as flocks swing over high Himalaya passes in Nepal, but this was the first record for a whooping crane kill.[29]

Eagles have probably taken other youngsters. In 1982, Drewien "strongly suspected" eagles were responsible for the disappearance of two well-grown and active young from territories. He knew that golden eagles oc-casionally killed and ate sandhills on Grays Lake. A similar event happened in the 1983 transplant season when five whooper chicks died within ten days of hatching. Drewien concluded that at least one of them was snatched up by a golden eagle that he had seen preying on waterfowl. American crows and northern ravens have also been implicated in egg destruction.[30]

The tenor of progress reports on the whooping crane experiment shows a roller-coaster-like quality about ADC effectiveness on Grays Lake. In some years, especially those with good water levels, which inhibit mammal access, fledging rates are satisfactory. In others, mostly drier years, optimism turns to despair. For seven months before the end of March 1986, for example, ADC tallied fifty-four coyotes and fourteen foxes on and around the immediate boundaries of Grays Lake. Aerial hunting, trapping, shooting, and M-44's destroyed many predators and continued in May and June when an additional fourteen animals were killed. Dry conditions nevertheless contributed to higher than usual egg predation. Selected foster parent sandhills lost clutches before whooper eggs arrived, and, on the very morning that fifteen were flown in, three coyotes and a red fox were shot from a helicopter. Drewien figured that a crash in the population of ground squirrels was causing hungry carnivores to push into the marshlands. That year only two juveniles survived to migrate. Similar problems and inclement weather occurred in 1987 when only two birds fledged.[31]

Wirescapes

Before 7:00 A.M. when the fleet of pickup trucks rumbles through Monte Vista, Colorado, only bluster from birds—sparrow chatter, starling whistling, and warbles from red house finches perched on poles—awakens this farm town. Mountain light blares across the southern end of this 100-mile-long tableland squeezed between the San Juan Mountains and the Sangre de Cristo range, whose peaks top 14,000 feet. Sharp light draws slivers of white from curbside snow. It has bleached the Coors sign on a nearby silo, for Monte Vista is a grain town and beer from vast irrigated "circles" of barley is its lifeblood. Premium barley used for brewing is also good for cranes. Up to twenty thousand sandhills crowd this plateau every October and November. They glean stubbles and gobble storm-blasted grain left unharvested, then, pushed by snow and cold, follow an air path above the sinewy Rio Grande into New Mexico's winter landscape.

In March the sandhill cranes return and pass north. Ten miles away near the 14,000-acre Monte Vista NWR,

winter ice cracks as water gurgles free peeling back the snow's white sheet to give hungry tall birds access to food. Acolytes attend the milling cranes. Larks teeter on fence wires, blackbirds fill cottonwoods with wheezy songs, and waterfowl swing down, perhaps ten thousand or more pairs of ducks feast on the grain that has been spilled or never harvested. After the cranes leave, ducks will remain and nest in this valley's wetlands.

Conversion of this mile-high country from greasewood and short grasses to irrigated crops has augmented crane foods. Battalions of sandhills turn yellow fields brown and fill the sky with their gutteral voices as they pass from roost sites to food and back again. A party of twenty or so snow geese, irregular visitors compared with hordes along the Rio Grande drop into a pond. Big raptors are still here. Roughlegs crouch on poles, bald eagles are menacing silhouettes in bare trees, a slim kestrel flicks raw air. Such predators pick over flocks of waterfowl, looking for sick or injured birds. They spot desert cottontails, jackrabbits, or small rodents amid patches of drier earth, competing with coyotes. They will also scavenge crane carcasses beneath wires that festoon this broad, flat upland.

In the evening, angled light shimmers from a metal web strung across the valley. Poles and wires march across grain fields and refuge lands. Transmission lines pack county roads. It is a wirescape that carries power to huge pipes set on wheels bigger than those on jumbo jets. Propelled by electricity, in spring these pipes trundle slowly across black earth, hosing water onto budding seeds in order to make the high desert bloom.

The switch to water-dependent crops provides more food for birds but brings dangers as well. Power lines snag big, lanky cranes, especially younger and less experienced individuals, as they fly from roost sites to feed and are forced to cross over the festoons of hard, cold metal that link pylon to pylon. In rain, fog, or snow, even knowledgeable birds may forget or fail to recognize blurred strands and be killed.

Disturbance in a nearby field as a farmer checks equipment may cause flocks to rise up; some birds flare upward and over the wires, a very few will flap hurriedly under them, but others beat into their deadly horizontal bands, often hitting the topmost strand that acts as a conductor for lightning strikes. At least three whoopers have died after hitting this type of thin, high wire, and, in all, seven have died in the San Luis Valley. There are certain "black spots" near Monte Vista that take a heavy toll on both types of cranes. With a species just getting started, like the whooping crane, mortality due to wires

MONTE VISTA

Magpie carries song
over a sleeping land.
Dabs cottonwood

with redwing chortle,
loops fence with
lark strum. Snow-

packed seed and shred
of grass sleep on,
until that bugle

fills the valley from
a flake of bird
whiter than winter.

He spins the dormant
hum into nature hymn
surely as the prayer

wheel turns. Pealing
his declaration to saffron
cranes who chant

their leader down on
snowcapped plain, he
glides through winter

door to grasp that
dappled sound from
magpie's throat, and

smiles a yellow blessing
from his eye that
melts the spring.

can inhibit the foster project's eventual success.

There is a paradox. The San Luis Valley attracts cranes because of increases in nutritious grains; however, expanded acreages demand more and more lines to bring power for irrigation, and these lines destroy cranes, waterfowl, and other birds that benefit from the extra food. The ironic twist in this picture involves the whooping crane. Monte Vista celebrates its "Whooping Crane Festival" every March by pulling in people to the lower end of the San Luis Valley. Townsfolk, local artists and entrepreneurs generate interest in the endangered cranes. They organize art exhibits and visits to the nearby refuge to see perhaps six or ten graceful white cranes that mingle with abundant cousins. Visitors with an interest in bird watching come from Denver, Albuquerque, or other distant urban centers. Farmers and ranchers join them, but unless methods are found to flag wires, manipulate their spacing or configuration on poles, or somehow make them more visible to flying cranes, the special festival's future is dim.

More than eighty species of birds from hummingbirds to whoopers have been involved in wire strikes or electrocutions in North America. Experts note that cranes, together with eagles, swans, and pelicans, crop up disproportionately in statistics. That these big, conspicuous birds are easier to spot on the ground than smaller passerines is one reason, but their large size, weight, and wing span also make them less maneuverable at low altitudes, thus more susceptible to death and serious injury from hitting power lines.

More attention is being turned toward mitigating damage from these and other wires by placing them away from flyways or physical features that concentrate migratory birds, most of which fly at less than 3,000 feet above ground level. Utility companies have experimented with various methods of illuminating obstructions, have redesigned pylons and wires to minimize risks, and have studied habitat modification to keep foraging birds away from dangerous obstructions.[32]

These recent breakthroughs are important for whooping cranes, especially the foster flock. At least eleven birds from Grays Lake, including two that fledged in 1976, have died or been incapacitated after hitting power lines (see Table 6). The U.S.-Canada flock has also lost five known members to wires. In addition to the first young male that Kuyt and others radio-tagged and monitored until it was mortally injured by a wire and died near Midnight Lake, Saskatchewan, in 1981 and Ms. Nyarling, found dead at Waco, Texas, the following year under yet another wire, an additional three birds at least have suffered injuries or death in the past thirty years.

Cranes fail to pick out these thin deadly cables in poor visibility, during high winds, or in short flights they make between roost and feeding areas, especially when large numbers may be moving. That is a major reason why the San Luis Valley is such a problem for both sandhill and whooping cranes. Thousands of greater sandhills congregate in barley fields bordered or in some cases transected by power lines. Secure wetland roosts lie within a mile or so; therefore, as dusk draws in, cranes finish gobbling up barley and flap off toward customary nighttime areas. Often it is quite dark when the last bunches of birds quit the stubbles, making wires harder and harder to see.

Drewien and Wendy Brown have studied at least sixteen hundred crane flights over power lines around Monte Vista NWR, noting that birds usually remain at low altitude in making short flights to feeding sites. Cranes can hit wires at such low heights and the risk of them doing so increases when birds are disturbed or panicked. They may be looking at the threat and not at the immediate flight path ahead or see it too late. In one "wild flush," a cameraman monitoring risks for a utility company actually filmed four sandhills hitting power lines in the Monte Vista area.

Brown and Drewien's conclusions from observations in this line-cluttered stopover are that cranes are more prone to hit wires than are waterfowl and that whooping cranes are more susceptible than sandhills due to their larger size and lower maneuverability. Inexperience with such obstacles and lack of familiarity with the region cause more juveniles than adults to become casualties. The removal of the static wire that lies topmost on the line and causes more strikes than do lower distribution wires may significantly reduce collisions. In their San Luis Valley study, Brown and Drewien's strike total dropped from twenty-five birds to eight birds with the static wire gone, then increased to eighteen again as a thicker wire was put back. The diameter of the wire did not appreciably decrease strikes. In other studies, some mostly with Japan's red-crowned cranes, the placement of colored markers, balls, or luminous tape on power lines reduced mortality by about 45 percent. If the birds can see these obstacles, they will certainly endeavor to avoid them.[33]

Hunting

The only area where hunters and cross-fostered whooping cranes regularly confront one another is in the

Table 6. Power-Line Strikes

76-17 Remains discovered under a power line 29 May 1977, near Lonetree, Wyoming.
76-15 So-called Ida; apparent victim died in San Luis Valley 18 March 1983.
79-4 Died from collision 14 April 1986 in Oxford Slough, Bannock County, Idaho.
80-17 Remains discovered near Monte Vista NWR 9 April 1981.
80-2 Apparently hit a line in San Luis Valley northwest of Alamosa in October 1982 but recovered sufficiently to continue migration; succumbed in New Mexico due to a possible leg injury and weakened condition. Last seen 20 January 1983.
83-9 Died from apparent line collision northwest of Monte Vista, May 1984.
83-13 Ten-month-old Patuxent no. 13 found dead two miles south of Alamosa, April 1984.
83-17 Died from apparent fence or line collision in San Luis Valley, March 1984.
83-14 So-called Ichabod; hit a line April 1984 near Grand Junction, Colorado; injured wing amputated, shipped to Patuxent on 2 May; died in food toxin epidemic, October 1987.
85-13 Juvenile male hit a line near source of Blackfoot River, Caribou County, Idaho; died in spite of intensive care, 2 October 1985.
87-5 Fall 1987 loss in San Luis Valley.

middle Rio Grande Valley of New Mexico, the cranes' wintering grounds. A great deal of effort has gone into planning and managing the annual snow goose hunt at Bosque del Apache NWR and into monitoring waterfowl hunting off the refuge each winter. Since the cross-fostering experiment began, two major areas of concern have developed: the possibility that whoopers might be shot, and the potential disturbance to the white cranes beyond the immediate zones for hunting.

Hunt supervision at Bosque has proven adequate to the task of protecting endangered cranes; none has been shot on the refuge. During the first year of the experiment (1975), the snow goose hunt lasted sixteen consecutive days, from 22 November to 7 December. Refuge personnel briefed hunters on crane and snow goose identification and then monitored the hunting area with its twenty blinds. When staff sighted whoopers in the area, they sounded a siren signaling a temporary stop to the hunt. This occurred on two occasions when chick 75-12, Ulcers, flew over blinds with its foster parents, earning its nickname from refuge personnel. While no whooper was shot, five sandhill cranes fell to the guns of one hunting party, who mistook them for snow geese. This misidentification brought home the need for hunters to know their birds as an integral part of hunt management.[34]

The following year, refuge staff expanded prehunt briefings and distributed brochures about hunting and crane identification. The same system of sirens was used again, but this time staff were forced to stop the hunt thirty-two times for wandering whoopers. Although no birds other than snow geese were shot, refuge observers had their hands full tracking the special cranes. Instead of consecutive days, the hunt was held over a longer period (20 November–19 December) but restricted to Saturdays, Sundays, Tuesdays, and Thursdays. The actual number of hunting days was thus similar to past years, but this fact was lost on the cranes, who responded as if it were a thirty-day hunt, leaving the refuge in large numbers. Unpredictable crane movement hampered identification, as did the whoopers' habit of sometimes flying among flocks of snow geese, often with their legs tucked in due to the unseasonably cold weather.

The 1977 Bosque NWR snow goose hunt returned to the format of consecutive days, sixteen in all. Staff introduced a number of management innovations to help ensure proper identification, and participants had to complete a special bird identification and training program. In addition, refuge staff briefed hunters each day. The system of sirens was replaced by a short-range AM radio station at refuge headquarters, to which each hunter tuned in to listen to Bosque Esther via portable radios provided by the refuge. Hunters were notified and cautioned when whoopers were present in the hunt area, but the hunt was not stopped. The grain fields on the northern portion of the refuge were excluded from the hunt area in 1977, providing cranes with a safe foraging area and obviating their need to leave the refuge so frequently.[35]

Efforts to educate hunters and to alert them to the need for care around whooping cranes have apparently paid off during refuge hunts and during waterfowl seasons off the refuge. Drewien credits refuge staff, state and federal wildlife agents, and, especially, hunters themselves for ensuring the safety of the big white birds without crippling hunting recreation. Off-refuge hunting has proven more dangerous for whooping cranes. To protect the birds during hunting seasons, authorities launched a publicity campaign designed to inform all prospective hunters and the public in general about the presence and significance of the foster flock. U.S. Fish and Wildlife Service agents and state enforcement officers patrol the Rio Grande Valley daily during hunting, watching for whoopers and contacting hunters. Despite several close calls, only one or two whooping cranes are suspected of having been shot.

During winter 1975–76, Drewien took note of three situations in which people shot at flocks of cranes containing whoopers. In 1977, a hunter who had passed the Bosque training course shot two sandhills just north of the refuge, on the pretext that he thought they were snow geese. Another man fired five shots at two whooping cranes near the refuge, again claiming that they were snow geese: the whoopers involved were 76-7 and 76-15. The former appeared unaffected and behaved normally the following day; 76-15, however, remained alone at its roost or in nearby brush for four days and was observed to be losing encounters with sandhills, unusual for this bird. After the fifth day, it appeared to have recovered and resumed normal feeding activities. Drewien believes a shotgun pellet may have hit the crane.[36]

On 3 January 1986, Patuxent no. 1, a 1979 bird, was found with blood on its breast feathers and limping badly at the Edeal Dairy near Los Lunas. Although apparently wounded in the lower breast, the bird recovered on its own. Mr. Edeal reported later that month that yet another hunter had taken a shot at this same bird but missed. That winter Patuxent no. 1 was mistaken for a "snow goose." One hunter asked permission to shoot it on the dairy's fields; however, the owner luckily recognized the "goose" as a whooping crane and turned him away. There was a third report of a hunter firing at a mixed flock of sandhills, whoopers, and snow geese. Patuxent no. 1 finally migrated safely out of the valley in spring.[37]

The related issue of disturbance has become an even more intractable problem. Through the years, refuge authorities have varied the timing and duration of the Bosque hunt, dividing it into two, then three, and then four periods in efforts to minimize disturbance and to bag more geese. Staff have planted corn and milo crops between crane roosts and hunt areas to lessen the temptation to forage further afield. Beginning in 1980, the New Mexico Game and Fish Department closed snow goose hunting off the refuge during all or part of the hunting period at Bosque so that the whoopers leaving the refuge would face fewer dangers.

A good deal of controversy remains, however, over the scattering effects of hunting. The whooping cranes not only distribute themselves throughout the middle Rio Grande Valley but in some cases also go far beyond (they have been sighted in Mexico, Arizona, and, reported but unconfirmed, West Texas). Drewien, while commending hunters and game officials for their efforts, believes that in past years hunting on the Bosque Refuge had caused whooping cranes to disperse and become isolated, thus making pair formation less likely. Crane coordinator Jim Lewis is more diplomatic: "We're dealing with a lot of unknowns . . . trying to find that balance point where we can control sandhills and snow geese . . . and still provide the environment the whoopers need to develop pair bonds." He points to having enough food on hand for the whoopers to remain in good health and, therefore, be less susceptible to disease. Some Audubon Society leaders accuse federal and state game authorities of catering to a minority of hunters. New Mexican game officials maintain that a ban on hunting would have little effect on whooper movements.[38]

Drewien seemed particularly vexed in 1986 when, in order to facilitate hunting, Bosque management decided not to flood the impoundment on Refuge Unit 18A. This was meant to force the geese that usually use the impoundment to seek wetlands farther south away from the refuge tour loop and into hunting areas. The impoundment has in past years also been the primary roosting and feeding site for cross-fostered whoopers and thus offers opportunities for socializing and potential pair-bonding. Without the impoundment, these opportunities, which are critical to the success of the program, are greatly reduced. Refuge management restored water to the impoundment by midwinter 1987.[39]

The issue of hunting sandhill cranes as well as geese in places frequented by whoopers had exacerbated an already delicate situation. In October 1986, no fewer than twenty-six whooping cranes existed in the Idaho flock. Twelve of them prepared to migrate from Grays Lake in late September, and all departed by 10 October. During the first two weeks of September, three permit hunts, begun in 1982, for sandhill cranes took place in Wyoming. Two whoopers turned up in or close to areas in which a total of 195 sandhills were shot, but closure of the hunt while white cranes were around obviated any further precautions. The presence of two whooping cranes drew few complaints from hunters.

During September and October, a total of twenty-three whoopers, including the single surviving juvenile, inhabited the San Luis Valley. A severe hailstorm on 22 September wrecked upstanding barley, and cranes, waterfowl, and other birds fed off this bonanza.

Between 16 and 31 October a special sandhill crane hunt was opened in the middle Rio Grande Valley, New Mexico, in order to reduce depredations on crops while minimizing effects on whoopers, which usually arrived in November. This new hunt specified that participants should be able to differentiate sandhill cranes from whoopers, use only steel shot, and adhere to a bag limit of three cranes. Authorities issued a total of 630 permits. Three hundred and forty-three sandhill carcasses were checked through monitoring stations. No whooping cranes were known to have been threatened, although three flew into the valley during the latter part of October. Six sandhills wore bands that hunters handed to state personnel, and five of the six birds were members of the Grays Lake population. In fact, Drewien reported that two brown cranes were sixteen years of age or older, and the oldest had been a foster parent for the whooping crane project in most years. Important biological data, obtained at considerable expense, were rendered obsolete with the death of no. 599-05063, which had nested on its territory close to the place where Drewien had banded it in 1970.[40]

Another habitat management and hunting-related issue came to a head in fall 1986. For several years the numbers of snow and Ross's geese, collectively called "light" geese, had skyrocketed in and around Bosque NWR. Reproduction in the Arctic around Queen Maude Gulf had been excellent and had brought fifty thousand or more light geese into the middle Rio Grande Valley. Crane numbers also grew, so that crops on federal and state areas grown specially for waterfowl had run out before the birds left on flights northward. Drewien and others became concerned about the impact of crowding and insufficient food, noting that periodic outbreaks of avian cholera in geese and to a lesser extent in cranes posed a serious threat to the birds. Farmers also stood to lose as geese and cranes had shifted to private grain lands in search of food, as they had the previous winter.

Federal and state authorities decided to increase grain production on state management areas but also manipulate habitat in order to reduce the numbers of waterfowl. In addition, they agreed to a 107-day light goose hunting season and hazed waterfowl from Bosque in order to move them farther south, even into Mexico.

Nature, it turned out, also helped. An extremely poor nesting season for light-colored geese in summer 1986 resulted in fewer numbers in New Mexico. The peak count at Bosque was 36,900, more than one-third lower than in the previous winter. An additional 19,000 cranes

Table 7. Disease and Poisoning

1982	15 July	Patuxent no. 2, a three-year-old, dies of avian tuberculosis in San Luis Valley.
1984	23 January	Male 82-13 captured on Bosque del Apache NWR dies of acute lead poisoning at Rio Grande Zoo, Albuquerque, New Mexico.
1985	21 January	83-15, a female, dies at Rio Grande Zoo, Albuquerque, of trauma associated with leg fracture after prolonged treatment for avian cholera.
1986	13 March	79-10, a male, dies of avian tuberculosis after capture on Belen State Refuge, New Mexico, 5 March.
	14 April	79-4, a male, collides with power line near Oxford Slough, Franklin County, Idaho, and necropsy reveals fine, small nodules on intestinal tract, suggestive of avian tuberculosis.
	14 May	Patuxent no. 5, 1982 whooper, captured near Monte Vista NWR, Colorado, 9 April, in weakened state, responds to treatment, then leg condition necessitates euthanasia: avian tuberculosis revealed by necropsy.
1987	September	Chick died in power line, showing avian tuberculosis.

inhabited wetlands between Albuquerque and Bosque NWR in mid-December. With more grains, fewer birds overall, and twenty whoopers in the mid-valley, problems of food availability diminished.[41]

Disease and Poisoning

Four Grays Lake whooping cranes have died from disease, and two others (up to and including 1987) that perished after colliding with power lines showed internal signs of illness. Another whooping crane succumbed to acute lead poisoning on Bosque del Apache NWR. Seven birds lost in six years, three of them in 1986, is a depressing statistic (see Table 7).

Patuxent no. 2 was the first documented case of avian tuberculosis in whooping cranes. This 1979 male whooper migrated from New Mexico in spring 1982 but remained in Colorado's San Luis Valley with a few sandhills after thousands of cranes had continued northward. The subadult frequented a small marsh on private lands about three miles southeast of Monte Vista refuge. Rod Drewien spied it in early June, noting how lethargic it seemed, but speculated that it was still too strong to be captured easily.

The bird's condition reportedly improved. Then, on the afternoon of 15 July 1982, refuge personnel picked up its body. The day before, they had watched Patuxent no. 2 limping from the marsh toward a barley bin. Thin and now weak, the crane had taken to walking 250 yards from a safe wetland to a source of grain and had collapsed close to the bin containing treated barley. The National Wildlife Health Laboratory in Madison, Wisconsin, which specializes in avian ailments, found *Mycobacterium avium*, an organism linked to tuberculosis, in the whooper's system. *Salmonella* also infected Patuxent no. 2. Medical experts ordered its skin incinerated as a health measure.[42]

Seven months after this first case of avian TB near Monte Vista NWR, a chick wintering on Aransas NWR came down with the same disease; then, almost two years later, avian TB struck three cranes in rapid succession, all in the foster population. The second occurrence also involved a 1979 male whooping crane. In late February 1986, Drewien received reports of a bird barely able to fly on Belen State Refuge, New Mexico. With assistance from Lance Asherin and Whooping Crane Coordinator Jim Lewis, Drewien captured the sick male and took it for treatment to Albuquerque Zoo.

On 13 March, male 79-10 died. A necropsy diagnosed avian TB. Barely a month had passed when another crane, 79-4, hit a transmission line in Idaho. The collision ruptured this male's liver, but Madison specialists found several nodules in its intestines and suspected tuberculosis. A postmortem showed 79-4, however, to be in fairly good health when it died.

A few days before whooper 79-4 died in Idaho, refuge staff in Monte Vista heard from a local farmer that a white crane was behaving "strangely." Weak and emaciated, Patuxent no. 5 showed no inclination to fly as Drewien and Lance Asherin closed in. Transported to Albuquerque Zoo, this 1982 male rallied, then its condition deteriorated. Leg problems incapacitated the crane, and after just over a month in captivity veterinarians put it out of its misery. Once again, laboratory tests turned up avian TB.[43]

All three 1986 deaths occurred in spring after whooping cranes had wintered along New Mexico's middle Rio Grande Valley. At that time, record numbers of light-colored geese flocked into the region. Such a spectacular buildup of cranes and, particularly, geese on Bosque and surroundings created a situation in which disease and stress associated with exceptional crowding could lead to waterbird mortality. Experts believe that's what happened. Drewien knew that food supplies grown for wildlife would not last. By mid-January, grain planted for birds in the northern half of the valley had run out. Geese and cranes moved on to private lands. Landowners harassed them and caused thousands of cranes to migrate early in search of food and less disturbance. With inadequate diet and natural resistance weakened, some whoopers became more prone to such diseases as avian TB and cholera.

The U.S. Fish and Wildlife Service and New Mexico Game and Fish Department decided to prevent, if possible, such problems in 1986–87 by opening a special sandhill hunt in the mid-valley and hazing geese from Bosque in order to keep water birds from remaining in such numbers. They also planned to increase grain production on state areas, even contracting for the entire crop at Los Lunas prison farm, in order to carry lingering geese and cranes, especially whoopers, through the winter in good health. The plan worked. When birds migrated in early 1987, they had not exhausted food supplies, reports of crop depredations decreased, and, most important, there were no whoopers behaving "strangely," stricken with a terminal illness.[44]

Crane veterinarian James Carpenter, who works daily with Patuxent birds, notes that, unlike mammals, birds usually show disease symptoms only after the ailment has progressed and they are seriously ill. Prevention, rather than treatment of disease, is the key for popula-

tions both in captivity and in the wild. Routine examination and tests in Patuxent's flock, for example, enable caretakers to check parasite levels that may increase dramatically and spark off an epidemic. Such assessments are not possible in wild birds; therefore, availability of ample food and water, good weather, and freedom from disturbance or crowding are crude measures by which biologists assess possibilities for disease outbreaks. When food runs short, with abrupt drops in temperature, typically in winter, waterfowl crowded on refuges run risks of contracting infectious diseases.[45]

Like avian TB, fowl cholera caused by *Pasteurella multocida* strikes down waterbirds on winter range and has stricken at least one whooping crane. A young female, 83-15, flew into Bosque NWR at sunset on 12 November 1984 after spending a summer quietly in western Wyoming. She had stopped for two weeks in Colorado's San Luis Valley en route to New Mexico. Two days later, 83-15 began behaving oddly. She remained on a roost site all day without flapping off with other cranes. Although she was alert, the whooper's condition deteriorated. During the evening of 28 November, Rod Drewien and refuge biologist Michael Hawkes moved in to capture the sick crane and with a backpack generator and spotlight dazzled her eyes long enough to use a large dip net as a restraint. Staff placed 83-15 in a special crate and drove immediately to Albuquerque Zoo, fearing avian cholera.

Eighty-three-fifteen had inhabited two places in which avian cholera had occurred. Sixty-five sandhill cranes had died earlier in 1984, mostly from avian cholera, on Monte Vista NWR. Sandhill cranes had returned to Colorado two weeks early that year, swinging down into a frigid, snow-filled plateau. They were starving. Grain had run short in New Mexico, in the very refuge that 83-15 made a home, and people harassed them elsewhere. Colorado authorities bulldozed snow off frozen stubbles, opened wells on refuge lands to flood areas, giving protection and drinking water. Emaciated, exhausted birds began to die. Refuge staff retrieved bodies from iced-in sleeping places or in frozen fields where cranes foraged incessantly in brutally cold weather. The 1984 cholera epidemic was the worst recorded among sandhill cranes.[46]

Avian cholera had struck Bosque, another spot in the crane flyway in which two previous outbreaks (in 1982 and 1983) claimed scores of geese when 83-15 touched down. In most respects 83-15 turned out to be a model patient. The crane showed little panic as people examined and treated her with broad spectrum antibiotics and ointment. Tests showed avian cholera; however, by mid-December, 83-15 was clinically recovered and attention turned to improving her overall health, especially body weight, which had sunk dangerously low. Frustrated by the whooper's unwillingness to consume a tempting array of morsels, caretakers force-fed her. A month later, 83-15's strength had rebounded. But on 21 January 1985, she could not stand; when she was forced upright, keepers were horrified to see her right leg dangling. As they set her leg, 83-15 died suddenly under anesthesia. Examination showed no sign of avian cholera.

Somehow, female 83-15 had run or flown into her enclosure and fractured her leg: another mishap had claimed one of Grays Lake's precious females. Cured of serious illness, she died from an accident before biologists freed her into the wild. A total of 22 sandhill cranes and 775 snow geese and Ross's geese died from avian cholera on Bosque refuge in 1985.[47]

Whoopers have died from lead poisoning. Eighty-two-thirteen, a male, dropped into Bosque wetlands in December 1983 after passing most of the previous month around Monte Vista NWR and New Mexico's mid-valley Los Lunas–Bernardo area, Miracles' old haunt. He had summered on Grays Lake. On 28 December a four-day goose hunt opened on Bosque NWR, and 82-13 and four whooper companions promptly flew out. He appears to have gone northward but was back on 5 January 1985, when Rod Drewien saw blood on a wing; 82-13 looked wounded and sick.

Crane biologists watched 82-13 carefully, hoping that he would pull through, but, after consultation with medical authorities around the country, Drewien spotlighted the ailing crane on 21 January and turned him over to bird vets from Albuquerque's Rio Grande Zoo.

An X-ray showed three shotgun pellets in the left thigh, plus a dense gritlike substance in his gizzard. Initial diagnosis of a gunshot injury led to antibiotics and high-protein foods forced into him. But, after recovering enough to attack a handler and further tests showed acute lead poisoning, 82-13 weakened quickly and died. A postmortem revealed his gizzard packed with lead fragments and pieces of stone and plastic. Forensic tests run by the FBI in Washington, D.C., proved that 82-13 did not die by picking up spent shotgun pellets or from being blasted. It is still unclear where the lead that killed him came from. The analysis speculated that it may have been a battery of some sort glittering in a field that 82-13 picked up and swallowed, or even a fishing sinker covered with a plastic coating.[48]

Numbers and Recruitment

Rod Drewien and others involved closely with the foster program express frustration and disappointment about the numbers of birds. Frustration is due to the fact that most known deaths to fledged cranes are due to humanly induced rather than natural factors. Power lines, fences, shooting, and incidental mishaps, such as 82-13's ingestion of lead, kill more fledged cranes than such natural factors as weather, predation, and disease. Frustration also arises from the deaths or disappearance of a disproportionately large number of females. Drewien is puzzled by this statistic and suggests that females seem less attracted back to natal areas than males, who can be depended on to home in to Grays Lake after three or four seasons and to defend a territory. Females migrate northward from New Mexico alone or in flocks of sandhills and disperse throughout crane summer range. Some of them, like Ulcers, don't tolerate the kind of crowding and jostling that sandhill cranes mete out and retire to valley ponds and marshes, becoming quiet and secretive.

Fundamentally, disappointment with the foster experiment stems from the issue of reproduction, or lack thereof. As of 1 January 1988, not one crane in the foster flock has paired successfully with another, established a territory, and nested. For more than a decade now, Drewien has watched cranes on Grays Lake, at stopover points, and on winter quarters at all times of day and in all weathers. Situations like those already described about the 1975 whooper cohort have occurred time after time: birds recognize one another, they associate, forage, appear to accept each other's company but fail to sustain or deepen relationships. Drewien admits ruefully that "maybe we've ended up with a mule!"

It may be difficult to determine if some actual behavioral mechanism, an imprinting factor, for example, has gone wrong or has not been triggered properly. So far, human efforts to assist with pair formation have involved the physical capture, transport, and release of sexually compatible individuals into Grays Lake.

In March 1986, U.S. Fish and Wildlife authorities approved a proposal to capture and transport as many as four female whooping cranes from summer areas to Grays Lake. The aim was to "enhance opportunities for pair formation" with a number of male cranes that, over the years, have demonstrated a proclivity to home back to their birthplace and set up territories. By returning females to Grays Lake, Drewien and others have tried to speed up the familiarization process on the grounds that cranes may not be encountering each other frequently enough or for long enough on winter areas in New Mexico. With a population of only twenty to thirty birds at any one time, potential partners may be too isolated to find each other.

Between 26 June and 2 August 1986, Drewien added the task of spotlighting errant females to his other duties of egg transplant and crane monitoring. He grabbed four birds thought to be females (not all had been banded or had had blood tests taken), carried them to an area within view of the headquarters on the eastern side of Grays Lake, and freed them close to five males, four of which occupied territories. All the new cranes remained near the release point until they migrated between 6 and 10 October 1986.

Interactions and associations between females and the resident males have interested observers. On thirty-six occasions over the summer, Drewien observed cranes together. One 1982 female moved into a male's preferred area and the "pair" flew about together, a new behavior "record" for Grays Lake. Instances of unison calls and joint foraging heartened Drewien, who was pleased to see that most transplanted birds left the valley with other whoopers. They failed, however, to sustain connections; ways parted in Colorado. Whooper 84-22, for example, whom Drewien had captured in Lincoln County, Wyoming, about twenty-five miles from Grays Lake, migrated with two other whoopers on 10 October but flew into northeast Colorado (near Hudson) and was seen alone before she continued on to the San Luis Valley.

In 1987, none of the translocated females returned to the Grays Lake release site, although one, Patuxent 17 (1984) did return to the western shore of the lake where Drewien had first captured her. Drewien was unable to locate 84-22 after April 1987, when the whooper was seen on Monte Vista NWR. He did, however, find a third bird in a most remote section of crane habitat within Yellowstone National Park and a fourth crane north of Grays Lake. On June 14, the biologist found the decayed body of this whooper close to Island Park Reservoir, Fremont County, Idaho.

In June and July 1987, Drewien's team captured four more cranes, one of which, Patuxent 17, he had grabbed the previous summer. He released them near males on Grays Lake. The cranes behaved as their counterparts had in 1986, keeping close to the release site, sometimes associating with other whoopers, and after a few days setting up routines for foraging and roosting. A project that showed initial promise has baffled observers, who are reassessing whether dispersion and isolation may be

critical factors that keep cranes from pairing.[49]

Females (and some males) scatter into a variety of aquatic habitats during summer months. A greater preference for wetlands compared with sandhills carries whoopers to water bodies in sagebrush flats, high marshes, small and large lakes, and valleys or creek bottoms in rugged country. One adult female (Patuxent no. 3), whom Drewien failed to capture in 1986 but did in 1987, summered in Hoback Basin, some fifty miles northeast of Grays Lake, feeding partly on grasshoppers on high mountain slopes at about 7,000 feet. With an erratic and unpredictable flight schedule, the crane successfully evaded two attempts to make her part of the first shipment back to Grays Lake but ran to the edge of its 3–4-acre marsh in July 1987 and was captured.

People wonder whether snagging such cranes earlier, in Colorado's San Luis Valley, for example, in March or April, would help sustain associations longer and lead to nesting. Adult male cranes usually turn up on Grays Lake from early to mid April, so there is a plan to introduce wild trapped females at that time; bringing them in when the nesting season is advanced may not be physiologically optimal for pair bonding.

Another consideration is to place two Grays Lake cranes in an enclosure on the refuge and "force" a pair bond. Behaviorist George Archibald believes that in captivity even cranes of different species will pair off. Holding whoopers together, then releasing them after a period in confinement may do the trick, though others are skeptical.

In observations of territory-holding males, Drewien has been struck by the strong urge in some to nurture chicks. In summer 1983, for example, seven of eight whoopers aged three or older reasserted areas that they had defended in 1982. One of them, 79-10, a territorial male, took over parental duties when a female sandhill crane nearby died entangled in a wire fence in late June. Drewien observed how 79-10 moved in with the surviving sandhill parent, who was left to raise two chicks. "The whooper often accompanied the family, giving alarm calls when humans or other danger appeared," reported Drewien, who saw the adult whooper feed one of the chicks. "This intermittent relationship ended in September when the male sandhill and surviving chick left the territory and staged for migration." A similar happening in July 1987 resulted in territorial male whooper 78-10 feeding a sandhill chick whose family he joined. The sandhill parents tolerated his interest.[50]

One way of capitalizing on this parenting urge is to introduce a captive-raised whooper chick into a male whooper's territory and monitor the situation. If a male reacts to a puppet-raised chick, according to Archibald, he will begin to feed it (through a safe enclosure fence, probably); then, as the bond develops, he will lead it to a staging area and guide it southward on migration. An extra bonus in this scenario is to introduce a female as well, so that the chick may become the focal point for both adults, who may share in the experience of rearing it. Not only will whoopers raise tiny whoopers but they may also pair bond as a result.

Such talk demonstrates that experts have not given up entirely on Grays Lake. Time, however, is running out and with such a variable fledging success, plus unexpected mortality especially from power lines, there is a big question mark about the future of free flying cranes in the Mountain West.

If the experimental whoopers are more mules than cranes, as Drewien half-jokingly suggests, the project is doomed; no manner of human tinkering will assist with misimprinted whoopers. Nobody seriously thinks they will hybridize, even though Patuxent's valiant Ghostbird shows his zest for life and produces quantities of semen. The answer may lie in the marshlands of Texas, where subadult whoopers associate for winter months and, as Mary Anne Bishop observed, gradually establish stronger and stronger bonds by habitually consorting, foraging, and traveling together. This process takes place over three or four winters and is why, given the skewed sex ratio, people have argued that physically placing Grays Lake cranes together could catalyze pair formation. On the other hand, single or widowed adults in the Aransas flock have paired off quickly. One or two cases have been noted of apparently unpaired individuals heading north and then breeding that same summer in Wood Buffalo. The issue of females "floating," Drewien's term for dispersion during summer, puzzles biologists. Nobody knows for sure which adult of a pair selects the nest site. They think that males may do this; at least, data, again from Aransas, suggest that male cranes return to an area near the winter territory maintained by their parents. They attempt to crowd in or establish a domain close to that prime winter station. Without influence from males who seek them out, females at Grays Lake must strike out on their own.

Nobody believes that Grays Lake's high elevation a mile and a quarter above sea level affects the failure of females to return. In fact, in 1986, Patuxent no. 3 lived even higher up than that. However, experts don't know what effects heights have on crane physiology; sandhills nest at Grays Lake, they argue, therefore, there is noth-

ing to prevent whoopers from following suit. The fact that few females return does not mean they avoid the place, just that their homing instincts, unlike males', may be different. Drewien has discovered that, as they mature, whoopers can be looked for in the same places year after year: individuals set up routines that work for them and then follow these rather assiduously.

Whether or not altitude affects crane physiology, there is little doubt that Grays Lake is near the western edge of the historic range of whooping cranes. Drewien, who has journeyed far and wide censusing cranes in the Mountain West and has pored over records of white cranes from Yellowstone Park south to Chihuahuan desert uplands and beyond, believes firmly that present routeways of foster birds are similar to ancestral ones. At one time whoopers occurred around Utah's Great Salt Lake, although we don't know in what numbers or in what density.

Likewise, in Florida, the possible site for a second experimental flock, whoopers undoubtedly occurred a century ago, but, as in the West, documentation is unusually sparse. Most clear evidence for nesting comes from Canada's prairie provinces and from a northern tier of U.S. Plains states into the Midwest. Louisiana also had its resident whoopers until about fifty years ago.

Why, it may be asked, have these regions in which prime habitat exists—some preserved in refuges—not become sites for repopulation? In other words, why was the Grays Lake program not initiated in some place where whoopers are known to have flourished? Those who know answer this question in two ways. First, they suggest that there are few, if any, states or provinces supporting strong constituencies of hunters who are amicable to having whoopers on their flyways. New Mexico, people explain, has soured on the whooper program because it has allegedly restricted hunting and slowed its extension into some regions, notably those areas in which sandhill and whooping cranes co-exist. Frustrated waterfowl hunters, together with landowners who have seen geese and cranes pilfer their grain, have come to dislike the endangered cranes. Such economic disbenefits and hunter lobbies spell doom for a similar experiment to be tried in the continent's heartland. Florida, as we have seen, has no goose or crane hunting; therefore, whoopers don't have an image problem. New Mexico is tired of them.

The second reason is linked to the first. In Louisiana, the saying goes, the only good cranes are those headed toward a gumbo cauldron. People argue that the Gulf state's traditions, especially pot hunting, are antithetical toward any whoopers planted back in White Lake, for example. Biologists who have worked in Louisiana are not as cynical. They point to rejuvenation of brown pelicans—though nobody eats them!—and speak of ways of accomplishing similar initiatives for whooping cranes. It is a matter of discussion and dialogue. Visitor use of Bosque, for example, has tripled since whoopers made it an important winter stopping place. Eighty-five thousand people may seem a small number, but Monte Vista capitalizes on the magnetism of white cranes. Visitation at Aransas has climbed, and local tour boat operators compete for a growing clientele wishing to see cranes along the Intracoastal Waterway. In 1986 and 1987, five boats regularly churned up and down the cut to float near whoopers.

Entrepreneurial initiative aside, and cranes certainly bring new dollars into local communities, watching and learning about this slender waif of indomitability have their own clean, simple, and shining value: we need the crane. It reminds us of nature's fecundity, its optimism, its will to persist and be full and complex, if only we will watch and listen. The crane bugles this statement to us. It is not hostile, it is not abject—a misshapen, brittle, pathetic broken thing—it is a wild bird with its own agenda that may or may not include us; that choice is ours. It is an animal that will be what it should be: a marvelous gesture toward life not death, a sign of our own gift, and the mark of reverence that we choose to revere in others.

Our ability to perceive quality in nature begins, as in art, with the pretty. It expands through successive stages of the beautiful to values as yet uncaptured by language. The quality of cranes lies, I think, in this higher gamut, as yet beyond the reach of words.

—ALDO LEOPOLD
A Sand County Almanac, p. 102

Conclusion

If the aim of the U.S. *Whooping Crane Recovery Plan* to reclassify the species from endangered to threatened is to succeed, a number of steps must be taken in order to sustain public interest and commitment and to conserve the species' habitat. Hunters, for example, must identify whoopers correctly and not mistake them for goose or sandhill crane targets. Likewise, reclaiming land for crops along the migration corridor and loss and contamination of wetlands in winter quarters must be curtailed in order to optimize the quality and quantity of space available for the cranes.

Access to wild whooping cranes has been a matter of juggling people's sympathy and interest with the bird's need for an environment in which it is neither disturbed nor molested. Over the past twenty-five years, the numbers of visitors on Aransas, for example, have increased sixfold, from about 13,000 who registered in 1961 to almost 70,000 in 1986. "Crane watchers" converge on the refuge from all over North America. Most come from the 2.5 million Texans who live within a few hours' drive—from Houston, Austin, and San Antonio. March is the most popular month. Balmy spring weather draws bird watchers, who climb an overlook and strain for a glimpse of Mustang Lake's crane family or visiting subadults. Excited reports filter back to the visitor center about a whooper "flock" or "flotilla" on the marshes, and staff smile politely, murmuring to themselves, "God bless those whooping pelicans."[1]

Aransas employees are concerned about visitors coming too close and disturbing the cranes. By taking one of four or five boats along the Gulf Intracoastal Waterway from Rockport, tourists can get much closer to whoopers than on the mainland. While this act of appreciation is good for crane promotion, such unrestricted access to winter territories strung out along that waterway tends to temporarily frighten off some birds, may result in conflicts between crane neighbors,

and may limit the procurement of food. Restrictions, however, are much easier to impose on approaches from the land than on water because Texas law declares that navigable waters are open to the public.

The idea of "critical habitat" helps mitigate some potential disputes between humans and cranes. Under Section 7 of the 1973 Endangered Species Act, a zone around Aransas NWR, which includes adjacent barrier islands and Welder Point, has been declared vital for the species. The law mandates that federal agencies must consult about any plans or activities that would affect crane welfare. Currently, eight additional areas are designated as critical habitat in seven states, mostly along the migration route to Canada and in the Rocky Mountain West. Section 7, however, applies only to actions by federal authorities or federally funded actions by other parties and not to state or private landowners. Along the migration corridor, many private landowners are well disposed toward saving the cranes and are prepared to cooperate with agencies by limiting human entry to feeding and roosting sites on farms and ranches.

Discussions between federal, regional, and state authorities, who have jurisdiction over areas used by whoopers, are directed toward resolving conflicts over land use. Such concerns about interagency impacts on whooping cranes go back in Aransas to the completion of the Gulf Intracoastal Waterway in 1940. Tom Stehn figures that almost 1,500 acres of important tidal marsh have been lost or degraded by this channel. He has pored over old photos and maps in order to measure the amount of wetland destroyed by the waterway itself and has estimated subsequent erosion caused by wave action from storms and boat traffic in an area that Stephenson once characterized as "the finest [of] whooping crane wintering grounds."[2]

In his early roseate spoonbill research, Bob Allen was fascinated by the huge, clanking *Matagorda,* a floating dredge that carved out the original navigable channel. On 15 April 1940, camped on Rattlesnake Point, the birdman spotted the goliath heading in his direction. The dredge came from the south, chewing and sucking its terrifying way, and would soon "be eating voraciously," said Allen, through the very spit of land on which he was camped. Curious about its work, Allen headed out to meet the dredge. Climbing aboard, he found that its operators had become enthusiastic birdwatchers, identifying flocks wheeling around the mixture of water, sand, and mud spewed from an outlet pipe. Gulls picked morsels from the slurry, curlews and godwits skeetered on new mud banks, but Allen's spoonbills and the ghostlike whooping cranes would have nothing to do with this behemoth.

Like Allen, manager Stevenson disliked the Intracoastal Waterway. In October 1939, he came across two families near Redfish Bay "not as yet disturbed by canal dredge, thank G—." One unexpected benefit developed, however, and the manager picked up on it. Barely had new islands comprised of spoil appeared when a host of seabirds selected them as nesting sites.[3]

According to Stehn's calculations, however, over the years about four times more habitat has been lost than gained by creation of the waterway. While creating islands, dredges' spoil has buried pristine marshlands; and, by slicing out this stretch of tidal flat and bay substrate, engineers effectively placed acre after acre off limits for cranes. The channel becomes rapidly too deep to wade in. Although recovery team members support a proposal for shifting the Intracoastal Waterway farther east into Mesquite Bay, it is unlikely to happen soon. One reason why the cut passed through marsh habitat in the first place was to facilitate maintenance and provide calmer water for shipping.[4]

Contamination remains an ever-present danger on the Intracoastal Waterway. Fortunately, no major petrochemical spill has occurred on the Aransas Refuge section when whoopers have been present. However, a U.S. Fish and Wildlife Service report on contaminants draws attention to "chronic low level discharges of hydrocarbons and heavy metals from oil and gas production, pipeline transportation, and oil tanker traffic" in that area. This 1986 report calls for close monitoring. Small oil spills or bilge pumpage date all the way back to 1941 in refuge documents. Light fuels evaporate and denser materials in small quantities disperse, but residues sink into sediments, and their possible entry into the food chain is a serious matter.[5]

Boat traffic on the Intracoastal Waterway disturbs cranes; so does hunting, both around the wintering grounds and along the migration track. There has been no actual proof that a crane has been shot on or near the Aransas Refuge for over twenty years; however, waterfowl hunters occupy blinds close to its borders. A survey by Texas Parks and Wildlife concluded that hunting has no "gross effects" on whooping crane distribution, although airboats ferrying hunters to blinds flush cranes as they blast past territories along the mainland shore.[6]

"Spot closures," or, as in the case of Blue–White's sojourn near El Campo, informal closure with careful monitoring, can effectively cope with any unusual overlaps between sandhill crane seasons and lingering whooping cranes. Three regions in Texas have been opened for sandhill crane hunting; normally, these seasons are staggered so that there is little likelihood that the two species would occur together. Most if not all whoopers are secure in the Aransas locality by the time sandhill hunting begins.

Other crane watchers are not as confident as Texas authorities that hunters and whooping cranes can be separated. Eight states on the Central Flyway through which whoopers migrate have opened seasons for sandhill cranes, and if North Dakota is at all indicative the trend is to expand hunting. In recent years as many as seven thousand people have bagged upward of thirteen thousand cranes annually. Sandhill crane specialists believe the fall flight of half a million birds is capable of sustaining such an offtake. Whooper advocates are less sanguine; they argue that misidentification is easy, especially in poor light, and as whoopers associate with sandhill crane flocks, especially on migration, risks of accidentally killing the wrong cranes are increased.[7]

Other concerns exist about the survival of whooping cranes migrating between Canada and the United States. Gary R. Lingle of the Platte River Whooping Crane Critical Habitat Maintenance Trust has identified a number of hazards, including crop pesticides, military activities, utility lines, and disease, all of which have received short shrift, he argues, in official documents. Lingle and others have publicized the importance of the Platte River as a stopover for whooping cranes. Ninety percent of whooper sightings in Nebraska have taken place within thirty miles of the Platte River, mostly between Lexington and Grand Island; and this stretch holds up to half a million sandhill cranes, who glean stubbles, visit wet meadows, and roost among braided channels where in fall and spring a few of their pale cousins may be spotted.

The "Platte River Bottoms," a 3-mile-wide, 53-mile-long strip of riparian land from Lexington to Denman, was designated as "critical habitat" for whooping cranes in the belief that the Platte River historically has been a major stopover for these birds about halfway into their journey from Canada to the Gulf coast. For the past fifteen years, the National Audubon Society has been actively involved with habitat preservation along this stretch. In 1974, the society acquired the Lillian Annette Rowe Bird Sanctuary, a 2,000-acre roost site consisting of channel and upland areas, east of Kearney, and used by passing whooping cranes.

Like other Plains states and provinces, Nebraska's wetlands, especially riparian areas along the Platte River, have dwindled substantially in recent decades. Similar losses in other places vary from 75 to 90 percent in central and south Saskatchewan to 35 percent in South Dakota. Crane conservationists aim to mitigate habitat loss and deterioration by reconstituting, at least along the Platte River, as has been mentioned, channel roosts, water meadows, and native grasslands, habitually preferred by both species of crane.[8]

Canada-U.S. Cooperation

An April 1985 "Memorandum of Understanding" between respective heads of the U.S. Fish and Wildlife Service and Canada's Wildlife Service clarified arrangements for whooping crane management. It formalized procedures that had been followed by the two nations since whooping crane egg transfers from Wood Buffalo to Patuxent began in 1967. The memorandum also streamlined efforts for population buildup by spelling out responsibilities and ways of minimizing conflict and redundancy between the United States and Canada. The memorandum recognized that all eggs or progeny from egg transfers are joint property of the two nations; it identified repositories for specimens and standardized postmortem and retrieval procedures. In sum, the agreement emphasized that experts from both nations should communicate fully and effectively on matters related to whooping crane survival.

In September 1986, the Canadian Wildlife Service released its own draft recovery plan (published in 1988). Broadly, its objectives are similar to those spelled out in its U.S. counterpart. According to the Canadian document, biological research and monitoring in Wood Buffalo are to continue and include investigation of nesting sandhill cranes who may be tapped as foster parents to increase whooper productivity.

Canadian sentiments, like those in the United States, lean toward expanding nesting range by foster techniques and manipulating clutches within Wood Buffalo to increase chick survival. For several years now, biologists have transferred some eggs from dependable breeders to the nests of pairs with eggs that do not contain live embryos.

There is also discussion about establishment of a captive flock in Canada, run along similar lines to Patuxent. The proposal is that some eggs would come from Wood Buffalo and subadults from Patuxent, at least for the first few years. A "round-up" of Grays Lake cranes, if people conclude that, for whatever reason, reproduction there is fundamentally impaired, is unlikely to contribute to the captive flock due to the possibility of disease in birds taken from the wild.[9]

Canadian researchers like Ernie Kuyt have developed a great deal of information about specific pairs and their breeding histories, territories, nest sites, and so on, down to the weight, size, coloration, and sex of chicks from year to year. Additionally, data about subadult distribution in summer and staging areas in early fall, notably in Saskatchewan, are filling out a picture for the entire wild flock.

Away from Canada, the status of the whooping crane is far less reassuring. The spectrum of problems faced by the "west flock" is a microcosm for North America, ranging from low fledging success because of predation and inclement weather to casualties from transmission lines. Most deaths after fledging are due to humanly induced hazards, such as fences and power lines. The most disheartening characteristic of this situation is that of more than 277 eggs set out on Grays Lake (1975–1987) none has resulted in independent breeding, despite human efforts to link-up potential mates.

Captive breeding among Patuxent whoopers has had its ups and downs and is limited by the need to inseminate birds artificially. Disease outbreaks can be devastating. In fall 1984, seven whoopers, including five females, died from eastern equine encephalitis—a mosquito-borne disease, previously unknown among whooping cranes. The incident decimated female brood stock as the best layers succumbed within a few days.

In fall 1987, another sixteen cranes, including three whoopers, died at Patuxent, puzzling staffers, who investigated a range of likely causes before settling on a fungal toxin that contaminated food. Ironically, Patuxent's cranes were supposed to represent insurance

ABOVE: **A three-day-old whooping crane chick fostered by sandhill crane parents, Grays Lake, June 1976. Photograph by Rod C. Drewien.**

LEFT: **Ten sandhill cranes lift over wires near Monte Vista NWR. Low-flying cranes, including whoopers, may be killed or seriously injured by failing to avoid entanglement with wires and fences. Photograph by author.**

against a disaster on Aransas, but the captive flock has proven more fragile than the wild one.[10]

Management Trends

Whooping crane biologists, conservation administrators, and other experts have generated enormous insight, expertise, and enthusiasm for saving this troubled species. Their sincere commitments of time and energy demonstrate just how seriously they understand their task. It is also clear that they regard management as vital for recovery.

Ideally, whoopers and humans would have no quarrel, but, obviously, we have severely limited the distribution and numbers of cranes. In theory, by policing our own activities, especially those that kill or disturb birds, and by setting aside habitat, we could leave the whooping crane to go about its life with minimal interference. No further action is called for as long as numbers trend upward. That conservation policy operated for the Wood Buffalo–Aransas flock, beginning in 1916 with the Migratory Bird Treaty Act, which prohibited hunting, through the mid-1960s. In practice, however, the population continued to decline, and, even after the establishment of the Aransas Refuge, numbers fluctuated, remaining dangerously low. In part, according to knowledgeable folk, this was because some people shot at cranes, ignoring legal restrictions, and continued to whittle away wetland habitat and disturb them.

"Hands on" is the other side of the conservation coin. Over the years crane proponents have argued for more management and manipulation. Patuxent provides a dramatic case of this philosophy. There we rear and breed captive cranes in hopes of eventually returning them to places that we consider appropriate. Patuxent whoopers experience only captivity and are wholly dependent on humans, who control their reproduction.

Between the poles of mostly hands off and entirely hands on lies a range of concerns that reflect our philosophy about cranes and affect how we approach them. For example, the likelihood of habitat contamination on the Aransas National Wildlife Refuge was important in sparking discussions about a second "insurance" flock and led to experiments with wild whoopers far removed from the Texas Gulf Intracoastal Waterway and nearby oil wells. In sum, concerns about indirect impacts beyond the jurisdiction of wildlife agencies dictated that as a matter of prudence decision makers should formulate policies for intervention. As Aransas cranes choose to remain in an increasingly disturbed and hazardous winter area, officials could minimize dangers and risks by restricting hunting and public access to their habitat; it also seems reasonable and wise to start another population away from threats of pollution or a late hurricane.

This activist policy has psychological payoffs. One feels better doing something rather than doing nothing. But when is something enough? Workers must consciously guard against impulses to do too much. They must also take care not to lose respect for their charges, reducing them to a "big white chicken" caricature. Conservation defined as "active management" has a reassuring ring, implying know-how and confidence in our ability to conserve through intervention: the biologist, like the doctor, knows what best to prescribe.

Similarly, the idea for a "new flock" suggests farsightedness, not a response to crises about which experts have a limited set of choices. But this idea also carries assumptions, namely, that we can have cranes do our bidding by manipulating essential characteristics of their biology. The idea for a "new flock," or "insurance cranes," gears people toward intervention. Such a hands-on approach involves the collection of data about key aspects of crane biology, such as reproduction, migration, food habits, and so on. Such information satisfies our curiosity about the "whys" and "hows" of crane behavior and distribution; it is part of our fascination with the world about us.

Banding is one way of obtaining scientific data about cranes. Scores of Grays Lake sandhills were banded as a necessary first step in planning and implementing the experimental whooping crane flock. Banding wild whoopers in Canada over the past decade has turned up important information about movements, behavior, longevity, pair formation, and productivity—useful in discussions about the preservation and management of habitat along the migration corridor and on the Texas coast. While justifying this manipulation of cranes because it allows us to identify specific individuals in specific situations and circumstances, we risk glossing over the fact that banding also costs cranes something. They risk accidental death or injury and bear the burden of pain and stress. Wearing colored leg markers disquiets a chick, at least initially. The artifact may come to affect the way we observe, so that we begin to see the color combination of bands and not the crane that wears them. For example, I have referred to favorite birds by the band colors because I know no other way of identifying individuals; but I must recognize that bands also exemplify human control and my impatience with mystery and demand for coherence.

It is easy to forget that a band is but a gadget; a tool that assists research. As these tools have become utilized and accepted, other choices of not applying them, which may be more expensive in time and money, become harder to promote or fund. Simply put, gadgets tend to be self-promoting. The dilemma is that, as numbers increase and because whoopers look alike and are naturally wary, perhaps there is no other way of telling cranes apart except by banding them, although Allen and some of his colleagues were said to be able to recognize certain birds. Recently, through his patient monitoring and long experience at close quarters with both crane species, Rod Drewien has absorbed a unique understanding of crane lore. Kuyt, Blankinship, Bishop, and Stehn have generated similar insights through painstaking observations.

The concern about banding is relatively minor compared with other hands-on issues that involve captivity and propagation. However, the knowledge that banding generates tends to lead to more questions that demand additional or different information. The U.S. and Canadian recovery teams understand this. In 1987, they discussed future banding and agreed to continue banding Wood Buffalo young through 1989. Beyond that breeding season, only a few chicks, probably from newly formed pairs, would carry colored leg markers; by then, note experts, most of the research goals used to justify banding will have been met.

Radio-tracking followed banding. As individual cranes came to be readily identified, their activities could be monitored more closely by attaching radios. In some people's minds such telemetry increased the risks of losing birds. In other words, the wild population conserved initially through indirect, largely noninterventionist means changes into a population that is increasingly manipulated and subject to risks from gadgets, although not perhaps to the degree of the "experimental flock" of fostered cranes. But is there a "nonexperimental" flock? Does "wild" cease to be "wild" through a little intervention here, by banding and radio tracking, or there, by swapping eggs in order to "improve" reproductive success?

Such questions have no simple answers. Banding has that neutral quality about it: it is a simple device that is capable of giving biologists important information. Obviously, cranes don't need it; they know who they are and how and where they live. We claim rights to their knowledge even though some cranes may suffer in giving it to us. Radio-tagged whooper chicks or subadults die; some may have been destined to do so irrespective of carrying bands and a transmitter, but experts regard them as potentially expendable in terms of collecting information that they could use to assist in the recovery of the species. We wanted to know how, when, and where they flew on seasonal migrations, and we were willing to weigh potential benefits against possible costs.

When we move along the spectrum of active intervention, manipulation, and management and consider egg collecting for shipment initially to Patuxent (1967) and then to Grays Lake (1975), the impacts and implications become more obvious. Whether one argues that captive rearing has benefited the whooper or not, initial justification for lifting eggs was because the species was *in extremis*. In the mid-1950s through the early 1960s, numbers were low and losses tended to offset gains. In 1953–54 there were twenty-four cranes; the same again in 1956–57. In 1958–59 there were thirty-two and the same number in 1962–63 when no young flew into Aransas. An average increase of less than one bird per year from the early 1950s through the early 1960s was not reassuring, particularly when aviculturists argued they could raise cranes in captivity. "Zoo-held" whoopers, like California condors, appeared a distinct attraction.

Fortunately, the situation has improved. The wild flock of 130 or so (April 1988) has tripled since 1967. Nevertheless, no one calls for discontinuing egg transfers; rather, people speak of a *second* captive flock, presumably in Canada, and a *second* experimental wild flock in the east, possibly in Florida. The premises have shifted, the new ones being laid out in the 1986 U.S. *Recovery Plan*—we are going to save the whooper in our way, through more and more direct management.

By our removing an egg from most nests, whooping cranes do not have the opportunity of rearing two chicks. Experts, however, acknowledge that in some wetter years (mid-1980s) it is quite possible that some parents would have guided twins to Texas, although refuge reports show that having two chicks in a family was an infrequent occurrence. Management incrementalism has directed eggs to Grays Lake and Patuxent. At the same time the Canada-U.S. flock has increased threefold from forty-three when egg transfers began, and some regard this recovery as having been actually enhanced by egg-napping. In this view, parents are able to devote more time and effort to rearing a single chick in a nesting habitat that is on the fringe of the northern limit for nesting and, therefore, may be marginal.

Whatever the merits of this argument, the point is that we have chosen to exert our control and have established ingenious procedures to enjoy whoopers in new places. In this move toward new flocks and captive propagation we play off whooper independence and unpredictability against human caring and nurture and risk losing sight of the objective of having more wild cranes. Currently, more cranes are alive than in any time during the past century; but some of them may be behaviorally maladjusted. Have we not blurred the distinction between hands off and hands on?

Cranes should not be locked away on some preserve and cushioned like pampered pets; nor should they be treated as relicts fit only for the zoo. No crane person sees it in those simplistic terms, but there has been a tendency to do something rather than not do something; the Endangered Species Act mandates that Fish and Wildlife Service personnel take active steps toward this species' recovery.

This is not a call to remystify cranes, but it is a plea to let them be birds with unfathomable qualities or behaviors that help define them. Certainly, they are not "little people" in the way that turn-of-the-century fanciers pictured birds in order to arouse popular sentiment for feeding, caring for, and studying different species; but they are like people as individuals and groups. Cranes acquire a set of social skills; they have a "language" and "customs" about which we have clues but little understanding. Mystery is there.

The real mark of intelligence, and the quality of love that reveals true humanness, is letting cranes be who they are and cherishing that unique identity which adds vibrancy as well as complexity to this world around us. A hands-off policy will not accomplish this any more than one of hands on. What is needed is judicious and solicitous management that aims to build up numbers of wild cranes. Crane experts understand this and constantly monitor the species' needs, mitigating hazards and working to maximize the availability of habitat. North America's example in helping the whooping crane is, therefore, a prototype for research and conservation in other countries. A positive assessment would conclude that the relatively small negative impact that banding has inflicted is outweighed by the information that has been gained.

More needs to be done. As humans, we tend to covet and claim far more than we cherish and care for. This may be because we seek to fill an empty spirit and we do not allow ourselves the time or patience required to forge a personal relationship with other things—mineral, vegetable, or animal. Whooping cranes offer that opportunity for personalization, for regaining a sense

Whoopers become accustomed to distant barge traffic along the Gulf Coast Intracoastal Waterway, Aransas NWR. Photograph from Entheos.

CRANES ON POINT PASTURE ROAD

They prance as two-
year-olds
     heady for the

gallops, the joy
of smooth
footfall. No

oxeye, spartina, live-
oak brush, endless
hock
     lifts, deliberate
steps to
find food
and eye
adults who
     punish
     territorial
transgressions.

They skeeter almost
as do
yearlings, all
legs unhitched to
anything, ready
     to race,
     gambol, above
all to dance

with blood-
curdling calls, white
whirls, wings
          drooping,
greeting right
mate in
right season.

Only to troop
back to
     rank
vegetation!

of honor for ourselves and for those things that surround us. Animals are especially important because they share in our being persons who urge consideration out of respect, not merely convenience. Walt Whitman says: "I think I could turn and live with animals, they are so placid and self-contain'd, I stand and look at them long and long." He points clearly to the damage of believing in a depersonalized world. The poet discloses the natural dignity of animals who neither "whine about their condition," nor grow "demented with the mania of owning things." It is the natural integrity of animals that astonishes Whitman, as they "show their relations to me and I accept them." That integrity attracts more and more like-minded people. The whooping crane invigorates in us a generosity of spirit and a sense of sharing—of being bound together in a moral order of tolerance, respect, and love. The quiet, honest look of the crane is a mirror of ourselves—a glance that in turn we must direct toward each other and at the pools of living fascination that embrace us.[11]

Spring Craneland

Cranes are restless. Eleven birds associate south of Matagorda Island's Cottonwood Bayou. Two spiral up and pass more than five minutes climbing in a tight circle before they plane back to the ground, wings outstretched, legs dangling. They land close to the pair whose lost chick, so-called Oklahoma, is at least 350 miles away across the Red River. These new parents have moved eight miles from their use area—they do not defend a territory—on San José Island, which should have been the youngster's first winter home. Perhaps they will pick up the stray female as they migrate through Oklahoma or Kansas or over Nebraska's Platte River, to which its winter companion sandhill cranes may have guided it. The chick is on the migration path for whooping cranes.

The Cottonwood Bayou family remains indifferent to this flock of subadults and new pairs. The trio stalks in the distance as younger cranes spread out in the foreground, forming a long line, and walk unconcernedly toward the back dunes. These cranes turn from one side to another as they pry morsels from the soft mud in the flats. Some wade across shallow leads, others step among dense stands of sea-oxeye. Most birds have wintered on this long, low barrier of sand and understand the intricate geography of these marshy places. One of them, an unpaired female, flew off fifty or so miles and joined sandhill cranes on the mainland. When her brown relatives migrated toward Canada she returned and is gobbling crabs, shrimp, and other marine delicacies with white companions.

Other birds mark the season's shift. A new flock of cinnamon-colored godwits probes the shallows beside the lanky cranes. Similarly hued curlews settle on a bankside. They stare about dolefully as though nature has punished them with such heavy sickle-shaped bills, but their rippling trills add freshness to the scene. Willets respond. They flicker above the grasses, flashing their black-and-white wings and yodel that it is time to nest in isolated spaces. New swallows dart north, old mergansers join a cloud of two hundred scaup, who will soon whir away from their winter haunt. Birds crisscross the open shoreline, stitching land and water together.

Three whooping cranes track west, flapping ponderously toward the mainland. They swing north above two territories whose owners stand stiffly watching them. Suddenly, a big crane from the Lobstick territory along Dunham Bay zooms in low and angry. He lands on the spot from which another intruding family has quickly launched itself. The strangers settle. Again the male lumbers upward and swings toward them head down, neck outstretched. The trespassers leave hurriedly, beating along the air track toward the uplands the other crane family had taken. The Lobstick male is triumphant. He stands tall, a bold five feet, while three hundred yards away his mate and white-toned chick forage seemingly unaware but probably confident of his victory.

All winter this whooper has worked to enlarge his space. This time he has pushed farther north than ever before. It is a precedent for next winter. It is also an act of assertiveness that body chemicals trigger during this season. Within a month, probably sooner, Lobstick will have gathered his family for the last time and climbed aloft to survey this impressive domain. Perhaps the same threesome to whom he has just shown aggression will circle up and together six cranes will set out on a two thousand and more mile journey to their nesting grounds.

South of Lobstick territory but north of Dunham Point, ten additional whoopers are gathered together. They are also subadults, not yet old enough to breed, and are in the process of establishing lifetime bonds. They are also trespassers. Unlike Lobstick, the adult owners demonstrate unusual tolerance toward them, often feeding within a few yards of immature cranes and only occasionally showing any overt hostility. Today, the proprietary pair stands quietly about one hundred yards away on the bay edge.

Today, we have encountered 71 different cranes, most in small flocks and family groups. Five years ago, this total would have comprised the entire Aransas flock. Yesterday, however, Tom Stehn counted 103 cranes in his survey from an airplane, including what he thought was a dead bird close to the edge of Dunham Bay. Fortunately, we have discovered that this "bird" is a piece of frayed, white plastic flapping in the marsh. But there is no sign of the chick that lived on Middle Sundown Bay. Its parents show up clearly against the green vegetation, but their youngster is not with them. It disappeared during a protracted spell of cold, wet weather about a month ago. The young whooper may have been sick or was surprised by a roving coyote or cunning raccoon. Such predators make short work of diseased or unwary animals. This chick is the only loss among the record number of whooping cranes fledged in 1986.

Stehn will be saddened to see his charges leave. For the past six months he has plotted their whereabouts and studied their movements. Soon, his whoopers will follow the geese and sandhills that wintered on this Gulf lowland. Crane movements, flights about the refuge, and flocking behavior suggest that the time for departure is drawing near. Soon whooping crane wingbeats will link this southern marsh to the arctic sky.

Wild things are truly alive
only in the place where they belong.
Away from that place they may bloom
like exotics, but the eye will search beyond them
for their lost home.

—J. A. BAKER
The Peregrine, p. 168

Epilogue

Late December 1988. The strong norther has brushed away rain clouds. A curlew lays down a russet slash on the heaving bay. Clear light helps birders, but they must concentrate on places less exposed to the rushing air and poke deep into oak mottes in order to spot the perching birds that with stockier shorebirds and water-fowl comprise the wintering species on Aransas National Wildlife Refuge. On foam-faced brine along the coastal waterway, people note the curlew as it charges past knots of bufflehead ducks bobbing crazily. Three Bonaparte's gulls also sweep by. White flashes sharpen their pointed wings that tuck air billows under them like the ski poles of slalom racers. Forster's terns swerve and flicker. They slam into wave edges but more often than not emerge with bills empty.

Whooping cranes know how to deal with these strong conditions. They wade hock deep in sloughs away from turbulence and forage in the lowest sections of the marshes. Today, forty or so are scattered in territories along the waterway. Biologist Tom Stehn remarks on how mobile they have become. A bumper crop of acorns and several planned burns on the uplands attract them. Up to a dozen at a time stalk newly blackened tracts and consume terrestrial foods on the peninsula.

Close to Ayres Cut, a crane family slants low across Sundown Bay. It menaces another group who bugle haughtily, then turns into the wind. Three whoopers gain height and begin to spiral. Soon they are lifted above the black dots of vultures. Turning clockwise then counter-clockwise with the youngster outside the circle, the family continues to climb and after several minutes are tiny glowing specks visible only through binoculars. They assume a tight arrowhead formation, track due west on set wings, and vanish.

Perhaps, although there is no precedent, they will join up with others off the Aransas Refuge. So far, Stehn has counted 137, but four have disappeared, so the total is about the same as last winter. With 17 banded young, most of which have reached Texas, people were hoping for a record 150 whoopers, but at least a dozen birds, mostly subadults, are unaccounted for and Tom fears that it is getting late for stragglers. Unlike spring 1987 when the wild flock left Texas and returned again without loss, fall 1988 has not been kind, although there have been no confirmed reports of injured or dead whooping cranes.

One noticeable absentee is nil–White, who has not come back to his North Sundown Island territory. Two subadults, both nil-White's progeny and familiar with the geography of this wetland, occupy their elder's domain. One of them, o–R, passed the entire spring and summer on Aransas. She loafs quietly near her sibling from last year. It is disturbing to realize that their parents, experienced and successful in crane ways, are missing. There has been no sign of nil–White's mate; Tom has failed to observe any single unbanded crane roaming that locality.

With the bold 1978 male missing, only three cranes survive from his banded cohort of ten. Only two are left from the ten cranes that Kuyt's team handled in 1977, the first year for banding. It may be that a whooper's life is not as long as experts predicted; at least evidence from the first two years of banding points in that direction. As if to compensate, however, some wild birds breed at an earlier age than was anticipated. In spring 1988, for the first time, egg-napper Ernie Kuyt discovered fertile eggs in the nest of a three-year-old female. Only males, such as Blue–White, had been known to nest at this age. Presently, B–W is guarding his first chick along the refuge shore of St. Charles Bay.

Blue–White's one-time associate, Bwsp–Bwsp (now nil–Bwsp, and paired), nested for the first time in 1988. She feeds her chick on Dunham Bay. So far, this new family has not ventured onto the barrier island chain that nil—Bwsp frequented as a subadult. [On 3 January 1989, a hunter fatally shot this female parent on the north end of San José Island, reportedly mistaking the whooping crane for a snow goose.]

Information about other old and new wanderers is fragmentary. So-called Oklahoma, WbW—o, spent a lengthy period on the Platte River in spring 1988 and, in company with sandhill cranes, turned up in Saskatchewan in late September. Tom has looked out for her but she may surpass Blue—White in passing a third winter away from Aransas Refuge. New information places her near the Red River in Oklahoma, close to the area in which she passed her first winter. Her younger sibling, so-called Amarillo, y/b—YbY, headed north into the Nebraska Sandhills in spring, but there has been no recent word about him.

Night herons scatter along the creek that gurgles out of Redfish Slough. Unused to human intruders, they are reluctant to quit their hidden domain of sea-oxeye, spartina, and saltgrass. Hunching momentarily in the shallow slough, they flap away ponderously and mill about as the wind hits them. Above, a pair of sandhill cranes hurtles past, betrayed in the high air by their throaty calls. Skeins of these brown cranes fan out to croplands beyond the refuge. They roost on Goose Lake; sometimes whoopers join them, but in general sandhills use the back areas—oak uplands on the peninsula where they feed on acorns, tubers, and grassland items. Here on the tidal flats they seem hesitant—out of place in this habitat for white cranes.

West of the Rockies it is whooping cranes that are out of place. Subjects of an experiment, Grays Lake whoopers mingle with their more numerous cousins. But in many instances the sandhills don't welcome them and tend to peck at chicks or drive them away.

A succession of dry summers has continued to plague productivity in this foster population. Predators gained access to the marsh as water levels have receded about midsummer, causing heavy losses among both sandhill and whooping crane chicks. Now, the entire Grays Lake whooper flock is down to a dozen or so birds; none have nested. Efforts to help pair individuals have gone unrewarded. Liaisons have occurred after captured and transplanted female whoopers have been set free in the territories of adult males, but such associations have proved temporary. Some birds have left Grays Lake together, then each has gone its way in Colorado or New Mexico. There are to be no further transplants of whooping crane eggs into Grays Lake, Idaho.

Attention has shifted to Florida. Plans are being fi-

nalized to place captive-born and parent-raised whooping cranes into the Kissimmee Prairie region. There are problems, some potentially serious, associated with a "third" flock; predators and diseases are two. However, techniques for soft, or gradual, release into the wild have proven successful with endangered Mississippi sandhill cranes and will be applied to whoopers. The greatest benefit is to establish a sedentary population of wild whooping cranes in a state that is ready to welcome and enjoy them, and to minimize risks from power lines, food shortages, and hunting that a migratory population experiences. The basic argument for this new initiative is "insurance," should a calamity befall the Wood Buffalo—Aransas population.

Insurance whooping cranes at Patuxent have not prospered, however. There are forty-six birds (early in 1989) in that captive flock, whose reproductive performance has been poor for several years. That fact and feed-related illnesses have caused experts to reassess the situation in the Maryland facility. They have decided to split up the captive flock, keeping some at Patuxent and sending others to the ICF at Baraboo, Wisconsin. In addition, Canadian Wildlife Service authorities have decided to establish their own captive flock and have invited zoos to make proposals for keeping and breeding whooping cranes.

Eggs from nests (31 in 1988) in Wood Buffalo National Park will go to increase the numbers of whoopers in captivity. If releases go ahead in Florida, it is imperative to have a sizeable number of young on hand in order to start up the new flock.

In fall 1988, Canadian researchers decided to terminate intensive often-exhausting efforts to band all known whooping crane chicks. Eleven years of data have built a window into the world of this white crane. Biologists know where they are and where they go, with whom they associate, and at what age they pair off and nest. But as individuals, the cranes continue to baffle us. Three families suddenly split up, the juvenile separating from its parents, on the Aransas Refuge prior to spring migration in 1988. Tracking data had shown that some adults guide their juvenile all the way back to the nest area in Canada; others separate from their youngster in Saskatchewan—or within a few days' flight of Wood Buffalo. Two subadults (both banded) failed to migrate at all and preferred to pass the summer subsisting on saltwater foods, thereby running risks from Hurricane Gilbert. One new pair that winters on Matagorda Island (one parent carries Y—b/b bands) seems unable to guide its chicks to the Gulf coast. Oklahoma was the first one that it lost and Amarillo was the second.

Banding has supplied us with a basic picture of whooper activities but does not help explain such peculiar patterns of behavior. Canadian experts should be congratulated for their willingness to recognize and accept limits to such methods of studying cranes. The large number of color-banded subadults will continue to furnish useful information for years to come, although unbanded birds will tend to make counts less accurate.

Aransas biologists monitor how the various crane families and pairs settle in for their winter sojourn. Although the total for 1988–89 is disappointing—a record loss from one season to the next—it is worth recalling that only two winters ago the wild flock topped one hundred for the first time in recorded memory. From 1983–84, whooper numbers in the migratory flock have grown a record 80 percent. We pay tribute to this species for such vitality and we must congratulate those human guardians who have committed themselves to furthering the recovery of this magnificent bird.

Appendix 1.
The Status of Cranes in the Genus *Grus*

NAME	STATUS
Common crane (*Grus grus*)	Two races; not listed as threatened or endangered.
Black-necked crane (*Grus nigricollis*)	Endangered, listed 14 June 1976.
Hooded crane (*Grus monarcha*)	Endangered, listed 2 December 1970.
Japanese or red-crowned crane (*Grus japonensis*)	Two races are proposed; endangered, listed 2 June 1970.
Whooping crane (*Grus americana*)	Endangered, listed 11 March 1967.
Sandhill crane (*Grus canadensis*)	Six races; Mississippi and Cuban both endangered, listed 14 June 1973 and 14 June 1976, respectively.
White-naped crane (*Grus vipio*)	Endangered, listed 14 June 1976.
Sarus crane (*Grus antigone*)	Two races; eastern one extirpated from much of its former range and considered endangered.
Brolga crane (*Grus rubicundus*)	Not listed as threatened or endangered.
Siberian crane (*Bugeranus* [formerly *Grus*] *leucogeranus*)	Endangered, listed 2 December 1970.

On the basis of behavior and vocalization, George Archibald has grouped the nine *Grus* cranes into three associations: *Canadensis* (sandhill), *Antigone* (sarus, brolga, and white-naped), and *Americana* (hooded, common, black-necked, Japanese, and whooping).

SOURCE: U.S. Fish and Wildlife Service, *Endangered and Threatened Wildlife and Plants*.

Appendix 2.
Whooping Crane Fact Sheet

1894
May — Last report of nesting in North Central United States, in Eagle Lake, Hancock County, Iowa.

1922 — Wood Buffalo National Park, Northwest Territories, Canada, established.

1922
May — Last confirmed nest and eggs in Canada's plains and aspen parkland zone, Muddy Lake, near Unity, Saskatchewan.

1937
31 December — Aransas National Wildlife Refuge, Texas, established by executive order.

1939
15 May — Last confirmed fledged young in United States, reported from White Lake marshes, Vermilion Parish, Louisiana.

1940
August — Severe storm scattered White Lake residents, reducing the population from thirteen to six birds. The final wild survivor, Mac, died at Aransas NWR, 1950.

1940
Fall — Wild population estimated at thirty-two (26 in Texas, 6 in Louisiana).

1941
Fall — Josephine, so-called Queen of the Whooping Cranes, displayed in Audubon Park Zoo, New Orleans, after being injured in Evangeline Parish. In captivity, she was paired with two males (Pete and Crip); laid fifty-two eggs, twelve hatched, four lived at Audubon Park Zoo where she died 13 September 1965—the last survivor from Louisiana's nonmigratory population.

1941–42
Fall/Winter — Aransas population dropped to sixteen individuals.

1949
October — Famous Crip captured on Aransas NWR, paired with Josephine 1950–1965 (to produce Rusty 1950); then paired with Rosie, 1966–1971, and Ektu, 1976–1979. He died in San Antonio Zoo, 27 March 1979.

1950 — Wild population thirty-one (all in Texas).

1952 — Robert Porter Allen published pioneer monograph, *The Whooping Crane*. The Aransas population fell back to twenty-one (same as in 1943–44).

1954 — Nesting grounds discovered at Wood Buffalo N.P.

1956 — Rosie captured near Lampasas, Texas; died at San Antonio Zoo, 16 June 1971 (produced Tex 1967).

1960 — Wild population thirty-six.

1964 — Injured Canus taken from Wood Buffalo; moved to Patuxent Wildlife Research Center, 1966; sired numerous progeny, including hybrid Ghostbird.

1967 — The species is included on the federal list of endangered species drawn up under the 1966 Endangered Species Act.

1967 — First airlift of six eggs from Wood Buffalo N.P. to National Wildlife Research Center, Patuxent, Maryland, for artificial incubation. Transfers continued in 1968, 1969, 1971, and 1974 to present.

1970 — Wild population fifty-seven (in Texas); fourteen captive cranes at Patuxent.

1973 — Endangered Species Act (as amended) authorized preparation of a whooping crane recovery plan.

| 1975 | Transplant of fourteen eggs from Wood Buffalo to Grays Lake National Wildlife Refuge, Idaho, for placement under sandhill foster parents; young fledged, including Miracles (died 1982). Egg shipments continued 1976 to 1988. |

1975 — One of the first eggs (3) *laid* at Patuxent by a seven-year-old female hatched out Dawn.

1976 — Five eggs laid at Patuxent, two sent to Grays Lake. Tex moved from Patuxent to the International Crane Foundation, Baraboo, Wisconsin.

1977 — Efforts made to band all chicks in Wood Buffalo.

1979 — First eggs from Patuxent fostered to fledging stage at Grays Lake.

1980 — Wild population ninety-eight (78 in Texas, about 20 in New Mexico); twenty at Patuxent.

1980 — First U.S. *Recovery Plan* published.

1982 June — Gee Whiz born at Baraboo from Tex "paired" with ICF Director George Archibald. Tex dies 22 June.

1984 — Seven birds, mostly females, died at Patuxent of equine encephalitis, an uncommon mosquito-spread virus.

1984 — Errant chick Blue–White passes his winter off Aransas NWR at El Campo, Texas.

1986 — Canada-U.S. wild flock tops one hundred on the wintering grounds in Texas.

1986 December — U.S. *Recovery Plan* (revised) published.

1987 September–October — Three whoopers and thirteen other cranes died at Patuxent from a fungus-produced toxin in feed grain.

1988 — U.S. Recovery Team approves draft criteria for a captive crane flock in Canada. The aim is to have birds on a site by 1990.

1988 May — Two birds at Patuxent died and twenty-seven other whoopers were affected by possible food-contaminated toxins.

1988 Summer — Thirty-two nests discovered in Wood Buffalo National Park contained sixty-two eggs. Twelve eggs were flown to Grays Lake National Wildlife Refuge, and fifteen others were sent to Patuxent. Seventeen chicks were banded in Canada. Forty-seven cranes existed at Patuxent.

Notes

Preface

1. Theodore S. Van Dyke, *Game Birds at Home*, pp. 139–145, 141 (first quotation), 144 (second and third quotations), 145 (fourth and fifth quotations).

Introduction

1. A. Rutgers and K. A. Norris (eds.), *Encyclopedia of Aviculture*, 1: 251; John Pollard, *Birds in Greek Life and Myth*, pp. 83–84, 104, 110–111, 181–183; Norman Douglas, *Birds and Beasts of the Greek Anthology*, pp. 99–102; Ernest Ingersoll, *Birds in Legend, Fable, and Folklore*, pp. 89, 94, 170, 237; George Cansdale, *Animals of Bible Lands*, pp. 158–159.

2. Edward A. Armstrong, *The Life and Lore of the Bird*, pp. 115, 221, 235, 241; idem, "The Crane Dance in East and West," *Antiquity* 7 (1943): 71–76; Dorothy Britton and Tsuneo Hayashida, *The Japanese Crane*, pp. 11–13, 48 ff; Harold P. Stern, *Birds, Beasts, Blossoms, and Bugs*, pp. 3, 11, 26, 29, 153–154.

3. Paul A. Johnsgard, *Cranes of the World*, pp. 3–10, 77, 85 (quotation); Lawrence H. Walkinshaw, *Cranes of the World*; Carey Krajewski, personal communication, 28 June 1988.

4. Johnsgard, *Cranes of the World*, pp. 8–9; Robert P. Allen, *The Whooping Crane*, pp. 3–5, 51–64.

5. Johnsgard, *Cranes of the World*, pp. 131–133, 151–158, 197–200; Vladimir E. Flint and A. A. Kistchinski, "The Siberian Crane in Yakutia," in *Crane Research around the World*, ed. James C. Lewis and Hiroyuki Masatomi, pp. 136–145; Walkinshaw, *Cranes of the World*, pp. 144–161, 197–216, 236–249, reports Siberian's whistling voice as less penetrating than that of any *Grus*.

6. George W. Archibald et al., "Endangered Cranes," in *Crane Research around the World*, ed. James C. Lewis and Hiroyuki Masatomi, pp. 1–12; Lawrence H. Walkinshaw, "The Sandhill Cranes," in ibid., pp. 151–162, and *Cranes of the World*, p. 1 and passim.

7. Allen, *Whooping Crane*; Faith NcNulty, *The Whooping Crane*; Robert P. Allen, *On the Trail of Vanishing Birds*, pp. 29–59 passim; idem, "Whooping Cranes Fight for Survival," *National Geographic* 116 (1959): 650–669.

8. James C. Lewis, "The Whooping Crane," in *Audubon Wildlife Report, 1966*, ed. Robert L. Di Silvestro, pp. 659–676; Robert L. Simison, "Whooping Cranes Get a New Friend in Bid to Survive," *Wall Street Journal*, 25 February 1985. Lewis was the leader of all whooping crane workshops convened on this continent (Texas 1978, Wyoming 1981, Nebraska 1985, and Florida 1988). He edited papers delivered at the fourth Crane workshop held at Grand Island, Nebraska, in March 1985, and co-edited the papers presented at Sapporo's International Crane Symposium, *Crane Research around the World* (1981), including in the publication additional essays written between 1974 and 1981. The first International Crane Workshop was held in Baraboo, Wisconsin, 1975; the second in Sapporo, Japan, 1980; the third in Bharatpur, India, 1983; and the fourth in Qiqihar, China, 1987.

9. U.S. Fish and Wildlife Service, *Whooping Crane Recovery Plan*, p. 62; James C. Lewis, personal communication, 2 October 1987 and 10 March 1988.

1. Aransas Cranes

1. Jean Louis Berlandier, *Journey to Mexico during the Years 1826 to 1834*, trans. Sheila M. Ohlendorf, Josette M. Bigelow, and Mary M. Standifer, 2: 390–393.

2. James C. Duval, *Early Times in Texas*, p. 24.

3. Hobart Huson, *Refugio*, 1: 8–9; T. J. Cauley, "Early Meat Packing Plants in Texas," *Southwestern Political and Social Science Quarterly* 9 (1929): 464–478; Euroda Moore, "Recollections of Indianola," in *Indianola Scrap Book*, p. 110 (quotation).

4. Huson, *Refugio*, 2: 162–163; Charles H. Stevenson, "The Preservation of Fishery Products for Food," *Bulletin of the United States Fish Commission* 18 (1898): 335–563, esp. 539.

5. "The Storm of August 20, 1886," in *Indianola Scrap Book*, p. 139.

6. Lelia Seeligson, "History of Indianola," in *Indianola Scrap Book*, p. 29 (quotation); advertisement, *Texas Field and National Guardsman* 13 (1911): 217; Vinton Lee James, *Frontier and Pioneer*, p. 47; Robin W. Doughty, *Wildlife and Man in Texas*, pp. 101–102.

7. Captains John and Ned Mercer, newspaper clippings containing accounts from diaries, 1871–1879, in *Corpus Christi Caller*, Barker Texas History Center, 4L401, University of Texas, Austin.

8. Captain Flack, *A Hunter's Experiences in the Southern States of America*, pp. 276–277; idem, *The Texan Rifle-Hunter, or Field Sports on the Prairie*, pp. 220–221. The term "bugle crane" used by market hunters appears in James O. Stevenson and Richard E. Griffith, "Winter Life of the Whooping Crane," *Condor* 48 (1946): 173.

9. George J. Durham, "Game in Texas," in *Texas Almanac for 1868*, pp. 92–96.

10. N.A.T., "Game in Texas," in *Burke's Texas Almanac and Immigrant Guide for 1881*, pp. 38–41.

11. George B. Sennett, "Notes on the Ornithology of the Lower Rio Grande of Texas, from Observations Made during the Season of 1877," *Bulletin of the United States Geological Survey* 4 (1878): 1–66, esp. 61; idem, "Further Notes on the Ornithology," ibid., 5 (1879): 371–440, esp. 435.

12. Henry P. Attwater, "South Texas Bird Notes," in Attwater Papers, Barker Texas History Center, University of Texas, Austin.

13. Allen, *Whooping Crane*, pp. 14, 19; Van Dyke, *Game Birds at Home*, p. 134.

14. Allen, *Whooping Crane*, pp. 83, 75–78.

15. Ibid., pp. 76, 79, 29–32.

16. Ibid., pp. 69, 12; John J. Lynch, "A Field Biologist," in *Flyways*, ed. A. S. Hawkins et al., p. 38.

17. Allen, *Whooping Crane*, pp. 11–12.

18. Ibid., pp. 13, 35; George A. McCall, "Some Remarks on the Habits, etc.," *Proceedings of the Philadelphia Academy of Sciences* 5 (1851): 213–224, esp. 223.

19. Allen, *Whooping Crane*, pp. 35–36.

20. Ibid., p. 37; Pierre M. F. Piagès, "A Journey through Texas in 1767," trans. Corinna Steele, *El Campanario* 16 (1985): 1–28, esp. 18, 24.

21. William Gray, *From Virginia to Texas, 1835*, p. 109.

22. J. L. Baughman, "Texas Natural History," *Texas Game and Fish* 9 (September 1951): 21; John Russell Bartlett, *Personal Narrative of Explorations and Incidents in Texas, New Mexico, California, Sonora, and Chihuahua*, 2: 526–527.

23. Harry C. Oberholser, *The Bird Life of Texas*, 1: 286–288; Oberholser (Harry C.) Papers: Bird Life of Texas, original manuscript, pp. 3000–3999, Whooping Crane, pp. 2834–2849, Barker Texas History Center, 4W218, University of Texas, Austin; John K. Strecker, "The Birds of Texas: An Annotated Check-List," *Baylor Bulletin* 15 (1912): 18; George B. Benners, "A Collecting Trip in Texas," *Ornithologist and Oologist* 12 (1887): 83.

24. Frederick Law Olmsted, *A Journey through Texas*, pp. 135, 224.

25. Oberholser Papers, p. 2843; Allen, *Whooping Crane*, pp. 35–36.

26. Oberholser, *Birds of Texas* 1: 286 (he does not list a source for J. D. Mitchell); Allen, *Whooping Crane*, pp. 35–36, 50; Oliver Davie, *Nests and Eggs of North American Birds*, p. 97; Arthur Cleveland Bent, *Life Histories of North American Marsh Birds*, pp. 219–231, esp. 221; Richard Banks, "The Size of Early Whooping Crane Populations" (Draft, 1978), U.S. FWS, Whooping Crane Coordinator, File, Albuquerque, New Mexico.

27. "Establishing the Aransas Migratory Waterfowl Refuge," *Federal Register* 3 (5 January 1938): 13, pursuant to Migratory Bird Conservation Act, 45 Stat. 1222—although not listed, this first crane average included a portion of Calhoun County; Arthur F. Halloran, "Aransas Refuge Biological Records—27 Years in Review—March 1964," Aransas Wildlife Refuge, Files, p. 5, notes fourteen birds for 1937–38 and eighteen for 1938–39, when official records also place an additional eleven cranes in Louisiana, totalling twenty-nine; however, Walkinshaw, *Cranes of the World*, p. 329, goes as low as perhaps twelve birds for winter 1937–38.

28. See McNulty, *Whooping Crane*, pp. 95–97, and Aransas National Wildlife Refuge (hereafter ANWR), Narrative Report, 1 May–31 August 1950, p. 4.

29. June C. McNeill, ANWR, Narrative Report, 1 November 1938–31 January 1939, p. 2; James O. Stevenson, "Refuge Weekly Itinerary and Report Activities," ANWR, Files, by date.

30. Stevenson, "Refuge Weekly Itinerary," 2 October 1938, p. 5.

31. Ibid., 20 October, 6 November, and 21 December 1938.

32. Stevenson, ANWR, Narrative Report, Fiscal Year 1939, dated 13 July 1939, pp. 3, 7–8.

33. McNeill, ANWR, Narrative Report, December 1938–January 1939, Aransas Camp BF-1, February–March 1939, and August–September 1939.

34. Arthur F. Halloran and Julian A. Howard, "Aransas Refuge Wildlife Introductions," *Journal of Wildlife Management* 20 (1956): 460–461; ANWR, Narrative Report, 3–31 October 1938, p. 7, and Narrative Report, Fiscal Year 1938–1939, p. 8; Leroy G. Denman to J. O. Stevenson, 4 March 1939, ANWR, Files; Arthur F. Halloran, "Management of Deer and Cattle on the Aransas National Wildlife Refuge, Texas," *Journal of Wildlife Management* 7 (1943): 204, states that Denman took over management of the ranch in 1919, whereas Denman's letter to Stevenson refers to a loan made to previous owner Cyrus Lucas "about 1918–1919" and a takeover "about 1923."

35. Halloran and Howard, "Aransas Refuge," pp. 460–461; Stevenson, ANWR, Narrative Report, 1 November 1938–31 January 1939.

36. Halloran and Howard, "Aransas Refuge," p. 461; Arthur F. Halloran, "Aransas Refuge Biological Records to 1967," ANWR, Files, pp. 17, 19, 21–22, and passim.

37. Halloran, "Biological Records to 1967," p. 1; McNulty, *Whooping Crane*, p. 41; Stevenson and Griffith, "Winter Life of the Whooping Crane," p. 172.

38. James O. Stevenson, "Will Bugles Blow No More?" *Audubon Magazine* 45 (1943): 134–139; Stevenson and Griffith, "Winter Life of the Whooping Crane," p. 168.

39. Stevenson, ANWR, Narrative Report, Fiscal Year 1940, pp. 6–7; idem, Weekly Itinerary, 27 October 1939 and 27 January 1940; idem, "Will Bugles Blow No More?" p. 139; Earl Craven, "The Status of the Whooping Crane on the Aransas Refuge, Texas," *Condor* 48 (1946): 37–39.

40. McNulty, *Whooping Crane*, pp. 54–57; Stevenson, Weekly Itinerary, 5 June, 1939, 1 April, 19 April, and 2 July 1940.

41. McNulty, *Whooping Crane*, pp. 54–55.

42. Allen, *Whooping Crane*, p. 87; idem, *The Flame Birds*, pp. 112–113.

43. Details of Aransas nesting appear in Allen, *On the Trail of Vanishing Birds*, pp. 119–134, and *Whooping Crane*, pp. 177, 186–195, and McNulty, *Whooping Crane*, pp. 90–106. Roy Bedichek, *Karankaway Country*, pp. 26–35, describes captive pair behavior at Aransas.

44. Julian A. Howard, ANWR, Narrative Report, 1 May–31 August 1950, pp. 3–4, and addendum, 6 April and 29 May 1950.

45. McNulty, *Whooping Crane,* p. 18.

46. Howard, ANWR, Narrative Report, 1 January–30 April 1950, pp. 3–5, etc.; McNulty, *Whooping Crane,* pp. 96–97, provides details of Mac's capture and shipment to Texas.

47. McNulty, *Whooping Crane,* pp. 102–106.

48. Robert P. Allen, "Report on the Whooping Crane," *Texas Game and Fish,* September 1953, p. 13.

49. ANWR, Narrative Report, September–December 1954, pp. 3, 8.

50. Allen, *On the Trail of Vanishing Birds,* pp. 79–118; McNulty, *Whooping Crane,* p. 126. Details about the "Photoflash" project can be followed in the *Victoria Advocate,* 21, 23, 30 August and 4 October 1955.

51. McNulty, *Whooping Crane,* pp. 131–146, 148; ANWR, Narrative Report, 1 May–31 August 1957, pp. 2–3.

52. McNulty, *Whooping Crane,* pp. 149–155.

53. Ibid., p. 159; Allen, *Whooping Crane,* pp. 163–165, 215, 217, speaks about providing aquatic foods through habitat management.

54. Robert H. Shields and Earl L. Benham, "Farm Crops as Food Supplements for Whooping Cranes," *Journal of Wildlife Management* 33 (1969): 811–817.

55. Ibid., pp. 812–814.

56. Ibid., pp. 814–815.

57. Ibid., pp. 815–817.

58. Allen, *Whooping Crane,* p. 34; Shields and Benham, "Farm Crops," p. 817; ANWR, Narrative Report, 1967, pp. 23–25.

59. U.S. Fish and Wildlife Service, *Recovery Plan,* p. 5.

60. ANWR, Narrative Report, 1970, pp. 19–22.

61. Ibid., p. 22; E. Frank Johnson, "Aransas Whooping Cranes," *Blue Jay* 34 (December 1976): 220–228.

62. ANWR, Narrative Report, 1971, p. 5, 1972, p. 2, and 1976, pp. 5–6.

63. ANWR, Narrative Report, 1976, p. 7, and 1977, p. 13.

64. ANWR, Narrative Report, 1980, p. 14.

65. ANWR, Narrative Report, 1970, pp. 2, 6, 17, 1971, p. 9, 1972, pp. 6, 22, and 1973, Appendix A; George W. Bomar, *Texas Weather,* p. 226.

66. David R. Blankinship, "Studies of Whooping Cranes on the Wintering Grounds," in *Proceedings of International Crane Workshop,* ed. James C. Lewis, p. 200.

67. Ibid., pp. 204–205.

68. Allen, *Whooping Crane,* pp. 117, 119; Blankinship, "Studies of Whooping Cranes," p. 205.

69. "Matagorda Island, Texas, Proposed as Added Habitat for Whooping Cranes," U.S. Department of the Interior news release, 29 November 1974.

70. ANWR, Narrative Report, August–October 1941, p. 4; Stevenson, "Will Bugles Blow No More?" p. 138; McNulty, *Whooping Crane,* pp. 49–51.

71. Texas House of Representatives, House Study Group, "Whooping Cranes and Space Ships: The Matagorda Island Controversy," 30 November 1981, p. 7.

72. Ibid., pp. 8–11.

73. "Three Agencies Agree on Management of Federal and State Lands on Matagorda Island, Texas," United States Department of the Interior news release, 9 November 1982; "Matagorda Island Wildlife Management Area," in ANWR,

Narrative Report, 1983; U.S. Fish and Wildlife Service, *Wetland Preservation Program, Category B., Texas Gulf Coast,* p. A-7.

74. Texas House of Representatives, "Whooping Cranes," p. 12; Daniel Benedict, "The U.S. vs. Texas: Which Shall Sponsor the Whooping Crane?" *Christian Science Monitor,* 28 July 1982; ANWR, Narrative Report, 1986, p. 3.

75. "Matagorda Island," *Grus Americana* 27, no. 2 (June 1988): 4; Tom Stehn, "Whooping Cranes during the 1987–1988 Winter," ANWR, August 1988, p. 24.

2. The 1980s

1. ANWR, Narrative Report, 1980, pp. 21 (quotation), 18–19, and 1969, pp. 7–8; Halloran, "Biological Records to 1967," pp. 11–14; ANWR, Narrative Report, 1986, pp. 29–49.

2. ANWR, Narrative Report, 1980, p. 19 (quotation), and 1969, p. 7; Halloran, "Biological Records to 1967," pp. 11–16; Wayne H. McAlister and Martha K. McAlister, *Guidebook to the Aransas Wildlife Refuge,* pp. 87–97; David Mabie, Texas Parks and Wildlife Department, Rockport, personal communication, 21 March 1988.

3. ANWR, Narrative Report, 1969, pp. 8–9, 1976, p. 7, and 1977, p. 13; McAlister and McAlister, *Guidebook,* pp. 90–92.

4. ANWR, Narrative Report, 1976, p. 6.

5. ANWR, Narrative Report, 1981, p. 24, 1982, p. 38, 1985, p. 41, and 1986, pp. 52–53.

6. ANWR, Narrative Report, 1981, p. 29, and 1983, pp. 22, 24; for whooper survival, see Ernie Kuyt and J. Paul Goossen, "Survival, Age Composition, Sex Ratio, and Age at First Breeding of Whooping Cranes in Wood Buffalo National Park, Canada," in *Proceedings 1985 Crane Workshop,* ed. James C. Lewis, pp. 230–244, esp. Table 1, pp. 233–234.

7. ANWR, Narrative Report, 1983, p. 22, and 1984, p. 32.

8. ANWR, Narrative Report, 1982, p. 34, and 1983, pp. 17, 24; Howard E. Hunt, Thomas V. Stehn, and R. Douglas Slack, "Whooping Crane Mortality during the Winter of 1982–83," in *Proceedings 1985 Crane Workshop,* ed. James C. Lewis, pp. 219–220.

9. ANWR, Narrative Report, 1984, pp. 35 (quotation), 36.

10. Ibid., p. 36.

11. ANWR, Narrative Report, 1985, pp. 30–31, 34, 35.

12. Ibid., pp. 37–38.

13. Ibid., p. 38.

14. Ibid., pp. 38–40; ANWR, Narrative Report, 1986, p. 35.

15. ANWR, Narrative Report, 1986, pp. 31, 33, 36–38.

16. Ibid., pp. 38–40.

17 Felix Sanchez, "Red Tide Killed 22 Million Fish, State Estimates," *Corpus Christi Caller,* 7 November 1986.

18. ANWR, Narrative Report, 1986, pp. 40–43; Tom Stehn, "Whooping Cranes during the 1986–1987 Winter," July 1987, pp. 3, 15–17, ANWR, Files. The red tide is discussed in Texas A&M University, Sea Grant College Program, *Red Tide in Texas,* p. 4, and University of Texas, Marine Science Institute, *Newsletter* 3 (January 1987): 1.

19. ANWR, Narrative Report, 1986, pp. 43–45, 47; Stehn, "Whooping Cranes during the 1986–1987 Winter," pp. 17–18.

20. ANWR, Narrative Report, 1986, pp. 46–47; Stehn, "Whooping Cranes during the 1986–1987 Winter," p. 6, and personal communication.

21. Tom Stehn, "Whooping Crane Juveniles Wintering Away from Aransas," 1987, p. 3, ANWR, Files.

22. Ibid., pp. 1–2; Bruce C. Thompson, *Whooping Crane Monitoring in Open Sandhill Hunting Zones in Texas, 1984–85 Season,* pp. 8–9, attachments 3, 4; *Texas Parks and Wildlife News,* 1 August 1985, p. 2; ANWR, Narrative Report, 1985, pp. 37, 41.

23. Michael Lange, "Two Whooping Cranes Wintering in Brazoria County during the 1985–1986 Season," pp. 1–16, San Bernard NWR, 1985, in ANWR, Files; ANWR, Narrative Report, 1986, pp. 31, 47.

24. Tom Stehn, personal communication; ANWR, Narrative Report, 1986, p. 47; Tom Curtis, "Wayward Bird Finds Companion," *Dallas Times Herald,* 9 March 1986.

25. Tom Stehn, personal communication, November 1987; Ernie Kuyt, personal communication, September 1987.

26. Mary A. Bishop, "The Dynamics of Subadult Flocks of Whooping Cranes Wintering in Texas, 1978–79 through 1982–83," M.S. thesis in Wildlife and Fisheries Science, Texas A&M University, 1984, pp. 69–71.

27. Rod Drewien, personal communication, 12 March 1987; Bishop, "Dynamics of Subadult Flocks," pp. 76–78.

28. ANWR, Narrative Report, 1986, p. 48.

29. R. Douglas Slack and Howard E. Hunt, "The Effects of Various Burning and Grazing Treatments . . . ," draft of FWS contract no. 14-16-0002-82-220, Texas A&M University, College Station, 1986, unpaginated, see Figs. 7 and 10.

30. Ibid., see recommendations section.

31. Bishop, "Dynamics of Subadult Flocks," pp. 69, 98–103.

32. Stehn, "Whooping Cranes during the 1985–1986 Winter," pp. 4–5, 13, and Fig. 6, and personal communication.

33. Blankinship, "Studies of Whooping Cranes," p. 201; Tom Stehn and E. Frank Johnson, "Distribution of Winter Territories of Whooping Cranes on the Texas Coast," in *Proceedings 1985 Crane Workshop,* ed. James C. Lewis, p. 191.

34. Stehn and Johnson, "Distribution of Winter Territories," p. 188; Stehn, "Whooping Cranes during the 1985–1986 Winter," pp. 9, 11; Craven, "Status of the Whooping Crane," p. 38.

35. Stehn and Johnson, "Distribution of Winter Territories," pp. 183, 191; Stehn, "Whooping Cranes during the 1985–1986 Winter," pp. 10–11; air census data for 1986–87 (especially January–February 1987), ANWR, Files; Stehn, personal communication, 1 April 1988.

36. Stehn, personal communication, April 1988.

3. Canada and Radio Tracking

1. Robert Porter Allen (ed.), *A Report on the Whooping Crane's Northern Breeding Grounds,* pp. 1–6, p. 6 (first and second quotations), p. 11 (third quotation); see also Allen, *On the Trail,* pp. 79–80; Robert H. Smith, "From Tundra to Tropics," in *Flyways,* ed. A. S. Hawkins et al., pp. 179–180, 179 (quotation). Smith's recollection of his 1952 sighting of young does not agree with a letter he wrote to Allen, which Allen quotes in his 1956 *Report,* p. 11. It seems that the first chicks were noted in the 30 June 1954 chance discovery, not in 1952.

2. McNulty, *Whooping Crane,* pp. 123–124; Allen, *On the Trail,* pp. 214–224, adds details of his activities around Fort Smith and first unsuccessful attempts to get into nest areas.

3. Ernie Kuyt, "Population Status, Nest Site Fidelity, and Breeding Habitat of Whooping Cranes," in *Crane Research around the World,* ed. James C. Lewis and Hiroyuki Masatomi, pp. 119–125, and "Recent Clutch Size Data for Whooping Cranes including a Three-Egg Clutch," *Blue Jay* 34 (1976): 82–83; N. S. Novakowski, *Whooping Crane Population Dynamics on the Nesting Grounds, Wood Buffalo National Park, Northwest Territories, Canada;* Goossen, "Survival, Age Composition," pp. 230–244, provide recent data on CNAs and subadult summer areas.

4. Kuyt, "Population Status," pp. 119–129; idem, "Clutch Size, Hatching Success, and Survival of Whooping Crane Chicks, Wood Buffalo National Park, Canada," in *Crane Research around the World,* ed. James C. Lewis and Hiroyuki Masatomi, pp. 126–129, esp. 128; Roderick C. Drewien, "Banding Whooping Cranes in Wood Buffalo National Park," paper delivered at Whooping Crane Conservation Association Annual Meeting, Regina, Saskatchewan, 3 October 1987.

5. Kuyt and Goossen, "Survival, Age Composition," pp. 230–244; Ernie Kuyt, "Banding of Juvenile Whooping Cranes and Discovery of the Summer Habitat Used by Nonbreeders," in *Proceedings 1978 Crane Workshop,* ed. James C. Lewis, pp. 109–111; idem, "Whooping Cranes at Wood Buffalo National Park," paper presented at Whooping Crane Conservation Association Annual Meeting, Regina, Saskatchewan, 2 October 1987.

6. Drewien, "Banding Whooping Cranes."

7. Marshall A. Howe, "Habitat Use By Migrating Whooping Cranes in the Aransas–Wood Buffalo Corridor," in *Proceedings 1985 Crane Workshop,* ed. James C. Lewis, pp. 303–311.

8. Ernie Kuyt, "Whooping Crane Tracking Report, Segments 1–8, NWT to Aransas National Wildlife Refuge, September–October 1981," Canadian Wildlife Service Report, 1982, pp. 7–8; idem, "The Far North," Part I, *Nature Society News,* reprinted in *North Dakota Outdoors* 45 (1982): 4–11, p. 9 (quotation); Stephen Labuda, "A Whooping Crane Migration Study," pp. 1–3, ANWR, Files; ANWR, Narrative Report, 1981, pp. 29–30; George Vandel, "Migration of Radio-Monitored Whooping Crane Family," draft, pp. 30–31.

9. Kuyt, "The Far North," Part I, pp. 8–9, p. 9 (quotation); ANWR, Narrative Report, 1981, p. 30; Labuda, "Whooping Crane Migration," pp. 1–2.

10. Kuyt, "The Far North," Part I, pp. 9–10; Labuda, "Whooping Crane Migration," pp. 2–3; ANWR, Narrative Report, 1981, p. 30 (quotation).

11. Labuda, "Whooping Crane Migration," p. 3.

12. Kuyt, "The Far North," Part I, pp. 10–11.

13. Ibid.

14. Ibid.; Labuda, "Whooping Crane Migration," pp. 3–4.

15. Labuda, "Whooping Crane Migration," pp. 4–5; Kuyt, "The Far North," Part II, pp. 11–13; ANWR, Narrative Report, 1981, p. 32.

16. Kuyt, "The Far North," Part II, p. 13; ANWR, Narrative Report, 1981, p. 32.

17. Labuda, "Whooping Crane Migration," p. 1.

18. Ibid., p. 2; Tom Stehn, "Tailing the Whoopers," *Texas Parks and Wildlife* 43 (March 1985): 21. There is some disagreement about the date of Ms. Nyarling's discovery. The U.S.

Fish and Wildlife Service, *Recovery Plan,* p. 126, lists "October 15 or 16, 1982."

19. Labuda, "Whooping Crane Migration," pp. 3–4; John P. Ward and Stanley H. Anderson, "Monitoring Study, Whooping Crane, Final Report, Fall 1983," p. 16; Ernie Kuyt, personal communication, 22 March 1988.

20. Labuda, "Whooping Crane Migration," p. 4 and appendix.

21. Tom Stehn, "A Whooping Crane Migration Study—Spring 1983," ANWR, Files, [pp. 1–2]; "Flight of the Whooping Crane," National Geographic Special, John Huston narrator, 1983.

22. Stehn, "A Whooping Crane Migration Study," [p. 4].

23. Ibid., [p. 5]; Ernie Kuyt, "Radiotelemetry-Assisted Studies of Whooping Cranes in Wood Buffalo National Park Prior to Migration, Autumn 1983," Canadian Wildlife Service Report, 1984, pp. 14–15, idem, "Northward Radio-Tracking of a Whooping Crane Family Migrating from the Aransas National Wildlife Refuge to Wood Buffalo National Park, April 1, 1983," Canadian Wildlife Service Report, 1986, pp. 58, 61–63.

24. Carol Dickinson, "A Whooping Crane Migration Study—Fall 1983," ANWR, Files, [p. 1]; L. S. Young, "Autumn Migration of Subadult Whooping Cranes," pp. 1–3, Whooping Crane Coordinator Files, Albuquerque.

25. Dickinson, "A Whooping Crane Migration Study," [pp. 2–4]; Young, "Autumn Migration of Subadult Whooping Cranes," pp. 6–10; Ward and Anderson, "Monitoring Study," p. 17.

26. Ward and Anderson, "Monitoring Study," pp. 52–55; Marshall A. Howe, "Distribution, Habitat Use, Behavior, and Survival of Migrating Whooping Cranes in the Great Plains," Table 1, [pp. 41–42], Patuxent Wildlife Research Center, n.d.

27. Kuyt, "Radio-Tracking of a Whooping Crane Family . . . April–May 1984," pp. 19, 30, 38, 52.

28. Ibid., p. 58; Howe, "Distribution, Habitat Use," pp. 21–22, 29.

29. Howe, "Habitat Use by Migrating Whooping Cranes," pp. 303–322; idem, "Distribution, Habitat Use," p. 9 and passim.

30. Howe, "Distribution, Habitat Use," pp. 11–15, 25–27; Brian W. Johns, "Whooping Cranes in Saskatchewan," paper delivered at WCCA Meeting, 2 October 1987; Ward and Anderson, "Monitoring Study," p. 22.

31. Kenneth J. Strom, "Protecting Critical Whooping Crane Habitat on the Platte River, Nebraska," *Natural Areas Journal* 5 (1985): 8–13; Paul J. Currier, Gary R. Lingle, and John G. VanDerwalker, *Migratory Bird Habitat on the Platte and North Platte Rivers in Nebraska.*

4. Propagation and Release

1. David R. Zimmerman, *To Save a Bird in Peril,* p. 81 (quotation); Hubert D. Astley, "The Cranes," *Avicultural Magazine* 5 (1907): 347–353; Jean Delacour, *The Living Air,* pp. 55–66.

2. James W. Carpenter and Scott R. Derrickson, "The Role of Captive Propagation in Preserving Endangered Species," in *1981 Proceedings of the Nongame and Endangered Wildlife Symposium,* ed. Ron R. Odum and J. W. Guthrie, pp. 109–113.

3. Whooping Crane Conservation Association, *Who, Why, When, and What;* idem, *1986 Who's Who: A Biographical Mini-Sketch;* Ray C. Erickson, "Whooping Crane Studies at the Patuxent Wildlife Research Center," in *Proceedings First International Crane Workshop,* ed. James C. Lewis, pp. 166–176; Fred G. Bard, personal communication, 2 October 1987.

4. Erickson, "Whooping Crane Studies," pp. 170–171; U.S. Fish and Wildlife Service, "Master Plan: Patuxent Wildlife Research Center, Laurel, Maryland."

5. Erickson, "Whooping Crane Studies," pp. 171–174. The 0.84 figure represents the average for thirty-one years before 1967; however, Erickson noted that some periods exceeded this, e.g., 1939–1948 when the average population increase from a much lower total number of birds averaged 8.3 percent annually, higher than 6.3 percent for the first five years of egg taking.

6. Zimmerman, *To Save a Bird,* pp. 79, 87.

7. Linda Charlton, "Captive Whooping Cranes Have Chick," *New York Times,* 30 May 1975; Lawrence Feinburg, "Dawn Heralds New Day for Whooping Cranes," *Washington Post,* 1 June 1975.

8. "Whooping Crane Chick Dies after 15-Day Life," *Washington Post,* 17 June 1975.

9. Erickson, "Whooping Crane Studies," p. 173.

10. U.S. Fish and Wildlife Service, *Recovery Plan,* pp. 34–35.

11. Ray C. Erickson, "Captive Breeding of Whooping Cranes at the Patuxent Wildlife Research Center," in *Breeding Endangered Species in Captivity,* ed. R. D. Martin, pp. 99–114; idem, "Transport Case for Incubated Eggs," *Wildlife Society Bulletin* 9 (1981): 57–60; "Use of Suitcase Incubator," worksheet, Patuxent Wildlife Research Center.

12. Erickson, "Captive Breeding," pp. 105–106 (quotation); Patuxent Wildlife Research Center Propagation and Laboratory Investigations Section, Endangered Species Research Branch, "Protocol for Hand-Rearing Crane Chicks (1987)," pp. 2–4. George F. Gee, "Crane Reproductive Physiology and Conservation," *Zoo Biology* 2 (1983): 199–213, states on p. 204 that hatching temperature is set for 37°C with a highest relative humidity of 75–80 percent.

13. Cameron B. Kepler, "Captive Propagation of Whooping Cranes: A Behavioral Approach," in *Endangered Birds,* ed. Stanley A. Temple, pp. 231–241.

14. Erickson, "Captive Breeding," p. 106.

15. James W. Carpenter and Scott R. Derrickson, "Whooping Crane Mortality at the Patuxent Wildlife Research Center, 1966–1981," in *Proceedings 1981 Crane Workshop,* ed. James C. Lewis, pp. 175–179.

16. Scott R. Derrickson and James W. Carpenter, "Whooping Crane Production at the Patuxent Wildlife Research Center, 1967–1981," *Proceedings 1981 Crane Workshop,* ed. James C. Lewis, pp. 190–198.

17. Kepler, "Captive Propagation," pp. 235–236; Johnsgard, *Cranes of the World,* pp. 26–27, 192–193.

18. Kepler, "Captive Propagation," pp. 236–238; U.S. Fish and Wildlife Service, *Recovery Plan,* p. 35; Gee, "Crane Reproductive Physiology," p. 205.

19. Kepler, "Captive Propagation," p. 238.

20. C. Larue, "Increasing Fertility of Crane Eggs," *Avicultural Magazine* 86 (1980): 10–15.

21. George F. Gee and Stanley A. Temple, "Artificial Insemination for Breeding Non-Domestic Birds," in *Symposium of the Zoological Society* (London) 43 (1978): 51–72.

22. George F. Gee, "Avian Artificial Insemination and Semen Preservation," in *Proceedings of the 1983 Symposium on Breeding Birds in Captivity,* ed. A. C. Risser and F. S. Todd, pp. 375–398.

23. Derrickson and Carpenter, "Whooping Crane Production," p. 193 (quotation).

24. George F. Gee, Murray R. Bakst and Thomas J. Sexton, "Cryogenic Preservation of Semen from the Greater Sandhill Crane," *Journal of Wildlife Management* 49 (1985): 480–484.

25. Jack Challem, "Lab Dusts for 'Genetic Fingerprints': Researchers Study Endangered Whooping Cranes," *Newsbulletin* (Los Alamos National Laboratory) 8 (25 March, 1988); reprinted in *Grus Americana* 27 (June 1988): 5; "For the Birds," *Scientific American* 258 (June 1988): 32–33.

26. Roderick C. Drewien, Whooping Crane Transplant Experiment, Grays Lake, Idaho, Cooperative Wildlife Research Unit, Progress Report No. 7, July–September 1976, p. 14, and No. 8, October–December 1976, pp. 21–22.

27. Roderick C. Drewien, Scott R. Derrickson, and Elwood G. Bizeau, "Experimental Release of Captive Parent-Reared Greater Sandhill Cranes at Grays Lake Refuge, Idaho," in *Proceedings 1981 Crane Workshop,* ed. James C. Lewis, pp. 99–111; Rod Drewien, personal communication, 10 May 1988.

28. Drewien, Derrickson, and Bizeau, "Experimental Release," pp. 99–111; Drewien, personal communication.

29. Elwood G. Bizeau, Thomas V. Schumacher, Roderick C. Drewien, and Wendy M. Brown, "An Experimental Release of Captive-Reared Greater Sandhill Cranes," in *Proceedings 1985 Crane Workshop,* ed. James C. Lewis, pp. 78–88.

30. Bizeau et al., "Experimental Release," pp. 85–88.

31. Stephen A. Nesbitt, "Notes on the Suitability of Captive-Reared Sandhill Cranes for Release into the Wild," in *Proceedings 1978 Crane Workshop,* ed. James C. Lewis, pp. 85–88.

32. Stephen A. Nesbitt, "Status of Sandhill and Whooping Crane Studies in Florida," in *Proceedings 1985 Crane Workshop,* ed. James C. Lewis, pp. 213–216; Mary Anne Bishop and Michael W. Collopy. "Productivity of Florida Sandhill Cranes on Three Sites in Central Florida," in ibid., pp. 257–263.

33. Phillip J. Zwank and Scott R. Derrickson, "Gentle Release of Captive, Parent-Reared Sandhill Cranes into the Wild," in *Proceedings 1981 Crane Workshop,* ed. James C. Lewis, pp. 112–116; Jacob M. Valentine, "Safeguarding Mississippi's Last Cranes," *ICF Bugle* 12 (1986): 2–3.

34. Jacob M. Valentine, "Recovery Plan for the Mississippi Sandhill Crane, *Grus canadensis pulla,*" and Attachment #1, 11 September 1986; Janet L. McMillen, David H. Ellis, and Dwight G. Smith, "The Role of Captive Propagation in the Recovery of the Mississippi Sandhill Crane," *Endangered Species Technical Bulletin* 12, nos. 5–6 (1987): 6–8; Phillip J. Zwank and Charlotte D. Wilson, "Survival of Captive, Parent-Reared Mississippi Sandhill Cranes Released on a Refuge," *Conservation Biology Journal* 1 (1987): 165–168.

35. Robert Horwich, "Reintroduction of Sandhill Cranes to the Wild," *ICF Bugle* 12 (1986): 1, 4–5, and personal communication, 28 June, 1987.

36. Horwich, personal communication, 28 June, 1987.

37. George W. Archibald and Debra L. Viess, "Captive Propagation at the International Crane Foundation, 1973–78," in *Proceedings 1978 Crane Workshop,* ed. James C. Lewis, pp. 51–73; George Archibald, personal communication, 27 June, 1987. Aspects of Archibald's biography appear in "ICF Tour Guide/Chick Parent Training Manual."

38. Georgette K. Maroldo, "Crip: The Constant Dancer," *Blue Jay* 38 (1980): 147–161, p. 158 (first quotation), p. 159 (second quotation).

39. "Fred and Tex," *Grus Americana* 18, no. 2 (June 1979): 3–4; "The Whoopers Arrive," *Brolga Bugle* [changed to *ICF Bugle* in 1982] 2 (Spring 1976): 1; "Easter Eggs," ibid. 3 (Spring 1977): 1; "Three Arrivals in White," ibid. 4 (Winter 1978): 1; Mike Putnam, "Aviculture Wrap-Up," ibid. 6 (October 1980): 2; George W. Archibald, "Gee Whiz! ICF Hatches a Whooper," *ICF Bugle* 8 (July 1982): 1, 4; Ron Sauey, "Of Cranes, and 'Coons, and Red-boned Hounds," ibid., pp. 1, 4. Faith McNulty, *Peeping in the Shell,* describes the hatching of the ICF male crane in a children's story.

40. International Crane Foundation, Guide to the Johnson Exhibit Pod.

41. Drewien, Whooping Crane Transplant Experiment, Progress Report No. 17, March 1981–March 1982, pp. 32–40.

42. Drewien, Whooping Crane Transplant Experiment, Progress Report No. 18, April 1982–April 1983, pp. 8–10.

5. Second Flock in Idaho

1. Cited by Peter T. Harstad and Max Pavesic, "The Lander Trail Report," in U.S. Fish and Wildlife Service, *Grays Lake NWR Master Plan,* 1982, Appendix, 9.19.

2. Roderick C. Drewien, "Ecology of Rocky Mountain Greater Sandhill Cranes," Ph.D. dissertation, University of Idaho, 1973, p. 152; Roderick C. Drewien and Elwood G. Bizeau, "Status and Distribution of Greater Sandhill Cranes in the Rocky Mountains," *Journal of Wildlife Management* 38 (1974): 720–742; James C. Lewis, "Sandhill Crane," in *Management of Migratory Shore and Upland Game Birds in North America,* ed. Glen C. Sanderson, pp. 4–43. Recent population estimates come from Roderick C. Drewien, Whooping Crane Cross-Fostering Experiment, Progress Report No. 86-2, March–April 1986, p. 4.

3. U.S. Fish and Wildlife Service, *Grays Lake NWR Master Plan.*

4. Drewien, Whooping Crane Egg Transplant Experiment, Report No. 1, pp. 1–7.

5. Drewien, Report No. 2, p. 2.

6. Ibid., p. 6.

7. Ibid., p. 1; idem, Report No. 1, p. 7, and Report No. 3, pp. 3, 9.

8. Drewien, Report No. 3, pp. 4–5, Tables 1 and 2; idem, Progress Report No. 4, pp. 1–2, Table 1 (hereafter P.R.).

9. Drewien, P.R. No. 4, pp. 5–7, 10–11.

10. Ibid., pp. 9, 12, 15, 16 (quotation).

11. Drewien, P.R. No. 5, pp. 1–3, 7, 9, 13.

12. Drewien, P.R. No. 6, pp. 1–2; P.R. No. 7, pp. 1–4.

13. Drewien, P.R. No. 5, p. 9 (quotation); P.R. No. 6, pp. 6–7; P.R. No. 7, pp. 2–3, Table 1.

14. Drewien, P.R. No. 6, p. 7; P.R. No. 7, pp. 4–5; P.R. No. 8, pp. 3, 27, 16, 13, 27; P.R. No. 9, p. 13.

15. Drewien, P.R. No. 8, p. 20; P.R. No. 9, pp. 3, 14; P.R. No. 8, p. 20; P.R. No. 9, p. 14.

16. Drewien, P.R. No. 9, pp. 9–10; P.R. No. 10, pp. 4–5.

17. Drewien, P.R. No. 10, pp. 5, 18, 6–8; P.R. No. 11, p. 3.

18. Drewien, P.R. No. 12, pp. 1, 19, 9–10; P.R. No. 13, pp. 22, 8, 10–12; P.R. No. 14, pp. 2–3.

19. Drewien, P.R. No. 12, pp. 1, 19; P.R. No. 13, pp. 2, 7–8, 10–12, 24; P.R. No. 14, pp. 2–4.

20. Drewien, P.R. No. 14, pp. 13–14, 25, 26; P.R. No. 15, pp. 32, 3, 15–17; P.R. No. 16, p. 17.

21. Drewien, P.R. No. 17, pp. 32, 34, 27; P.R. No. 16, p. 33; P.R. No. 17, pp. 3–4, 6–7, 26, 32–35.

22. Drewien, P.R. No. 17, pp. 35–41; P.R. No. 16, p. 17; P.R. No. 17, pp. 24–25, 6–10, 69–72.

23. Drewien, P.R. No. 18, pp. 6–8; P.R. No. 17, p. 34; Drewien, personal communication, 2 October 1987.

24. Rod Drewien, "Whooping Crane Foster Parent Experiment," paper delivered at Whooping Crane Conservation Association, Regina, Saskatchewan, 2 October 1987; U.S. Fish and Wildlife Service, Recovery Plan, pp. 41–43.

25. Roderick C. Drewien et al., "The Whooping Crane Cross-Fostering Experiment: The Role of Animal Damage Control," in Proceedings of the Eastern Wildlife Damage Control Conference, pp. 7–8; Drewien, P.R. No. 11, p. 5.

26. Drewien et al., "Whooping Crane Cross-Fostering," pp. 10–11, 13, 16–17; Drewien, P.R. No. 11, pp. 4–10.

27. Drewien et al., "Whooping Crane Cross-Fostering," p. 10; Drewien, P.R. No. 13, pp. 13–14, and P.R. No. 14, pp. 5–8, 15, 11.

28. Drewien, P.R. No. 14, p. 19; P.R. No. 15, pp. 19–27.

29. Drewien, P.R. No. 15, pp. 29–30; Ronald M. Windingstad, Harry E. Stiles, and Roderick C. Drewien, "Whooping Crane Preyed Upon by Golden Eagle," Auk 98 (1981): 393–394; Jean-Marie Thiolley, "La Migration des Grues a travers l'Himalaya et la Predation par les Aigles Royaux," Alauda 47 (1979): 83–92.

30. Drewien, P.R. No. 18, p. 16; Drewien and Brown, P.R. No. 19, pp. 14–15.

31. Drewien, P.R. No. 86-2, p. 7; P.R. 86-3, pp. 3–4; P.R. 86-4, p. 3; Jim Lewis, personal communication, September 1987.

32. Oak Ridge Associated Universities, A Proceedings: Impacts of Transmission Lines on Birds in Flight.

33. Wendy M. Brown, Roderick C. Drewien, and Elwood G. Bizeau, "Mortality of Cranes and Waterfowl from Powerline Collisions in the San Luis Valley, Colorado," in Proceedings 1985 Crane Workshop, ed. James C. Lewis, pp. 128–136.

34. Drewien, P.R. No. 4, pp. 13–15.

35. Drewien, P.R. No. 8, pp. 8–15; P.R. No. 12, pp. 11–13.

36. Drewien, P.R. No. 4, p. 14; P.R. No. 12, 15–16.

37. Drewien, P.R. No. 86-1, pp. 2, 4; P.R. No. 86-2, p. 7.

38. Drewien, P.R. No. 86-1, p. 2; Nolan Hester, "Whoopers in Trouble," Impact (Albuquerque Journal Magazine), 24 February 1987, pp. 4–7, 14.

39. Drewien and Brown, P.R. No. 86-5, pp. 1–3, 7–8; P.R. No. 86-6, pp. 12–14.

40. Drewien and Brown, P.R. No. 86-5, pp. 1, 6–7; P.R. No. 86-6, pp. 3, 13–14.

41. Drewien and Brown, P.R. No. 86-6, pp. 3, 8–13.

42. Drewien, P.R. No. 18, pp. 2–3, 64–65.

43. Drewien, P.R. 86-1, p. 5; P.R. 86-2, pp. 5–6; P.R. 86-3, pp. 2, 42–44.

44. Drewien and Brown, P.R. 87-1, pp. 1–2.

45. James W. Carpenter, "An Outline of the Treatment and Control of Crane Parasites," in Proceedings 1978 Crane Workshop, ed. James C. Lewis, p. 103.

46. S. Bret Snyder et al., "Pasteurella Multocida Infection in a Whooping Crane Associated with an Avian Cholera Outbreak," in Proceedings 1985 Crane Workshop, ed. James C. Lewis, pp. 149–155; Jon D. Kauffeld, "An Avian Cholera Epizootic among Sandhill Cranes in Colorado," ibid., pp. 145–148; Bosque del Apache NWR, "Annual Narrative Report, Calendar Year 1984," pp. 17–18, 23.

47. Snyder et al., "Pasteurella Multocida," pp. 150–151; Bosque del Apache National Wildlife Refuge, Annual Narrative Report, Calendar Year 1985, pp. 14, 24.

48. Bosque del Apache NWR, Annual Narrative Report, Calendar Year 1984, pp. 16–18; Drewien and Brown, P.R. No. 19, Table 1, p. 21; Drewien, "Whooping Crane Foster Experiment"; James C. Lewis, personal communication, March 1988.

49. Drewien, P.R. 86-3, pp. 5–7; P.R. 86-4, pp. 5–8; Drewien and Brown, P.R. 86-5, pp. 3–6; P.R. 87-3, pp. 2–4; P.R. 87-4, pp. 3–4; Drewien, "Whooping Crane Foster Experiment."

50. Drewien and Brown, P.R. No. 19, pp. 10–11 (quotations), and P.R. 87-4, p. 3.

Conclusion

1. ANWR, Narrative Report, 1969, p. 24, noted 13,000 registered visitors in 1961, whereas, the report for 1986, p. 80, reported 69,071, a 12 percent increase over the previous year despite the presence of red tide in early fall. Also see McAlister and McAlister, Guidebook, pp. 4–5.

2. Tom Stehn, "Impacts of the Gulf Intracoastal Waterway on the Endangered Whooping Crane," paper delivered at 1988 Crane Workshop, February 1988, p. 1; ANWR, Narrative Report, Fiscal Year 1940, pp. 6–7.

3. Allen, The Flame Birds, p. 133; ANWR, Refuge Weekly Itinerary," 22–29 October, 16 November 1939; ANWR, Narrative Report, February–April 1940, May–July, 1949, and May–July 1941, p. 3 (quotation).

4. Stehn, "Impacts of the Gulf Intracoastal Waterway," pp. 3–6, 8; U.S. Fish and Wildlife Service, Recovery Plan, pp. 71–72, 75–76.

5. U.S. Fish and Wildlife Service, Preliminary Survey of Contaminant Issues of Concern on National Wildlife Refuges, p. A-140 (quotation); Stehn, "Impacts of the Gulf Intracoastal Waterway," pp. 12–13.

6. Bruce Thompson and Ron George, "Minimizing Conflicts between Migratory Game Bird Hunters," in Proceedings 1985 Crane Workshop, ed. James C. Lewis, pp. 58–68.

7. Ibid., pp. 59–61, 67; Harvey W. Miller, "Hunting in the Management of Mid-Continent Sandhill Cranes," in Proceedings 1985 Crane Workshop, ed. James C. Lewis, pp. 39–46; Paul M. Konrad, "Expanded Sandhill Crane Hunting in the Dakotas and Oklahoma Threatens Endangered Whooping Cranes," in ibid., pp. 69–77.

8. Gary R. Lingle, "Status of Whooping Crane Migration Habitat within the Great Plains of North America," in *Proceedings 1985 Crane Workshop,* ed. James C. Lewis, pp. 331–340, esp. p. 338; U.S. Fish and Wildlife Service, *Recovery Plan,* p. 103; Currier, Lingle, and VanDerwalker, *Migratory Bird Habitat;* Strom, "Protecting Critical Whooping Crane Habitat."

9. Canadian Wildlife Service, "A Draft Plan for the Conservation of Whooping Cranes in Canada," September 1986, Appendix 1, "Memorandum of Understanding," pp. 35–42, p. 18 (quotation); James C. Lewis, personal communication, 10 March 1988.

10. Canadian Wildlife Service, "Draft Plan," p. 11 (Table 1, Composition of WBNP Whooping Cranes, 1966–1985).

11. I am indebted for these sentiments to an important statement made by Erazim Kohak (*The Embers and the Stars: A Philosophical Inquiry into the Moral Sense of Nature,* pp. 210–214), who drew my attention to Whitman's *Song of Myself* in regard to animals. I am indebted to James C. Lewis for his details about banding, personal communication, 10 March 1988.

Bibliography

Advertisement. *Texas Field and National Guardsman* 13 (1911): 217.

Allen, Robert P. *The Flame Birds*. New York: Dodd, Mead, 1947.

———. *On the Trail of Vanishing Birds*. New York: McGraw-Hill, 1957.

———. "Report on the Whooping Crane." *Texas Game and Fish*, September 1953, p. 13.

———, ed. *A Report on the Whooping Crane's Northern Breeding Grounds*. Supplement to Research Report No. 3, *The Whooping Crane*. New York: National Audubon Society, 1956.

———. *The Whooping Crane*. Research Report No. 3. New York: National Audubon Society, 1952.

———. "Whooping Cranes Fight for Survival." *National Geographic* 116 (November 1959): 650–669.

Aransas National Wildlife Refuge. Annual Narrative Report. Refuge Files.
3–31 October 1938.
1 November 1938–31 January 1939.
Fiscal Year 1938–1939.
Fiscal Year 1939.
February–April 1940.
Fiscal Year 1940.
May–July 1941.
August–October 1941.
May–July 1949.
1 January–30 April 1950.
1 May–31 August 1950 and addendum.
September–December 1954.
1 May–31 August 1957.
1967.
1969.
1970.
1971.
1972.
1973.
1976.
1977.
1980.
1981.
1982.
1983.
1984.
1985.
1986.

———. Annual Report. Civilian Conservation Corps, Aransas Camp BF-1. Refuge Files.
December 1938–January 1939.
February–March 1939.
August–September 1939.

———. Leroy G. Denman to J. O. Stevenson, 4 March 1939. Refuge Files.

———. "Nesting of Josephine and Crip." Aransas Log, May 1950. Refuge Files.

Archibald, George W. "Crane Taxonomy as Revealed by the Unison Call." In *Proceedings First International Crane Workshop*, ed. James C. Lewis, pp. 225–239.

———. "Gee Whiz! ICF Hatches a Whooper." *ICF Bugle* 8 (July 1982): 1, 4.

———. "Methods for Breeding and Rearing Cranes in Captivity." In *1974 International Zoo Yearbook*, 14: 147–155. London: Zoological Society of London, 1974.

Archibald, George W., et al. "Endangered Cranes." In *Crane Research around the World*, ed. James C. Lewis and Hiroyuki Masatomi, pp. 1–12.

Archibald, George W., and Claire M. Mirande. "Population Status and Management Efforts for Endangered Cranes." *Transactions of the 50th North American Wildlife and Natural Resources Conference* 50 (1985): 586–602.

Archibald, George W., and Roger F. Pasquier, eds. *Proceedings 1983 International Crane Workshop*. Baraboo, Wis.: International Crane Foundation, 1987.

Archibald, George W., and Debra L. Viess. "Captive Propagation at the International Crane Foundation, 1973–78." In *Proceedings 1978 Crane Workshop*, ed. James C. Lewis, pp. 51–73.

Armstrong, Edward A. "The Crane Dance in East and West." *Antiquity* 7 (1943): 71–76.

———. *The Life and Lore of the Bird: In Nature, Art, Myth, and Literature*. New York: Crown, 1975.

Astley, Hubert D. "The Cranes." *Avicultural Magazine* 5 (1907): 347–353.

Attwater, Henry P. "South Texas Bird Notes." Attwater Papers, Barker Texas History Center, University of Texas, Austin.

Baker, J. A. *The Peregrine*. London: Collins, 1967.

Banks, Richard. "The Size of Early Whooping Crane Populations." Draft, 1978. Fish and Wildlife Service, Whooping Crane Coordinator File, Albuquerque, New Mexico.

Bard, Fred G. [Canadian Wildlife Service (retired)]. Personal communication, 2 October 1987.

Bartlett, John Russell. *Personal Narrative of Explorations and Incidents in Texas, New Mexico, California, Sonora, and Chihuahua*. 2 vols. Chicago: Rio Grande Press, 1965.

Baughman, J. L. "Texas Natural History." *Texas Game and Fish* 9 (September 1951): 14–16.

Bedford, Duchess of. "Cranes at Woburn Park." *Avicultural Magazine* 6 (1907): 26.

Bedichek, Roy. *Karánkaway Country*. Austin: University of Texas Press, 1950.

Benedict, Daniel. "The U.S. vs. Texas: Which Shall Sponsor the Whooping Crane?" *Christian Science Monitor*, 28 July 1982.

Benners, George B. "A Collecting Trip in Texas." *Ornithologist and Oologist* 12 (1887): 83.

Bent, Arthur Cleveland. *Life Histories of North American Marsh Birds*. Bulletin 135, U.S. National Museum [1925], pp. 219–231. New York: Dover, 1963.

Berlandier, Jean Louis. *Journey to Mexico during the Years 1826 to 1834*. Trans. Sheila M. Ohlendorf, Josette M. Bigelow, and Mary M. Standifer. 2 vols. Austin: Texas State Historical Association, 1980.

Biederman, B. M., et al. "Genome of the Whooping Crane." *Journal of Heredity* 73 (1982): 145–146.

Binkley, Clark S., and Richard S. Miller. "Population Characteristics of the Whooping Crane, *Grus americana*." *Canadian Journal of Zoology* 61 (1983): 2768–2776.

Bishop, Mary A. "The Dynamics of Subadult Flocks of Whooping Cranes Wintering in Texas, 1978–79 through 1982–83." M.S. in Wildlife and Fisheries Science, Texas A&M University, College Station, 1984.

Bishop, Mary A., and David R. Blankinship. "Dynamics of Subadult Flocks of Whooping Cranes at Aransas National Wildlife Refuge, Texas, 1978–1981." In *Proceedings 1981 Crane Workshop*, ed. James C. Lewis, pp. 180–189.

Bishop, Mary Anne, and Michael W. Collopy. "Productivity of Florida Sandhill Cranes on Three Sites in Central Florida." In *Proceedings 1985 Crane Workshop*, ed. James C. Lewis, pp. 257–263.

Bizeau, Elwood G., Thomas V. Schumacher, Roderick C. Drewien, and Wendy M. Brown. "An Experimental Release of Captive-Reared Greater Sandhill Cranes." In *Proceedings 1985 Crane Workshop*, ed. James C. Lewis, pp. 78–88.

Blaauw, F. E. *A Monograph of the Cranes*. Leiden: Brill, 1897.

Blankinship, David R. [biologist]. Personal communication, 25 November 1986.

———. "Studies of Whooping Cranes on the Wintering Grounds." In *Proceedings First International Crane Workshop*, ed. James C. Lewis, pp. 197–206.

Bomar, George W. *Texas Weather*. Austin: University of Texas Press, 1983.

Bosque del Apache National Wildlife Refuge. Annual Narrative Report, Calendar Year 1985. Bosque del Apache, New Mexico.

Boyce, Mark S. "Time-Series Analysis and Forecasting of the Aransas/Wood Buffalo Whooping Crane Population." In *Proceedings 1985 Crane Workshop*, ed. James C. Lewis, pp. 1–9.

Boyce, Mark S., and Richard S. Miller. "Ten-Year Periodicity in Whooping Crane Census." *Auk* 102 (July 1985): 658–660.

Britton, Dorothy, and Tsuneo Hayashida. *The Japanese Crane: Bird of Happiness*. Tokyo: Kodansha International, 1981.

Brown, Wendy M., Roderick C. Drewien, and Elwood G. Bizeau. "Mortality of Cranes and Waterfowl from Powerline Collisions in the San Luis Valley, Colorado." In *Proceedings 1985 Crane Workshop*, ed. James C. Lewis, pp. 128–136.

Canadian Wildlife Service. *Canadian Whooping Crane Recovery Plan*. Ottawa: Minister of Supply and Services, 1987.

———. "A Draft Plan for the Conservation of Whooping Cranes in Canada." Ottawa, 1986.

Cansdale, George. *Animals of Bible Lands*. London: Paternoster Press, n.d.

Carpenter, James W. "Cranes (Order Gruiformes)." In *Zoo and Wild Animal Medicine*, ed. Murray E. Fowler, pp. 316–326.

———. "Diseases in Captive Cranes Caused by Mycotoxin-Contaminated Feed." Paper delivered at Fifth North American Crane Workshop, Kissimmee Prairie, Florida, 22–25 February 1988.

———. "An Outline of the Treatment and Control of Crane Parasites." In *Proceedings 1978 Crane Workshop*, ed. James C. Lewis, pp. 101–108.

——— [Endangered Species Program, Patuxent Wildlife Research Center]. Personal communication, June 1987; December 1987; February 1988.

———. "Species Decline: A Perspective on Extinction, Recovery, and Propagation." *Zoo Biology* 2 (1983): 165–178.

Carpenter, James W., and Scott R. Derrickson. "The Role of Captive Propagation in Preserving Endangered Species." In *1981 Proceedings of the Nongame and Endangered Wildlife Symposium*, ed. Ron R. Odum and J. W. Guthrie, pp. 109–113.

———. "Whooping Crane Mortality at the Patuxent Wildlife Research Center, 1966–1981." In *Proceedings 1981 Crane Workshop*, ed. James C. Lewis, pp. 175–179.

Cauley, T. J. "Early Meat Packing Plants in Texas." *Southwestern Political and Social Science Quarterly* 9 (1929): 464–478.

Challem, Jack. "Lab Dusts for 'Genetic Fingerprints': Researchers Study Endangered Whooping Cranes." *Newsbulletin* (Los Alamos National Laboratory) 8 (25 March 1988); reprinted *Grus Americana* 27 (June 1988): 5.

Charlton, Linda. "Captive Whooping Cranes Have Chick." *New York Times*, 30 May 1975.

Craven, Earl. "The Status of the Whooping Crane on the Aransas Refuge, Texas." *Condor* 48 (1946): 37–39.

Currier, Paul J., Gary R. Lingle, and John G. VanDerwalker. *Migratory Bird Habitat on the Platte and North Platte Rivers in Nebraska*. Grand Island: Platte River Whooping Crane Critical Habitat Maintenance Trust, 1985.

Curtis, Tom. "Wayward Bird Finds Companion." *Dallas Times Herald*, 9 March 1986.

Davie, Oliver. *Nests and Eggs of North American Birds*. Columbus, Ohio: Hahn and Adair, 1886.

Delacour, Jean. *The Living Air: The Memoirs of an Ornithologist*. London: Country Life, 1966.

Derrickson, Scott R., and James W. Carpenter. "Whooping Crane Production at the Patuxent Wildlife Research Center, 1967–1981." In *Proceedings 1981 Crane Workshop*, ed. James C. Lewis, pp. 190–198.

Dickinson, Carol. "A Whooping Crane Migration Study—Fall 1983." Aransas National Wildlife Refuge, Refuge Files.

Didiuk, Andrew. "Whooping Cranes in Manitoba?" *Blue Jay* 34 (1976): 234–236.

Doughty, Robin W. *Wildlife and Man in Texas*. College Station: Texas A&M University Press, 1983.

Douglas, Norman. *Birds and Beasts of the Greek Anthology*. London: Chapman and Hall, 1928.

Drewien, Roderick C. "Banding Whooping Cranes in Wood Buffalo National Park." Paper delivered at Whooping Crane Conservation Association Annual Meeting, Regina, Saskatchewan, 3 October 1987.

———. "Ecology of Rocky Mountain Greater Sandhill Cranes." Ph.D. dissertation, University of Idaho, 1973.

——— [biologist, Idaho Cooperative Wildlife Unit and U.S. Fish and Wildlife Service]. Personal communication, 1 October 1986; 12 March 1987; October 1987; February, 1988; etc.

———. Whooping Crane Cross-Fostering Experiment.
Progress Report No. 86-1, January–February 1986.
Progress Report No. 86-2, March–April 1986.
Progress Report No. 86-3, May–June 1986.
Progress Report No. 86-4, July–August 1986.

———. Whooping Crane Egg Transplant Experiment, Grays Lake, Idaho, Cooperative Wildlife Research Unit, College of Forestry and Range Sciences, University of Idaho, Moscow.
Report No. 1, May–June 1975.
Report No. 2, July 1975.
Report No. 3, August and September, 1975.

———. "Whooping Crane Foster Parent Experiment." Paper delivered at Whooping Crane Conservation Association Annual Meeting, Regina, Saskatchewan, 2 October 1987.

———. Whooping Crane Transplant Experiment.
Progress Report No. 4, October–December 1975.
Progress Report No. 5, January–March 1976.
Progress Report No. 6, April–June 1976.
Progress Report No. 7, July–September 1976.
Progress Report No. 8, October–December 1976.
Progress Report No. 9, January–March 1977.
Progress Report No. 10, April–June 1977.
Progress Report No. 11, July–September 1977.
Progress Report No. 12, October–December 1977.
Progress Report No. 13, January–June 1978.
Progress Report No. 14, July–December 1978.
Progress Report No. 15, January–November 1979.
Progress Report No. 16, November 1979–March 1981.
Progress Report No. 17, March 1981–March 1982.
Progress Report No. 18, April 1982–April 1983.

Drewien, Roderick C., et al. "The Whooping Crane Cross-Fostering Experiment: The Role of Animal Damage Control." In *Proceedings of the Eastern Wildlife Damage Control Conference*, pp. 7–8.

Drewien, Roderick C., and Elwood G. Bizeau. "Status and Distribution of Greater Sandhill Cranes in the Rocky Mountains." *Journal of Wildlife Management* 38 (1974): 720–742.

Drewien, Roderick C., and Wendy Brown. Whooping Crane Cross-Fostering Experiment.
Bi-Monthly Progress Report No. 86-5, September–October 1986.
Bi-Monthly Progress Report No. 86-6, November–December 1986.
Bi-Monthly Progress Report No. 87-1, January–February 1987.
Bi-Monthly Progress Report No. 87-2, March–April 1987.
Bi-Monthly Progress Report No. 87-3, May–June 1987.
Bi-Monthly Progress Report No. 87-4, July–August 1987.

———. Whooping Crane Cross-Fostering Experiment Progress Report No. 19, April 1983–November 1983.

Drewien, Roderick C., Scott R. Derrickson, and Elwood G. Bizeau. "Experimental Release of Captive Parent-Reared Greater Sandhill Cranes at Grays Lake Refuge, Idaho." In *Proceedings 1981 Crane Workshop*, ed. James C. Lewis, pp. 99–111.

Durham, George J. "Game in Texas." *Texas Almanac for 1868*. Galveston: Richardson, 1868.

Duval, James C. *Early Times in Texas*. Austin: Steck-Vaughn, 1967.

E. A. Engineering, Science and Technology, Inc. "Migration Dynamics of the Whooping Crane with Emphasis on Use of the Platte River in Nebraska." Report prepared for Interstate Task Force on Endangered Species. Lincoln, 1985.

"Easter Eggs." *Brolga Bugle* [changed to *ICF Bugle* in 1982] 3 (Spring 1977): 1.

Erickson, Ray C. "Captive Breeding of Whooping Cranes at the Patuxent Wildlife Research Center." In *Breeding Endangered Species in Captivity*, ed. R. D. Martin, pp. 99–114. London: Academic Press, 1975.

———. "A Federal Research Program for Endangered Wildlife." *Transactions of the Thirty-Third North American Wildlife and Natural Resources Conference* 33 (1968): 418–433.

———. "Propagation Studies of Endangered Wildlife at the Patuxent Center." *1980 International Zoo Yearbook* 20 (1980): 40–47.

———. "Transport Case for Incubated Eggs." *Wildlife Society Bulletin* 9 (1981): 57–60.

———. "Whooping Crane Studies at the Patuxent Wildlife Research Center." In *Proceedings First International Crane Workshop*, ed. James C. Lewis, pp. 166–176.

Erickson, Ray C., and Scott R. Derrickson. "The Whooping Crane." In *Crane Research around the World*, ed. James C. Lewis and Hiroyuki Masatomi, pp. 104–118.

"Establishing the Aransas Migratory Waterfowl Refuge." *Federal Register* 3 (5 January 1938): 13.

Faanes, Craig A. *Bird Behavior and Mortality in Relation to Power Lines in Prairie Habitats*. U.S. Fish and Wildlife Technical Report 7. Washington, D.C.: Government Printing Office, 1967.

Feinburg, Lawrence. "Dawn Heralds New Day for Whooping Cranes." *Washington Post*, 1 June 1975.

Flack, Captain. *A Hunter's Experiences in the Southern States of America.* London: Longmans Green, 1866.

————. *The Texas Rifle-Hunter, or Field Sports on the Prairie.* London: Maxwell, 1866.

"Flight of the Whooping Crane." National Geographic Special. John Huston, narrator. 1983.

Flint, Vladimir E., and A. A. Kistchinski. "The Siberian Crane in Yakutia." In *Crane Research around the World,* ed. James C. Lewis and Hiroyuki Masatomi, pp. 136–145.

"For the Birds." *Scientific American* 258 (June 1988): 32–33.

Fowler, Murray E., ed. *Zoo and Wild Animal Medicine.* 2d ed. Philadelphia: W. B. Saunders, 1986.

"Fred and Tex." *Grus Americana* 18 (June 1979): 3–4.

Gee, George F. "Avian Artificial Insemination and Semen Preservation." In *Proceedings of the 1983 Symposium on Breeding Birds in Captivity,* ed. A. C. Risser and F. S. Todd, pp. 375–398.

————. "Crane Reproductive Physiology and Conservation." *Zoo Biology* 2 (1983): 199–213.

———— [Endangered Species Program, Patuxent Wildlife Research Center]. Personal communication, December 1986; February 1988.

Gee, George F., and Stanley A. Temple. "Artificial Insemination for Breeding Non-Domestic Birds." *Symposium of the Zoological Society* (London) 43 (1978): 51–72.

Gee, George F., Murray R. Bakst, and Thomas J. Sexton. "Cryogenic Preservation of Semen from the Greater Sandhill Crane." *Journal of Wildlife Management* 49 (1985): 480–484.

Gray, William. *From Virginia to Texas, 1835: Diary of Col. Wm. F. Gray.* Houston: Fletcher Young, 1965.

Halloran, Arthur F. "Aransas Refuge Biological Records to 1967" (update of 1964 Report). Aransas National Wildlife Refuge, Refuge Files.

————. "Management of Deer and Cattle on the Aransas National Wildlife Refuge, Texas." *Journal of Wildlife Management* 7 (1943): 203–216.

Halloran, Arthur F., and Julian A. Howard. "Aransas Refuge Wildlife Introductions." *Journal of Wildlife Management* 20 (1956): 460–461.

Harstad, Peter T., and Max Pavesic. "The Lander Trail Report." Idaho Museum of Natural History, Pocatello, 1966. In U.S. Fish and Wildlife Science, *Grays Lake NWR Master Plan,* 1982.

Hawkins, A. S. et al., eds. *Flyways: Pioneering Waterfowl Management in North America.* Washington, D.C.: U.S. Fish and Wildlife Service, 1984.

Hester, Nolan. "Whoopers in Trouble." *Impact (Albuquerque Journal Magazine),* 24 February 1987, pp. 4–7, 14.

Horwich, Robert [biologist]. Personal communication, 28 June 1987.

————. "Reintroduction of Sandhill Cranes to the Wild." *IFC Bugle* 12 (1986): 1, 4–5.

Howe, Marshall A. "Distribution, Habitat Use, Behavior, and Survival of Migrating Whooping Cranes in the Great Plains." Draft, n.d. Patuxent Wildlife Research Center, Laurel, Maryland.

————. "Habitat Use by Migrating Whooping Cranes in the Aransas–Wood Buffalo Corridor." In *Proceedings 1985 Crane Workshop,* ed. James C. Lewis, pp. 303–311.

Hunt, Howard E., Thomas V. Stehn, and R. Douglas Slack. "Whooping Crane Mortality during the Winter of 1982–83." In *Proceedings 1985 Crane Workshop,* ed. James C. Lewis, pp. 219–220.

Huson, Hobart. *Refugio: A Comprehensive History of Refugio County from Aboriginal Times to 1953.* 2 vols. Woodsboro, Tex.: Rooke Foundation, 1953.

Ingersoll, Ernest. *Birds in Legend, Fable, and Folklore.* London: Longmans Green, 1923.

International Crane Foundation. "Guide to the Johnson Exhibit Pod." Baraboo, Wisconsin. Mimeo.

————. "ICF Tour Guide/Chick Parent Training Manual." Baraboo, Wisconsin. Mimeo.

International Wild Waterfowl Association, Inc. *Proven Methods of Keeping and Rearing Cranes in Captivity.* Salt Lake City: Game Bird Breeders' Gazette, 1962.

James, Vinton Lee. *Frontier and Pioneer: Recollections of Early Days in San Antonio and West Texas.* San Antonio: Privately published, 1938.

Johns, Brian W. "Whooping Cranes in Saskatchewan." Paper delivered at Whooping Crane Conservation Association Annual Meeting, Regina, Saskatchewan, 2 October 1987.

Johnsgard, Paul A. *Cranes of the World.* London: Croom Helm, 1983.

Johnson, E. Frank. "Aransas Whooping Cranes." *Blue Jay* 34 (December 1976): 220–228.

Kauffeld, Jon D. "An Avian Cholera Epizootic among Sandhill Cranes in Colorado." In *Proceedings 1985 Crane Workshop,* ed. James C. Lewis, pp. 145–148.

Kepler, Cameron B. "Captive Propagation of Whooping Cranes: A Behavioral Approach." In *Endangered Birds: Management Techniques for Preserving Threatened Species,* ed. Stanley A. Temple, pp. 231–241.

Kohak, Erazim. *The Embers and the Stars: A Philosophical Inquiry into the Moral Sense of Nature.* Chicago: University of Chicago Press, 1984.

Konrad, Paul M. "Expanded Sandhill Crane Hunting in the Dakotas and Oklahoma Threatens Endangered Whooping Cranes." In *Proceedings 1985 Crane Workshop,* ed. James C. Lewis, pp. 69–77.

Krajewski, Carey [University of Wisconsin Zoological Museum, Madison]. Personal communication, 28 June 1988.

Kuyt, Ernie. "Banding of Juvenile Whooping Cranes and Discovery of the Summer Habitat Used by Nonbreeders." In *Proceedings 1978 Crane Workshop,* ed. James C. Lewis, pp. 109–111.

————. "Clutch Size, Hatching Success, and Survival of Whooping Crane Chicks, Wood Buffalo National Park, Canada." In *Crane Research around the World,* ed. James C. Lewis and Hiroyuki Masatomi, pp. 126–129.

————. "The Far North." Part I and II. *Nature Society News.* Reprinted North Dakota Outdoors 45 (1982): 4–13.

————. "Northward Radio-Tracking of a Whooping Crane Family Migrating from the Aransas National Wildlife Refuge to Wood Buffalo National Park, April 1, 1983." Canadian Wildlife Service Report, Edmonton, 1986.

———— [biologist, Canadian Wildlife Service]. Personal communication, 2 October 1987; 22 March 1988.

————. "Population Status, Nest Site Fidelity, and Breeding Habitat of Whooping Cranes." In *Crane Research around the World,* ed. James C. Lewis and Hiroyuki Masatomi, pp. 119–125.

————. "Radiotelemetry-Assisted Studies of Whooping Cranes in Wood Buffalo National Park Prior to Migration, Autumn 1983." Edmonton: Canadian Wildlife Service, 1984.

————. "Radio-Tracking of a Whooping Crane Family Migrating from the Aransas National Wildlife Refuge to West-Central Saskatchewan, April-May 1984." Canadian Wildlife Service Report, Edmonton, 1986.

————. "Recent Clutch Size Data for Whooping Cranes including a Three-Egg Clutch." *Blue Jay* 34 (1976): 82–83.

————. "Report on Removal, Examination, and Transfer of Whooping Crane Eggs from Wood Buffalo National Park, 27–31 May 1988." Canadian Wildlife Service Report, Edmonton, 1988.

————. "Whooping Cranes at Wood Buffalo National Park." Paper presented at Whooping Crane Conservation Association Annual Meeting, Regina, Saskatchewan, 2 October 1987.

————. "Whooping Crane Tracking Report, Segments 1–8, NWT to Aransas National Wildlife Refuge, September–October 1981." Canadian Wildlife Service Report, Edmonton, 1982.

Kuyt, Ernie, and J. Paul Goossen. "Survival, Age Composition, Sex Ratio, and Age at First Breeding of Whooping Cranes in Wood Buffalo National Park, Canada." In *Proceedings 1985 Crane Workshop,* ed. James C. Lewis, pp. 230–244.

Labuda, Stephen. "The Impact of Man on the Blackjack Peninsula of the Texas Coastal Bend." Aransas National Wildlife Refuge, Refuge Files, 1975.

————. "A Whooping Crane Migration Study." Aransas National Wildlife Refuge, Refuge Files, 1983.

Lange, Michael. "Two Whooping Cranes Wintering in Brazoria County during the 1985–1986 Season." San Bernard National Wildlife Refuge, 1985. Aransas National Wildlife Refuge, Refuge Files.

Larue, C. "Increasing Fertility of Crane Eggs." *Avicultural Magazine* 86 (1980): 10–15.

Leopold, Aldo. *A Sand County Almanac.* New York: Ballantine, 1970.

Lewis, James C. [Whooping Crane Coordinator, Fish and Wildlife Service]. Personal communication, 2 October 1987; 10 March 1988; etc.

————, ed. *Proceedings First International Crane Workshop.* Stillwater: Oklahoma State University Press, 1976.

————, ed. *Proceedings 1978 Crane Workshop.* Fort Collins: Colorado State University Printing Service, 1979.

————, ed. *Proceedings 1981 Crane Workshop.* Tavernier, Fla.: National Audubon Society, n.d.

————, ed. *Proceedings 1985 Crane Workshop.* Grand Island, Neb.: Platte River Whooping Crane Habitat Maintenance Trust and U.S. Fish and Wildlife Service, 1987.

————. "Reintroduction of Whooping Cranes to Eastern North America." Paper delivered at Fifth North American Crane Workshop, Kissimmee Prairie, Florida, 22–25 February 1988.

————. "Sandhill Crane." In *Management of Migratory Shore and Upland Game Birds in North America,* ed. Glen C. Sanderson, pp. 4–43. Washington, D.C.: International Association of Fish and Wildlife Agencies, 1977.

————. "The Whooping Crane." In *Audubon Wildlife Report, 1966,* ed. Roger L. Di Silvestro, pp. 659–676. New York: National Audubon Society, 1986.

Lewis, James C., and Hiroyuki Masatomi, eds. *Crane Research around the World.* Proceedings of the International Crane Symposium at Sapporo, Japan, in 1980, and Papers from the World Working Group on Cranes, International Council for Bird Preservation. Baraboo, Wis.: International Crane Foundation, 1981.

Lingle, Gary R. "Status of Whooping Crane Migration Habitat within the Great Plains of North America." In *Proceedings 1985 Crane Workshop,* ed. James C. Lewis, pp. 331–340.

Lynch, John J. "A Field Biologist." In *Flyways: Pioneering Waterfowl Management in North America,* ed. A. S. Hawkins et al., pp. 35–40.

Mabie, David [Texas Parks and Wildlife, Rockport]. Personal communication, 21 March 1988.

McAlister, Wayne H., and Martha K. McAlister. *Guidebook to the Aransas Wildlife Refuge.* Victoria, Tex.: Mince Country Press, 1987.

McCall, George A. "Some Remarks on the Habits, etc., of Birds Met within Western Texas between San Antonio and the Rio Grande in New Mexico . . . ." *Proceedings of the Philadelphia Academy of Sciences* 5 (1851): 213–224.

McMillen, Janet L., David H. Ellis, and Dwight G. Smith. "The Role of Captive Propagation in the Recovery of the Mississippi Sandhill Crane." *Endangered Species Technical Bulletin* 12 (1987): 6–8.

McNulty, Faith. *Peeping in the Shell: A Whooping Crane Is Hatched.* New York: Harper and Row, 1986.

————. *The Whooping Crane: The Bird That Defies Extinction.* New York: Dutton, 1966.

Maroldo, Georgette K. "Crip: The Constant Dancer." *Blue Jay* 38 (1980): 147–161.

"Matagorda Island." *Grus Americana* 27 (June 1988): 4.

Mercer, Captains John and Ned. Newspaper clippings containing accounts from diaries, 1871–1879, in *Corpus Christi Caller.* 4L401, Barker Texas History Center, University of Texas, Austin.

Miller, Harvey W. "Hunting in the Management of Mid-Continent Sandhill Cranes." In *Proceedings 1985 Crane Workshop,* ed. James C. Lewis, pp. 39–46.

Miller, Richard S., Daniel B. Botkin, and Roy Mendelssohn. "The Whooping Crane (*Grus americana*) Population of North America." *Biological Conservation* 6 (April 1974): 106–111.

Moore, Euroda. "Recollections of Indianola." In *Indianola Scrap Book,* pp. 94–132 (facsimile reproduction). Port Lavaca, Tex.: Calhoun County Historical Survey Committee, 1974.

N.A.T. "Game in Texas." *Burke's Texas Almanac and Immigrant Guide for 1881*. Houston: Burke, 1880.

Nesbitt, Stephen A. "Notes on the Suitability of Captive-Reared Sandhill Cranes for Release into the Wild." In *Proceedings 1978 Crane Workshop*, ed. James C. Lewis, pp. 85–88.

———. "Status of Sandhill and Whooping Crane Studies in Florida." In *Proceedings 1985 Crane Workshop*, ed. James C. Lewis, pp. 213–216.

Novakowski, N. S. *Whooping Crane Population Dynamics on the Nesting Grounds, Wood Buffalo National Park, Northwest Territories, Canada*. Canadian Wildlife Service Report Series No. 1. Ottawa: Canadian Wildlife Service, 1966.

Oak Ridge Associated Universities. *A Proceedings: Impacts of Transmission Lines on Birds in Flight*. Oak Ridge, Tenn.: Oak Ridge Associated Universities, 1978.

Oberholser, Harry C. "Bird Life of Texas," original manuscript. Oberholser Papers, 4W218, Barker Texas History Center, University of Texas, Austin.

———. *The Bird Life of Texas*. Ed. Edgar B. Kincaid, Jr. 2 vols. Austin: University of Texas Press, 1974.

Odom, Ron R., and J. W. Guthrie, eds. *1981 Proceedings of the Nongame and Endangered Wildlife Symposium*. Game and Fish Division, Technical Bulletin, WL5. Athens, Ga.: Georgia Department of Natural Resources, 1981.

Olmsted, Frederick Law. *A Journey through Texas; or, a Saddle-Trip on the Southwestern Frontier*. Austin: University of Texas Press, 1978.

Piagès, Pierre M. F. "A Journey through Texas in 1767." Trans. Corinna Steele. *El Campanario* 16 (1985): 1–20.

Pollard, John. *Birds in Greek Life and Myth*. Plymouth: Thames and Hudson, 1977.

"Possible Cause Identified in Deaths of Cranes at Patuxent Wildlife Research Center." *Endangered Species Technical Bulletin* 12 (1987): 7.

Putnam, Mike. "Aviculture Wrap-Up." *Brolga Bugle* [changed to *ICF Bugle*] 6 (October 1980): 2.

"Red Tide." University of Texas Marine Science Institute *Newsletter* 3 (January 1987): 1–2.

"Regional News—Region C." *Endangered Species Technical Bulletin* 13 (June–July 1988): 8.

Risser, A. C., and F. S. Todd, eds. *Proceedings of the 1983 Symposium on Breeding Birds in Captivity*. Los Angeles, 1984.

Robbins, Tom. *Even Cowgirls Get the Blues*. Boston: Houghton Mifflin, 1976.

Rutgers, A., and K. A. Norris, eds. *Encyclopedia of Aviculture*. London: Blandford Press, 1970.

Sanchez, Felix. "Red Tide Killed 22 Million Fish, State Estimates." *Corpus Christi Caller*, 7 November 1986.

Sauey, Ron. "Of Cranes, and 'Coons, and Red-boned Hounds." *ICF Bugle* 8 (July 1982): 1, 4.

Seeligson, Lelia. "History of Indianola." In *Indianola Scrap Book*, pp. 23–37 (facsimile reproduction). Port Lavaca, Tex.: Calhoun County Historical Survey Committee, 1974.

Sennett, George B. "Further Notes on the Ornithology of Texas." *Bulletin of the U.S. Geological Survey* 5 (1879): 371–440.

———. "Notes on the Ornithology of the Lower Rio Grande of Texas, from Observations Made during the Season of 1877." *Bulletin of the U.S. Geological Survey* 4 (1878): 1–66.

Shields, Robert H., and Earl L. Benham. "Farm Crops as Food Supplements for Whooping Cranes." *Journal of Wildlife Management* 33 (1969): 811–817.

Simison, Robert L. "Whooping Cranes Get a New Friend in Bid to Survive." *Wall Street Journal*, 25 February 1985.

Slack, R. Douglas, and Howard E. Hunt. "The Effects of Various Burning and Grazing Treatments . . ." Draft. Texas A&M University, College Station, 1986. Aransas National Wildlife Refuge, Refuge Files.

Smith, Robert H. "From Tundra to Tropics." In *Flyways: Pioneering Waterfowl Management in North America*, ed. A. S. Hawkins et al., pp. 177–184.

Snyder, S. Bret, et al. "*Pasteurella Multocida* Infection in a Whooping Crane Associated with an Avian Cholera Outbreak." In *Proceedings 1985 Crane Workshop*, ed. James C. Lewis, pp. 149–155.

Stehn, Tom. "Impacts of the Gulf Intracoastal Waterway on the Endangered Whooping Crane." Paper presented at 1988 Crane Workshop, Kissimmee Prairie, Florida, February, 1988.

——— [biologist, Aransas National Wildlife Refuge]. Personal communication, Fall 1986; Spring and Fall 1987; Spring and Fall 1988; Winter 1989.

———. "Tailing the Whoopers." *Texas Parks and Wildlife* 43 (March 1985): 18–21.

———. "Whooping Crane Juveniles Wintering Away from Aransas." Aransas National Wildlife Refuge, Refuge Files, 1987.

———. "A Whooping Crane Migration Study—Spring 1983." Aransas National Wildlife Refuge, Refuge Files.

———. "Whooping Cranes during the 1986–1987 Winter." Aransas National Wildlife Refuge, Refuge Files, July 1987.

———. "Whooping Cranes during the 1987–1988 Winter." Aransas National Wildlife Refuge, Refuge Files, August 1988.

Stehn, Tom, and E. Frank Johnson. "Distribution of Winter Territories of Whooping Cranes on the Texas Coast." In *Proceedings 1985 Crane Workshop*, ed. James C. Lewis, pp. 180–196.

Stern, Harold P. *Birds, Beasts, Blossoms, and Bugs: The Nature of Japan*. New York: Abrams, 1976.

Stevenson, Charles H. "The Preservation of Fishery Products for Food." *Bulletin of the United States Fish Commission* 18 (1898): 335–563.

Stevenson, James O. "Refuge Weekly Itinerary and Report Activities." 2 October 1938; 5 June 1939; 27 October 1939; 27 January 1940; 1 April 1940; 19 April 1940; 2 July 1940. Aransas National Wildlife Refuge, Refuge Files.

———. "Will Bugles Blow No More?" *Audubon Magazine* 45 (1943): 134–139.

Stevenson, James O., and Richard E. Griffith. "Winter Life of the Whooping Crane." *Condor* 48 (1946): 160–178.

"The Storm of August 20, 1886." In *Indianola Scrap Book*, p. 139 (facsimile reproduction). Port Lavaca, Tex.: Calhoun County Historical Survey Committee, 1974.

Strecker, John K. "The Birds of Texas: An Annotated Check-List." *Baylor Bulletin* 15 (1912): 3–69.

Strom, Kenneth J. "Protecting Critical Whooping Crane Habitat on the Platte River, Nebraska." *Natural Areas Journal* 5 (1985): 8–13.

Stroud, Richard K., Charles O. Thoen, and Ruth M. Duncan. "Avian Tuberculosis and Salmonellosis in a Whooping Crane (*Grus americana*)." *Journal of Wildlife Diseases* 22 (January 1986): 106–110.

Swenk, Myron H. "The Present Status of the Whooping Crane." *Nebraska Bird Review* 1 (October 1933): 111–129.

Temple, Stanley A., ed. *Endangered Birds: Management Techniques for Preserving Threatened Species.* Madison: University of Wisconsin Press, 1977.

Texas A&M University, Sea Grant College Program. *Red Tide in Texas.* College Station: Sea Grant College Program, 1986.

Texas House of Representatives, House Study Group. "Whooping Cranes and Space Ships: The Matagorda Island Controversy." Interim News, No. 67–8, November 30, 1981, Austin. Mimeo.

Texas Parks and Wildlife News, 1 August 1985, p. 2.

Thiolley, Jean-Marie. "La Migration des Grues à travers l'Himalaya et la Predation par les Aigles Royaux." *Alauda* 47 (1979): 83–92.

Thompson, Bruce C. *Whooping Crane Monitoring in Open Sandhill Hunting Zones in Texas, 1984–85 Season.* Special Administrative Report, Texas Parks and Wildlife Department, Federal Aid Project W-103-R. Austin: Texas Parks and Wildlife, 1985.

Thompson, Bruce, and Ron George. "Minimizing Conflicts between Migratory Game Bird Hunters." In *Proceedings 1985 Crane Workshop,* ed. James C. Lewis, pp. 58–68.

"Three Arrivals in White." *Brolga Bugle* [changed to *ICF Bugle*] 4 (Winter 1978): 1.

U.S. Fish and Wildlife Service. *Endangered and Threatened Wildlife and Plants, January 1, 1986.* Washington, D.C.: Government Printing Office, 1986.

———. *Fisheries and Wildlife Research 1980.* Denver: Government Printing Office, 1981.

———. *Grays Lake NWR Master Plan.* N.p., 1982.

———. "Illness Strikes Rare Cranes at Patuxent Wildlife Research Center." News release, 30 September 1987.

———. "Master Plan: Patuxent Wildlife Research Center, Laurel, Maryland." Watertown, Mass.: Saski Associates, 1980. Mimeo.

———. "Matagorda Island, Texas, Proposed as Added Habitat for Whooping Cranes." News release, 29 November 1974.

———. *Patuxent Wildlife Research Center.* Washington, D.C.: Government Printing Office, n.d.

———. *The Platte River Ecology Study: Special Research Report.* Jamestown, N.D.: Fish and Wildlife Service, 1981.

———. *Preliminary Survey of Contaminant Issues of Concern on National Wildlife Refuges.* N.p.: Fish and Wildlife Service, 1986.

———. "Protocol for Hand-Rearing Crane Chicks (1987)." Patuxent Wildlife Research Center, Propagations and Laboratory Investigations Section, Endangered Species Branch, Laurel, Maryland.

———. "Three Agencies Agree on Management of Federal and State Lands on Matagorda Island, Texas." News release, 9 November 1982.

———. "Use of Suitcase Incubator." Worksheet. Patuxent Wildlife Research Center, Laurel, Maryland.

———. *Wetland Preservation Program, Category B., Texas Gulf Coast.* Albuquerque: Fish and Wildlife Service, 1981.

———. *The Whooping Crane.* Biological Services Program, FWS/OBS-80/01.3, March 1980. Washington, D.C.: Government Printing Office, 1981.

———. *Whooping Crane Recovery Plan.* Albuquerque: Fish and Wildlife Service, 1980, 1986.

University of Texas, Marine Science Institute. *Newsletter* 3 (January 1987).

Valentine, Jacob M. "Recovery Plan for the Mississippi Sandhill Crane, *Grus canadensis pulla*." Fish and Wildlife Service, Atlanta, 1984. Mimeo.

———. "Safeguarding Mississippi's Last Cranes." *ICF Bugle* 12 (1986): 2–3.

Vandel, George. "Migration of Radio-Monitored Whooping Crane Family from Fort Smith, N.W.T., Canada, to Aransas National Wildlife Refuge, Texas, Fall 1981." Draft. Whooping Crane Coordinator Files, Albuquerque.

Van Dyke, Theodore S. *Game Birds at Home.* New York: Fords, Howard and Hulbert, 1895.

Victoria Advocate, 21, 23, 30 August, 4 October 1955.

Walkinshaw, Lawrence H. *Cranes of the World.* New York: Winchester Press, 1973.

———. "The Sandhill Cranes." In *Crane Research around the World,* ed. James C. Lewis and Hiroyuki Masatomi, pp. 151–162.

Ward, John P., and Stanley H. Anderson. "Monitoring Study, Whooping Crane, Final Report, Fall 1983." Wyoming Cooperative Fishery and Wildlife Research Unit, Laramie, 1984.

"The Whoopers Arrive." *Brolga Bugle* [changed to *ICF Bugle*] 2 (Spring 1976): 1.

"Whooping Crane Chick Dies after 15-Day Life." *Washington Post,* 17 June 1975.

Whooping Crane Conservation Association. *Who, Why, When, and What.*

———. *1986 Who's Who: A Biographical Mini-Sketch.*

Windingstad, Ronald M., Harry E. Stiles, and Roderick C. Drewien. "Whooping Crane Preyed Upon by Golden Eagle." *Auk* 98 (1981): 393–394.

Young, L. S. "Autumn Migration of Subadult Whooping Cranes." Missoula, Montana Cooperative Wildlife Research Unit, October 1984. Whooping Crane Coordinator Files, Albuquerque.

Zimmerman, David R. *To Save a Bird in Peril.* New York: Coward, McCann and Geoghegan, 1975.

Zwank, Phillip J., and Scott R. Derrickson. "Gentle Release of Captive, Parent-Reared Sandhill Cranes into the Wild." In *Proceedings 1981 Crane Workshop,* ed. James C. Lewis, pp. 112–116.

Zwank, Phillip J., and Charlotte D. Wilson. "Survival of Captive, Parent-Reared Mississippi Sandhill Cranes Released on a Refuge." *Conservation Biology Journal* 1 (1987): 165–168.

Index